Human Rights and Reform

Human Rights and Reform

Changing the Face of
North African Politics

SUSAN E. WALTZ

University of California Press

BERKELEY   LOS ANGELES   LONDON

University of California Press
Berkeley and Los Angeles, California

University of California Press, Ltd.
London, England

© 1995 by
The Regents of the University of California

Library of Congress Cataloging-in-Publication Data
Waltz, Susan Eileen.
    Human rights and reform : changing the face of North African
politics / Susan E. Waltz.
        p.   cm.
    Includes bibliographical references and index.
    ISBN 0-520-20003-9 (alk. paper)—ISBN 0-520-20254-6 (alk. pa-
per : pbk.)
    1. Human rights—Morocco.   2. Human rights—Tunisia.   3. Hu-
man rights—Algeria.   4. Morocco—Politics and government.   5. Tunisia—Politics and government.   6. Algeria—Politics and government.   I. Title.
    JC599.A365W35   1995
    323'.0961—dc20   94-48264
                                                                   CIP

Printed in the United States of America
9 8 7 6 5 4 3 2 1

Contents

Preface

The North African states of Morocco, Tunisia, and Algeria had all won political independence by 1962, but this did not usher in the halcyon days many had dreamed of and hoped for. Over the past thirty years, governments or their agents have been responsible for blatantly contrived political trials, "disappearances," political assassinations, and the torture and imprisonment of opponents. Human rights practices raised concern both at home and abroad, and in the late 1970s, individuals from within the region began to organize national human rights groups. This book is an effort to tell their story and understand their place in North African politics.

"Human rights" is often framed as a moral issue of vital concern to those with humanitarian or idealistic interests but only marginally related to the world of politics, where interest in order, security, and power prevails. That is not my approach. My understanding is that all human rights activists have an interest in the way power is used, and human rights groups in North Africa, the Maghrib, are essentially political actors. They are different from other kinds of political actors, however, in that they neither vie for spoils within the political system nor attempt to overthrow that system. Rather, they work from within a recognized game of national politics to change its operating rules. Neither saints nor revolutionaries, they are political actors with a stake in the system, seeking reform.

This book is thus a comparative study of North African politics in the second half of the twentieth century, viewed from the perspective of an important, but understudied, set of political actors. The analysis of their efforts and speculation about their impact depends, not simply on their own actions or the responses they have elicited from those in power, but also on the historical and cultural context in which they operate. Accordingly, a substantial portion of the book is devoted to an analysis of national politics that takes into account the power of both state and society. In each case I have traced political structures back to a precolonial period, both to combat enduring misconceptions that political life in North Africa began with the arrival of the French and to emphasize the very deep roots of certain political patterns. Deeply seated structures serve as both context and target for the work of human rights groups; moreover, they condition the strategies developed by the groups themselves.

Current academic interests in democratization and social movements provide some of the conceptual underpinnings of my analysis. This book is a product of its time both in terms of the concepts it uses and the phenomenon it studies. Scholarship generally follows the march of history, and in due course the academic interests that frame the study will fade. Indeed, developments in eastern Europe and the former soviet republics have already caused enthusiasm for democratization to wane, and students of the Middle East are now less sanguine about prospects of democratization in that region than they were even a few years ago. Recognizing that events will in time overtake this book, I would point readers to the questions it raises about the nature of political structures and the way they are shaped and transformed. This, I believe, will be its most enduring feature. In writing this book I hope to record an important moment in North African history, but it is also my intent to offer a comparative view of political developments and to present an analytical framework that will accommodate a long view of politics in the Maghrib.

My analysis and conclusions are critical of contemporary leaders and policies they have pursued, but I do not intend the book to be hostile. In the course of writing it, I have come to appreciate the difficulties of political restructuring for all concerned. Set patterns are not easily altered, and power is not readily surrendered, or shared, by those who hold it. Nor should it necessarily be. Political philosophers have long wrestled with questions about who should hold political power, and a case can be made even for the despot or an oligarchical class that makes difficult political decisions to ensure stability and enhance prosperity. But power is also seductive. Lord Acton is so often quoted because the truth he offered resonates with experience: power corrupts, and absolute power corrupts absolutely. Despite legal commitments to the contrary, North African leaders have not refrained from abusing the powers they hold.

In the preparation of this book I have incurred many debts, the oldest of which is an intellectual debt to John McCamant. Long before it was intellectually fashionable, he asked questions about human rights, repression, dominance, and resistance. I was fortunate to be his student. At about the same time, Charles Micaud introduced me to the Maghrib, and I also wish to acknowledge at the outset the impact that has had on my life. Over the past twenty years, North Africans have taught me much about compassion, generosity, duty, and the depth of human connection; my life is richer for having crossed theirs.

In writing the book I owe the greatest debt to participants in the North African human rights movement themselves. In trips to the region or as they visited the United States, from 1989 to 1993, I interviewed more than two dozen individuals actively involved in the creation and/or the continuing function of Maghribi groups. Some spoke guardedly; others were more candid in their assessment of the human rights movement and its place in politics. Collectively, those I interviewed provided rich insights, without which the book would undoubtedly have taken a different direction. It is thus with regret that I have decided not to acknowledge them by name in these pages or to cite interviews with them in the text. Many of these individuals are quite prominent in political life and relatively immune to persecution, and in any case are willing to assume risks. Some would surely appreciate recognition. Others, though, are more vulnerable, and I wish to avoid making their lives more difficult. As I write, many human rights activists in Algeria live in fear of their lives; a member of the Moroccan Association of Human Rights was tried and convicted for crimes of opinion in 1993; and in Tunisia human rights lawyers who have defended Islamists are followed by plainclothesmen, and their telephone lines are monitored. Activists in international human rights organizations are less subject to such pressures, so I very gratefully acknowledge here an interview accorded me by Maître Daniel Jacoby, president of the International Federation of Human Rights, and the assistance in locating documents and verifying facts extended to me by researchers at Amnesty International's International Secretariat and Maryam Elahi at AIUSA's Washington office.

Universities make research of this sort possible, and at various stages Florida International University made generous contributions to the research and writing effort, as did the Office of International Studies and Programs at Michigan State University while I was on sabbatical leave in 1991–92. The American Institute for Maghrib Studies supported some of my travel to North Africa, and I have been grateful for the periodic use of its research facilities at the Centre d'études maghrébines à Tunis. I have also benefited from the support of a wide circle of friends, family, and colleagues, and regret not being able to mention them all by name. I would, however, like to acknowledge the contributions of Karen Dainer-Best, Darden Pyron, and Ralph Clem, who provided encouragement at critical moments along the way. Miraan Sa, Jody Pavilack, Dan Pierce, and Cheryl Grimshaw helped prepare the manuscript, and I am grateful for their able assistance. For their comments on individual chapters or the entire manuscript, I am indebted to Damian Fernandez, Ann Mayer, Jill Crystal, John Ruedy, Henry Munson, Liz Hodgkin, John McCamant, Marguerite Rollinde, Nicholas Onuf, and Mohiaddin Mesbahi. Their insights and suggestions strengthened both the analysis and its presentation. Any remaining errors and omissions are, of course, my responsibility alone.

The costs of writing this book have been borne primarily by two people, Jack Smith and Dan Pierce. Dan's wisdom and understanding by far exceed his years; I am grateful for his patience, his impatience, and his readiness to celebrate. As my partner, Jack has been a thoughtful critic and dear friend throughout the enterprise; without him, quite simply, this book would never have been.

List of Abbreviations

AI	Amnesty International
AIS	Armée islamique de salut (Army of Islamic Salvation, Algeria)
ALN	Armée de libération national (National Liberation Army, Algeria)
AMDH	Association marocaine des droits de l'homme (Moroccan Association of Human Rights)
ANP	Armée nationale populaire (National Popular Army, Algeria)
ASDHOM	Association pour la défense des droits de l'homme au Maroc (Association for the Defense of Human Rights in Morocco)
CDT	Confédération démocratique des travailleurs (Morocco)
CGT	Confédération générale des travailleurs (General Confederation of Workers, Tunisia)
CNRA	Comité national de la révolution algérienne (National Committee of the Algerian Revolution)
CNS	Compagnies nationales de sécurité (National Security Units, Algeria)
CRUA	Comité révolutionnaire d'unité et d'action (Revolutionary Committee of Unity and Action, Algeria)
ENA	Etoile nationale algérienne (Algerian National Star)
FDIC	Front pour la défense des institutions constitutionnelles (Front for the Defense of Constitutional Institutions, Morocco)

FFS	Front des forces socialistes (Front of Socialist Forces, Algeria)
FIDH	Fédération internationale des droits de l'homme (International Federation of Human Rights)
FIS	Front Islamique de Salut (Islamic Salvation Front, Algeria)
FLN	Front de libération nationale (National Liberation Front, Algeria)
GIA	Groupe islamique armée (Armed Islamic Group, Jama'a al-islamiyya al-musallahah, Algeria)
GPRA	Gouvernement provisionnel de la république algérienne (Provisional Government of the Algerian Republic)
HCE	Haut conseil d'état (High State Council, Algeria)
HRC	Human Rights Committee (United Nations)
ICCPR	International Covenant on Civil and Political Rights
ICESCR	International Covenant on Economic, Social, and Cultural Rights
LADDH	Ligue algérienne pour la défense des droits de l'homme (Algerian League for the Protection of Human Rights)
LADH	Ligue algérienne des droits de l'homme (Algerian League of Human Rights)
LMDH	Ligue marocaine des droits de l'homme (Moroccan League of Human Rights)
LTDH	Ligue tunisienne des droits de l'homme (Tunisian League of Human Rights)
MDS	Mouvement des démocrates socialistes (Movement of Socialist Democrats, Tunisia)
MNA	Mouvement national algérien (Algerian National Movement)
MNP	Mouvement national populaire (National Popular Movement, Morocco)
MP	Mouvement populaire (Popular Movement, Morocco)
MPDC	Mouvement populaire démocratique et constitutionnel (Democratic and Constitutional Popular Movement, Morocco)
MTI	Mouvement de la tendance islamique (Ittijah al-Islami, Islamic Tendency Movement, Tunisia)
MTLD	Mouvement pour la triomphe des libertés démocratiques

	(Movement for the Triumph of Democratic Liberties, Algeria)
OADP	Organisation pour l'action démocratique et populaire (Organization of Democratic and Popular Action, Morocco)
OMDH	Organisation marocaine des droits de l'homme (Moroccan Organization of Human Rights)
OS	Organisation spéciale (Special Organization, Algeria)
PA	Parti d'action (Action Party, Morocco)
PAGS	Parti avant-garde socialiste (Avant-Garde Socialist Party, Algeria)
PCM	Parti communiste marocain (Moroccan Communist Party)
PDC	Parti démocratique constitutionnel (Democratic Constitutional Party, Morocco)
PDI	Parti démocratique et de l'indépendance (Democratic Party of Independence, Morocco)
PI	Parti Istiqlal (Independence Party, Morocco)
PLI	Parti des libéraux indépendents (Liberal Independents' Party, Morocco)
PLS	Parti de libération et socialisme (Liberation and Socialism Party, Morocco)
PND	Parti national démocratique (National Democratic Party, Morocco)
PPA	Parti du peuple algérien (Algerian People's Party)
PPS	Parti du progrès et du socialisme (Party of Progress and Socialism, Morocco)
PRS	Parti de la révolution socialiste (Party of the Socialist Revolution, Algeria)
PSD	Parti destourien socialiste (Socialist Destourian [Constitutional] Party, Tunisia)
PUP	Parti d'unité populaire (Party of Popular Unity, Tunisia)
RCD	Rassemblement constitutionnel démocratique (Democratic Constitutional Rally, Tunisia)
RNI	Rassemblement national des indépendants (National Rally for Independence, Morocco)
RSP	Rassemblement socialiste progressiste (Socialist Progressive Rally, Tunisia)
SM	Securité militaire (Military Security, Algeria)

SN   Sûreté nationale (National Security, in Algeria, Tunisia,
            and Morocco)
SNL   Syndicat national des lycéens (National Syndicate of
            Secondary Students, Morocco)
UC   Union constitutionnelle (Constitutional Union, Morocco)
UDHR   Universal Declaration of Human Rights
UDU   Union des démocrates unionistes (Union of Democratic
            Unionists, Tunisia)
UGAT   Union générale des agriculteurs tunisiens (General Union
            of Tunisian Farmers)
UGTT   Union générale des travailleurs tunisiens (General Union
            of Tunisian Workers)
UNEM   Union nationale des étudiants marocains (National Union
            of Moroccan Students)
UNFP   Union nationale des forces populaires (Natinal Union of
            Popular Forces, Morocco)
UNTT   Union nationale des travailleurs tunisiens (National
            Union of Tunisian Workers)
USFP   Union socialiste des forces populaires (Socialist Union of
            Popular Forces, Morocco)
UTAC   Union tunisienne d'artisanat et de commerce (Tunisian
            Union of Crafts and Commerce)

PART I

Human Rights and the Politics of Change

Politics has been defined as a matter of who gets what, when, and how, and accordingly, the game of politics may be discussed in terms of the rules that govern the allocation of political values. Political analysis generally begins with recognition of the parameters of a political game, and analysts make their task one of identifying operational rules and the moves that can be made within their bounds. By definition, "illegal moves" lie beyond the scope of regular political play and so for the most part escape scrutiny.

That is not to suggest that rules are never challenged. Revolutionary movements offer only the most dramatic evidence of efforts to change the rules of the political game. Most systems harbor some players, or would-be players, who contest existing structures, but more often than not, their actions are without consequence. Through political repression or legal constraints they are excluded from play, and the game goes on.

Some players inevitably persist, however, and a combination of contextual factors that include social and economic conditions, political leadership, the history of political institutions, and the power of the zeitgeist may carry reform or revolutionary efforts to fruition. In the 1980s, such possibilities captured imaginations around the globe. Voices were raised against authoritarian rule, and repressive governments fell. Scholars wrote tomes on the process of democratization, which in a fundamental sense involves changing the rules of the game.

A vision of democratizing reform and expanding possibilities of participation touched North Africa, as it did other regions, and this book traces the efforts of one set of actors inspired by the possibilities of structural transformation. Human rights groups in North Africa have spearheaded a democratization movement, but ironically, their efforts have not received the attention they merit. Their position in the game of politics, whether as monitors or as challengers of the rules, puts them beyond a scope of vision focused on established structures and conventional players. Human rights activists have not been conventional players, but their contribution to the North African games of politics has been substantial. Part I of this book develops an analytical framework that allows their efforts to come into focus.

1 Introduction

Attention to the possibility of democratic transformation that has gripped scholars in recent years initially swept unnoticing past the Middle East. In consequence, interesting developments in Middle Eastern societies were neglected. Although the region as a whole remains characterized by authoritarian rule, by the late 1980s there was evidence of a growing concern about the linkage between governed and governors.[1] In November 1989, Jordan held its first full legislative election in more than twenty years. The popularly chosen parliament began to exercise atrophied muscle by investigating allegations of corruption in government agencies, referring several of them for judicial investigation. Following dissolution of the Kuwaiti parliament in 1986, Kuwait saw a popular expansion of its *diwaniyya,* a system of informal networks that generally promoted the sharing of interests within occupation groups. *Diwaniyya*s in the late 1980s evolved into political fora where the "guest audience" frequently numbered in the hundreds. Parliament was restored in 1992, and the new legislature promptly formed a human rights committee. In Egypt, associational life began to expand, and the concerns of intellectual critics increasingly found voice.[2] Within the greater Middle East, democratization seemed in the late 1980s to stand its best chance in the Maghrib, where the forced departure of Tunisia's President Habib Bourguiba focused attention on political problems, and where just a year later, turmoil provoked by economic crisis called the viability of Algeria's social contract into question. Expectations of democratization were raised high across the region.

In the interim, the euphoria has waned; skepticism has in large measure replaced the optimism of the late 1980s. All the same, societal pressures for democratization remain stronger than at any time in the recent past. Among elites in and out of power, questions of structural change still pro-

3

voke animated debate. Into the 1990s, across the Maghrib, small groups of individuals, most of them professionals, found themselves meeting in homes or restaurants specifically to discuss matters of public policy and political action. Their relatively quiet, but persistent, efforts to effect liberalizing political change merit close examination. It is to such efforts that this book directs attention.

Efforts, of course, are not to be confused with results. Regardless of expressed concerns and accompanying efforts, democratic transition is far from a certain outcome in the contemporary Maghrib. Many forces are at work, and the ventures of democratically oriented elites are only one among them. An eventual transition is far from assured, but likewise, it cannot be precluded. From the vantage of this book, the outcome of the present ambiguous situation is less critical than understanding pressures for structural change and how they are articulated. Even the truncated stories of failed or incomplete transitions can reveal much about the impetus for structural reform. Studies of accomplished democratic transitions have pointed up weak areas in our understanding of the process by which change is initiated. Little is known, for example, of the tactical decisions made by opposition elites, who in many situations have provided the impulse and the framework for democratization. As useful as it is to identify the conditions under which their actions are likely to be successful, of equal relevance are the factors that make them decide to act. An investigation of the exertions of opposition elites as actions are planned and executed affords a different perspective than that presented in post hoc studies of achieved transitions. Retrospective studies that project backward from successful transitions may screen out false starts and negative outcomes. Such an approach is appropriate when the focus is on the success of structural transformation; it necessarily yields fewer insights into the impetus for action that initiates a transition and carries it forward. A close-up, in situ view offers an opportunity to observe crafting in progress and apply analytic tools to help understand the process of democratization.

What is to be understood as "democracy" in a region where there are few indigenous referents? Even in the abstract, consideration of democratization is problematic, for the meaning of the word *democracy* itself is subject to dispute. The historical evolution of democracy and democratic theory from classical Athens to the contemporary period has given rise to a variety of governmental forms and theoretical models. With choices as extreme as those represented by Karl Marx and John Stuart Mill, democratic thought is like a tree with many grafted branches: the varieties of fruit may be only distantly related. Dominant perspectives alternatively emphasize representation and participation, and historical combinations have been myriad. What at root serve as the common denominator to different perspectives are twin notions of popular choice and accountability, although exactly who constitute the responsible citizenry remains at issue.[3] In a work commonly recognized as a central referent for democratic theory, Robert Dahl posits as defining characteristics of democracy, or polyarchy, the right to participate and the right to oppose. For Dahl, the noteworthy advantage of democracy does not lie in the particular policies it may produce, for in their content democratically produced policies may differ little from those arrived at by other political means. Democracy's major virtue is found, rather, in the protection from massive coercion it extends to those who enjoy the franchise.[4]

Form rather than content affords this protection from tyranny. Building on Joseph Schumpeter's argument that democracy is best seen as a political method, or institutionalized competition, democracy at its core is a set of agreed-upon rules for resolving conflict. Conflict is inherent in politics, and democracy distinguishes itself in recognizing that fact, enshrining rules that establish the parameters of acceptable—and unacceptable—political activity. Within the established bounds, uncertainty of outcome in political struggle is the hallmark of democratic process. Inherent uncertainty introduces an added measure of anxiety into democratic politics, but it is the source of the system's strength. The fact that the game is not fixed in advance keeps at the table many players who otherwise might retire in dismay, disgust, or indifference. Losing one round in democratic politics does not preclude winning the next, and vice versa.

The North African societies at the heart of this book, or at least important segments within them, have been clamoring for increased access to decision-making structures and increased influence on outcomes. In Tunisia, the Movement of Socialist Democrats (MDS) for many years carried this banner, and for the past decade, Islamists have most vocally contested the monopolistic control of power. Likewise, the proliferation of parties in Algeria after political liberalization in spring 1989 attested to widespread, albeit fragmented, interest in access to power. In Morocco, where multipartyism has long been constitutionally enshrined, but the role of parties has been circumscribed, organized labor pressed for political change. In 1990 it shifted its attention away from economic demands to concern for the political rights to organize, strike, and criticize government policy without fear of reprisal.

As Maghribi regimes flirt with the idea of democracy, the strongest proponents of liberalizing change have sounded their voices most often from the wings, at some distance from the seats of power. Their commitment to institutionalized democracy—and the possibility of political defeat—goes untested, but their demands and their commentary have helped shape a debate among elites about the nature of democratic governance. Criticism of personalism and monopolistic, single-party rule sets the measure of such discussions, and it has become as much a part of popular political culture in Tunisia and Algeria as has acknowledgment of the monarch's hold over the political system in Morocco. While some have focused narrowly on openly contested national elections, others have argued that democratization is a process that to be effective must extend beyond multipartyism and open elections to respect for the independence of law.

As either product or ongoing process, democracy requires active cultivation. Even in well-established democracies, the continuous reproduction of democratic rule both in the polity at large and in smaller organizational groupings is far from automatic.[5] In societies struggling to establish avenues of participation and structures of accountability, the opportunities for failure abound, and outcomes are highly uncertain. Returns on democratization may be both unevenly distributed and slow to show themselves; as a structure of governance, democracy will likely prove more cumbersome than the alternatives. Guiseppe DiPalma notes that arriving at a working democracy requires not simply the proper raw materials, but considerable craftsmanship, and the mastery of the craftsman becomes that much more critical absent congruent elements of political culture to provide even indirect support. "When . . . countries arrive on the threshold of democracy without those structural or cultural qualities deemed important [for sustaining democracy], when [they] arrive under conditions of harried and divisive mobilization, then the task of crafting should be the more crucial and challenging. Whatever the historical trends, whatever the hard facts, the importance of human action in a difficult transition should not be underestimated."[6] The shape and durability of the outcome is a function, not only of advantageous contextual conditions, but of particular judgments made at particular junctures with more or less political skill.

The shapers of governance structures everywhere include the universal suspects of politics: old elite families, bourgeois industrialists, the military, sectarian groups and religious leaders, labor unions, and political parties. Although the salience of given players varies according to national history, the Maghribi countries of Tunisia, Algeria, and Morocco offer examples of the full panoply of actors and actions. The region has known reform, revolution, and stagnation; its era of twentieth-century independence opened on a newly formed republic, a revolutionary socialist state, and one of the world's oldest ruling monarchies. The prominence of such national leaders as Habib Bourguiba, Hassan II, and Houari Boumediene has tended to obscure the more ordinary and less visible effects of mobilization parties and the relatively quiet bargains struck by elites, but in the ongoing lives of their polities, these political forces have molded the patterns of contemporary political culture. Clientelism, factionalism, and governmental centrism have all helped shape the political process, building institutions and developing patterns that, if far from being to the satisfaction of all, have nevertheless resulted in a high degree of order and continuity. The dynamics of the political process as they have evolved over the past thirty years are explored in Chapters 3–6 of this book. At this point, it need simply be noted that, in the long view and by comparison either to sub-Saharan Africa or the eastward reaches of the Middle East, the three states of Morocco, Algeria, and Tunisia have been noteworthy for the upper hand they have kept over popular disruptions.

All the same, basic tensions have not dissipated, and neither have the problems of polity formation been fully resolved. On the contrary, the prospect of chronic economic difficulties has raised serious questions about Maghribi states' continued ability to satisfy their citizens, and the rise of Islamist ideology over the past two decades is indicative at very least that views differ as to how the polity might be organized. To a significant degree, Maghribi states consolidated their powers by embracing a welfare function. With the greater demands of a larger, more educated, and urbanized population and a concomitant scarcity of resources, however, the expectation of state strength has become a political liability. Yesterday's state functioned effectively with limited popular access, doling out services and subsidies where desirable or expedient and exercising political repression elsewhere. Today's state, with relatively limited resources, faces a fundamental challenge of participation. The old game leaves too many would-be players on the margin, threatening social cohesion. Total abandonment of established patterns threatens chaos, and statesmen do well to move with caution. Yet where the established political game enters another iteration of demand and unsatisfying response, perhaps with superficial modifications intended to placate marginalized players, the results are ever more disappointing. Maghribi statesmen today face the serious challenge of injecting flexibility and resilience into the institutions crafted a generation ago. The contemporary political challenge is to alter, without entirely scrapping, the rules of the game.

A conceptual distinction between metapolitics and relational politics points up the critical nature of the choices at hand.[7] *Relational politics* denotes the efforts of players within an established framework to affect a political outcome. These are the moves—advances, retreats, alliances, and compromises—that determine the distribution of political goods. The analysis of relational politics customarily assumes the basic stability of the social, economic, and institutional parameters within which players operate. That is, variation is expected within the formal and informal structures of a reasonably well-anchored political system; the terms of the struggle are uncontested and figure largely as background, contextual variables. Where events occur to undermine the efficacy of existing arrangements, those erstwhile contextual variables are brought center stage. *Metapolitics* refers to the political dynamics of efforts to set and alter the rules and parameters of political contests. Regime transformation necessarily involves alteration of the system itself and entails efforts to reset the operating political parameters. It is the nature of a transition to call into question old arrangements. In such periods, actors old and new seek to satisfy interests, carrying out the business of relational politics, but they are also engaged in efforts to establish "rules and procedures whose configuration will determine likely winners and losers in the future."[8] Transitions are more than just an old contest with new actors. To a significant degree, they engage energies in an effort to create a new political game.

Uprooting established patterns of political interactions and redirecting social energies is a daunting task. Inevitably, the attention of actors and observers alike is directed to formal structures—constitutions, parliaments, courts, and electoral systems. Formally articulated structures represent only the tip of the iceberg of politics, however, and they are difficult enough to change even with an expressed popular mandate. Informal patterns anchored in a society's political culture present an even greater challenge, insofar as their foundation and perpetuation are rarely examined by those enmeshed in them. Culture provides a social frame of reference, and as such it is commonly perceived as an extension of the natural order. Culture's power to orient energies is enhanced by the fact that it is reproduced without being articulated and thus remains unquestioned. The invisibility of patterns to those who operate within a culture—and even more so, the invisibility of their roots—leaves those patterns resistant to change. Structural forces work on culture as wind and water work on stone, but continuity is the lawful expectation of culture. Even revolutionary political change, or structural transformation, must eventually reconcile itself with patterns of socialization reproduced in small parochial units.[9] Appreciation in recent decades of the monumental proportions of the task of transformation has led many observers to doubt the probability, if not the possibility, of far-reaching political change in the direction of democratization in societies with a long history of authoritarian rule.

The power of political patterning notwithstanding, an impulse toward important political change is readily apparent in North Africa. As already noted, the rise and spread of Islamism across the Maghrib and the proliferation of political associations signal shifting, and sometimes contradictory, frameworks of political interaction. Change must be considered as more than hypothetical—without being inevitable. It has been argued that modernity ineluctably drives cultures toward tolerance and cultural flexibility, an adaptive response to the rapidity of change and recognition of the diversity imposed by technologies that have reduced cultural isolation.[10] To the extent that modernity is a ubiquitous social force, democracy—with the emphasis on form rather than content—appears more consonant with cultural flexibility than authoritarian structures. From that vantage, some have argued that democracy is the political form of choice, and of history.[11] In fact, nothing is less certain. Human responses at both personal and social levels often fly in the face of wisdom, and history. The crafting of democracy is fraught with uncertainties; opportunities to slip abound. However desirable, democratic forms do not simply appear. They must be worked with skill, and given the formidable difficulties of political engineering, democracy is far from assured as the product of current political demand. Indeed, there are few indications that those who now clamor for access to the structures of governance would, if in power themselves, be inclined to share that power. The rhetoric employed to contest monolithic structures of power opens up the possibility of democratizing change, but transformation is hardly guaranteed.

If democracy in its essence is a set of rules that leave open the question of political victory, how are such rules established? Who or what social groups have the capacity to direct structural transformation? In the Maghrib, social and political structures that might assist in the birthing of democratic rule are themselves weak or compromised. Ruling parties cling fiercely to their power; opposition parties are fragmented and weak. With few exceptions, the industrial bourgeoisie has no base independent of government. There is little history of pluralism; such associations as do exist steer carefully clear of politics. Labor unions, the notable exception, are dwarfed by political parties in Morocco and co-opted by central power structures in Algeria and Tunisia.

Among the conventional players, only the courts offer some promise. Through powers of adjudication, courts may ideally function as referees in the game of politics. That function turns on trust and good faith, however, and requires impartiality of the referee. The willingness of courts to accept evidence extracted under torture, or falsified testimony, compromises that requisite impartiality. Courts across the Maghrib are not universally compromised, but neither is the full independence of the judiciary established. In recent years, courts have begun to exercise their powers more fully, and over time they may be expected to play an important role in limiting arbitrary power. In August 1991, for example, a Moroccan court refused to convict Islamist students charged with petty theft and "insults to bureaucrats" (*outrage à fonctionnaire*) on grounds of insufficient evidence. With the government's blessing a few months later, the Algerian Constitutional Council struck down a provision of the 1991 electoral code allowing men to procure the vote(s) of their spouse(s). It remains that at the present juncture a court system that in the past has been compromised in the most critical cases cannot bear responsibility, ex nihilo, for the safeguarding of a democratic polity.

If the "who" of democratic transition is problematic, the "how" is no more obvious. Bargaining strategies have been suggested as one important avenue to structural reform. Recent experiences in Tunisia and Algeria, however, have failed to establish viable working rules of democratic procedure. Tunisia's 1988 National Pact, intended to oversee a transition to a democratic contest, was discredited within months. Islamists, included in the negotiation of the pact, were denied formal access to the electoral system, and stringent rules of candidacy exacerbated the problems of new parties trying to compete. The ruling party's complete sweep of the legislative contest in 1989 confirmed cynics in their belief that it did not intend to share power, and the once-celebrated pact faded from Tunisia's political landscape.

In Algeria, Prime Minister Sid Ahmad Ghozali's difficulty in late 1991 in selling parliament a package of electoral reforms that would credibly guarantee an open electoral contest further illustrates the problems inherent in bargaining among the elite as a path to democratizing reform. In an open political market, competition for spoils may well entail establishing rules for their distribution. However, where the outcome of an eventual contest is or appears to be embedded in those rules themselves, mistrust in the immediate term of the democratic intent of at least one important player may overshadow longer-term interest in opening up the political system. Bargaining strategies are unreliable as a route to open contest and may be as likely to sabotage democratization as to promote it.

Government-led liberalization seems no more trustworthy as a sure path to democracy. Liberalization may signal the need of an authoritarian regime to reach beyond the bounds of its coalition for additional support, but it may also simply be the means by which an authoritarian regime buys time for itself. Political succession, economic crisis, or manifest loss of legitimacy signaled by popular protest may provide the impetus for liberalizing measures intended to establish or bolster legitimacy. The political need for legitimacy cannot, however, be depended upon to sustain liberalization. Legitimacy is certainly useful to a regime, in that it reduces the need for coercive measures, but as Adam Przeworski notes, many regimes manage to establish and maintain a hold on power through fear, or the simple lack of alternatives.[12] Liberalization seemed critical to establish the legitimacy of Zine el Abidine Ben Ali's claim to power in the aftermath of the bloodless coup that removed Habib Bourguiba from office in 1987. In time, however, with the military and security apparatuses under firm control and any threat from the legal opposition minimized, political liberalization has become less compelling for the regime.

It is against this backdrop of increased demand for access to the political system and a mixed response from the regimes that hold the reins that the emergence of a North African human rights movement takes on political significance. Since the mid 1970s, an organized commitment to the protection and promotion of human rights has taken shape across the Maghrib. In the three countries of Morocco, Algeria, and Tunisia, six human rights groups now pressure their governments to exercise their authority within the bounds of law. The Tunisian League of Human Rights, founded in 1977, is in many regards the doyen of the Maghribi movement. It was not the first such group to appear, that title having been claimed by the Istiqlal Party's Moroccan League of Human Rights as early as 1972, but it was the first politically independent group. Political unrest shook Tunisia within a year of the league's founding, seriously testing the league's commitment to its cause in the face of risk to its own members. The league passed that test, and for several years was the only consistently audible Maghribi voice raised in defense of human rights and protesting at their violation. A Moroccan Association of Human Rights, initially affiliated with the Socialist Union of Popular Forces (USFP) was formed in 1979, but like the LMDH, it maintained a low profile. Three Algerian groups, since narrowed to a pair, joined the field in the mid 1980s. Their commitment, too, was tested by events of October 1988. Finally, the emergence of the politically independent Moroccan Organization of Human Rights in December 1988 dissociated human rights from partisan contest and in the process gave new purpose to Morocco's two party-affiliated organizations.

As watchdogs over the practices of their governments rather than as contestants for political gain, the Maghribi human rights groups have established themselves as important political players. By the mandate they have fashioned, they are seeking to change the rules of the game rather than to assure a given political outcome. To the extent that they resist engaging in direct political contest, relational politics, they free themselves to monitor, and shape, metapolitical forces. They play politics at a different level, but one that may be more germane, ultimately, to the development of democratic governance. In this region, which has neither folk tradition nor national historical tradition on which to draw for guidance through a transition from authoritarian rule, human rights groups have become political players of critical importance precisely because their single goal is to see the rules of the political game rewritten.

History will have to judge the measure of their success. This book can only document their efforts. The story of the Maghribi human rights movement is complex, and can be divorced neither from the context of local political struggles nor from the larger international framework through which it took shape. Nor, for that matter, can it be entirely extricated from the personal affiliations and rivalries of some of its central characters. Desire for political change of the sort advocated by rights groups is a matter of conscience, which is often born of accidentally acquired and morally troubling knowledge. There is a considerable leap from knowledge to action, however. This study is an attempt to understand the process by which individual knowledge is crystallized into political action and the elements that contribute, more or less explicitly, to calculated expectations of success.

In these introductory pages, I have argued that human rights groups challenge the rules of the political games across North Africa, and that in so doing they perform a "metapolitical" function. Their experience is a prism through which to view democratizing efforts across the Middle East, and, indeed, in other regions where private concerns have overshadowed public rules in political contests. The very existence of these groups represents a challenge to entrenched authority; their mere survival is worthy of note, and any appreciable impact they have had requires explanation.

Several factors have enhanced the efforts of human rights groups and have protected their members; in Chapter 2, readers are directed to the most important of these. Evaluating both the process of crafting structural change and the extent of change itself, however, demands closer attention to the contexts in which the human rights groups operate. Only with a baseline in mind can we appreciate either the objectives that are being pursued or the dialogue that has been opened with governments. Chapters 3–6 accordingly examine the underpinnings of political culture in the Maghrib and outline the frameworks of political games as they were historically developed and have been played across the Maghrib on a country-by-country basis. Chapter 7 traces the emergence of politically independent human rights groups in all three countries, while Chapters 8 and 9 consider the contemporary period more closely to explore the dynamics of their internal operations and interactions with the governments of the Maghrib. The story of Maghribi human rights groups would be incomplete, and an analysis of their political function would be seriously flawed, without attention to the role actors from beyond the Maghrib have played. Outside, international parties have helped protect human rights groups, and they have also brought their own pressures to bear on all of the governments of the Maghrib. In Chapter 10, the dynamics between individual groups and the governments whose practices they challenge are fitted within the context of what has been called "post-international politics." Public policy and political processes are no longer simply a matter of domestic concern in North Africa, assuming they ever were. Chapter 11, finally, assesses the net effect of all these pressures on political systems in the Maghrib.

The bulk of this book is about making and playing political games, which for some is effectively a matter of life and death. Political games are not easily created or undone, and the task of constructing a game fair to all players taxes even the most skillful and the most committed. It is thus important to reiterate that this is a book about efforts. The question of success is left to the end of the book, and beyond.

2 The Political Power of Human Rights

By content alone, the message of human rights groups directly confronts vested authority. It is noteworthy that in the West, the two principal human rights documents—the French Déclaration des droits de l'homme et du citoyen and the U.S. Bill of Rights—were drafted explicitly to limit the arbitrary powers of government. Both documents seek to protect individual liberties against the oppression of those who govern, and both assure due process of law for those accused of wrongdoing. So long as authority has effective control in a nondemocratic regime, it is difficult to imagine that such groups will be appreciated. In many ways, they present as direct an assault as abusive authority ever faces. As Jack Donnelly puts it, "Respecting human rights is extremely inconvenient for a government, even in the best of circumstances. And the less pure the motives of those in power, the more irksome human rights appear."[1]—And the more irksome groups that lobby for human rights appear, it might be added.

That such groups have survived, in operation, more than a decade is in itself a political development of significance in the Maghrib.[2] The North African human rights dossier includes socioeconomic concerns as well as a gamut of civil and political rights abuses, among them torture and ill-treatment, "disappearances," political imprisonment, fair trials, incommunicado *garde-à-vue* detention, and restrictions on freedoms of association and press. That activists may claim some success in advancing their cause is even more noteworthy and merits the attention of both scholars and policy makers.

The contribution of human rights groups to Maghrib politics stems directly from the historically unique position they occupy. They have been able to draw on protective resources that interest groups cannot so readily claim: a strong moral component, effective international support, and the ability to adopt political tactics that while maintaining their effectiveness minimizes their political threat to vested authorities. These unique shields have created a special place for human rights groups within the framework of national politics.

THE MORAL CLAIM

The basic texts from which human rights activists derive a mandate may be religious or secular in origin, but worldwide the fundamental argument by which they take up their charge is a normative one. Preambular clauses to principal human rights texts refer to natural rights and human dignity, enshrining an ideal of justice that incorporates equality and fairness in law. In international law, such texts arise from sources designated "general principles." While not recognized as a major source of international law, arguments from general principle have, for example, undergirded the legal imposition of United Nations sanctions against South Africa's apartheid regime. Retrospectively, they have been invoked to explain and justify the abolition of the international slave trade and traffic.

The principal human rights documents of our time, drafted in the aftermath of the Nazi holocaust, have clear moral origins. The Universal Declaration of Human Rights (UDHR), passed without dissenting vote by the UN General Assembly on December 10, 1948, justifies its creation in part as a reaction to the "barbarous acts which have outraged the conscience of mankind." Without specifying either a philosophical or a legal definition of "rights," the UDHR's thirty articles establish a common understanding of ideas and expectations about the relationship between governments and citizens and about the socioeconomic basis of human dignity. The two main treaties derived from the Declaration, the International Covenant on Civil and Political Rights (ICCPR) and the International Covenant on Economic, Social, and Cultural Rights (ICESCR), alternatively proclaim the rights of full participation in the political processes of state and government and elevate basic welfare needs to the status of rights. Rather than reflecting an existing Hobbesian reality, human rights instruments aim to create a new, more idealistic reality, setting "a common standard of achievement" by which the world is expected to abide. Inherent moral considerations and the claim to universality reduce human rights groups' risk of reprisals from hostile authority, even though immunity from persecution can never be guaranteed where fundamental rights are not fully protected by law. The limited protection enjoyed by human rights groups may not be fully reliable, but the appeal to principles beyond the narrow scope of self-interest does afford a certain liberty of speech and action. The appeal to principles, and by extension the moral power of human rights groups, is strengthened by the claim of universality. Because of the controversy it poses and its centrality to the work of North African human rights groups, the notion of universality must be treated at some length here.

Human rights texts—the UDHR and the international covenants—do not simply claim to be a moral guide for our times, an amalgam of worldwide normative standards. The UDHR lays broader claim to universality, applicable to "all members of the human family," "all peoples and all nations." Accession to the UN Charter entails acceptance of the UDHR, and members at least nominally pledge themselves to achieve universal respect for and observation of human rights and fundamental freedoms. That act is facilitated, it must be acknowledged, by the fact that the legal status of the Declaration alone is unclear. In consequence, states rarely stumble over it, and even the covenants are observed more by lip service than in practice. By the end of 1993, nearly two-thirds of the UN's 188 member nations had acceded to or ratified the two main covenants, which took force in 1976, but only 72 states had ratified the more constraining Optional Protocol, enabling the ICCPR's Human Rights Committee to receive and consider plaints from individual citizens of party states.

From the perspective of governments, tacit acknowledgment of the UDHR and even accession to principal treaties may hold little meaning, but for groups promoting respect for human rights, the existence of the UDHR and derivative treaties holds great significance. They establish, philosophically at least, the limits of sovereignty over questions of human rights. By the principle of universality, human rights can be considered as a collective good belonging not to a single nation but to the international family of humankind. If the "good" is seen not in terms of the state's own mission but as the collective welfare of humankind, national governments are shown to protect narrower interests—those of the state. Policies and practices that fall below standard invite censure at the least. A Lockean logic transposed on the international system might even suggest that a government failing to guarantee fundamental human rights has not earned legitimacy, so that it becomes the duty of a global citizenry to contest its rule. Such an outcome is, in fact, suggested by the language of the Universal Declaration: " . . . it is essential, if man is not to be compelled to have recourse, as a last resort, to rebellion against tyranny and oppression, that human rights should be protected by the rule of law."

The North African human rights groups at the center of this book and the governments under which they operate both accept the principle of universality. Were the contest over political structures and dynamics limited to those two sets of actors, the discussion of moral and legal underpinnings that lend strength to the human rights movement might well end here. The resurgence of Islam as a political force, however, along with continuing questions about the role of Islamic law and practice in everyday life, have engaged human rights groups in a broader debate that requires more extensive discussion.

A universalist view of human rights adopts the position that a single set of human rights principles applies to all societies, and that all governments are obliged to bring their laws and practices into conformity with those principles. That position is contested by relativists, who argue the multiplicity of acceptable human rights standards and see them as inevitable in a culturally diverse world. Critics of a universalist position point with justification to the fact that the UDHR's roots essentially lie in the Western tradition, and that at the time of its drafting, few of what are now known as states of the developing world were in a position to offer substantive input. A "universal" declaration composed today might arguably look very different from the one acclaimed forty years ago. At the June 1993 World Conference on Human Rights, in their final pronouncement, states unanimously reaffirmed the principle of universality and inseparability of rights, but not before several of them had registered counterconcerns about the preservation of sovereign control over domestic matters.

Human rights activists defend themselves against relativist arguments adduced both by scholars sensitive to charges of parochialism and nationalist actors with a stake in defending cultural patrimony. The argument of universal and/or absolute rights versus culturally relative standards is one of particular relevance in cultures with claim to Muslim heritage and the Shari'a tradition of law. It is indeed worth noting that Saudi Arabia was one of the eight UN members who in 1948 chose to abstain from the General Assembly vote on the UDHR.

Several scholars have recently addressed the intellectual opposition of universal and relativist positions and shed light on the underpinnings of the argument. Richard Falk, for example, notes that cultural relativists who orient themselves toward societal tradition, religious teachings, and the primacy of cultural settings implicitly or explicitly favor a view that cultural attitudes automatically deserve deference. Their defense of local practice generally overlooks elements that undergird repressive, dominating, and exploitative practices. At the same time, Falk is critical of "secular fundamentalists" conditioned by the European Enlightenment who promote a rational social and political order that by its nature includes a "vestigial distaste for any intrusion on the terrain of human rights by recourse to religion, tradition, and emotion."[3] Alison Renteln is likewise critical of universalist arguments that quickly slide into absolutism. They are, in her view, representations of thinly disguised ethnocentrism, "insofar as Western ideas are presumed to be ubiquitous."[4] She argues that neither the universality of rights nor their absolute nature can be inferred from a select number of documents of Western origin; valid arguments of universality depend instead on manifestations of similar principles in diverse cultural contexts.

Rhoda Howard has recently responded to this argument, noting with irony that if cultural standards are inferred from prevalent attitudes and practices, the West itself could not be said to endorse or respect human rights.[5] Human rights is a fairly young idea in Western political thought, and moreover, the notion of a monolithic "Western" culture is itself problematic. Properly speaking, contemporary human rights ideals come from two separate intellectual traditions in the West, and Western political history is replete with examples of human suffering occasioned by the blatant disregard of noble principles. Slavery and slave trade are only the most ignominious examples; the oppression of religious, racial, and ethnic minorities and the repression of those who advocated workers' rights, women's rights, or an alternative political doctrine are all part of Western history. Howard contends that efforts to reconcile modern human rights norms with cultural practices worldwide in order to establish universality are bound to fail. We do better, she argues, to acknowledge that ethical questions may legitimately be addressed, abstractly and philosophically, in a way that transcends the diversity of cultures.[6] Amplifying the argument and making a poignant appeal for cross-cultural application of the UDHR, Reza Bashari writes: "We should resist all impulses to mythologize authenticity. . . . Power, domination, and inequality are the issues."[7] His claim that "the insistence on the universality of human rights standards is a political demand for the protection of individuals in the contemporary world of the modern states and capitalist, market economies"[8] echoes Falk's suggestion that a largely fruitless debate could be resolved if human rights attention were to be focused squarely on human suffering and human "intolerables."[9]

In endorsing the notion of universality, human rights groups across the Maghrib have not felt compelled to surrender any claim to an Islamic heritage. To the contrary, they have sought to emphasize elements embedded in their culture that condemn "intolerables" and sanction the protection of human rights (*huquq al-insan*). They frequently note that the principle of mutability extends to Islamic law as to other legal systems. What distinguishes the Islamic tradition, and by extension politics in the Arabo-Muslim world, is the starting position that Shari'a is the speech of God rather than positive law, and that the corpus of religious law is inextricably linked to political practice. Within the framework of Islam, the ability to create new law is constrained, but Shari'a may be made relevant in a contemporary world through interpretation. Islamic law, like international law, derives from several sources. Most important is the Qur'an itself, the word revealed to the Prophet Muhammad from 610 to his death in 632. Originally maintained as an oral tradition, it was eventually preserved in written form. In addition, the Sunna (tradition) of the Prophet, preserved in collections of *hadith* (sayings) of the Prophet, served as a source of law, amplifying and expanding the limited legal principles set forth in the Qur'an. A variety of techniques were employed by the jurists of Islam to develop legal rules based on these sources. One of the most important of these was *qiyas*, or analogical reasoning. Solutions to legal problems that were subsequently ratified by a consensus, or *ijma'*, of legal scholars were regarded by most Muslims as definitive. The degree to which Muslims remained free to ignore the solutions worked out by the early jurists and to engage in independent interpretation of the sources (*ijtihad*) has been a matter of dispute in the course of Islamic legal history.

Following the Islamic legal tradition, "Islamic" human rights documents and texts that have proliferated since the promulgation of the UDHR in 1948 share the common approach of testing contemporary provisions and concepts against the Qur'an and Sunna or, alternatively, comparing and analyzing religious texts against each other to generate a body of Islamic "rights."[10] Islamic thought about human rights is developed strictly through deductive reasoning and as such stands in fundamental contrast to the Western tradition. It is important to recognize, however, that even within the framework of textual exegesis, there is room for substantial interpretation, and substantial discretion.[11] Scholars working within the tradition of Islam differ on such important rights-related issues as the status of the individual,[12] equality, and duty.[13] Moreover, with time there has been legal as well as social attrition of certain practices sanctioned by the holy writ. Slavery, for example, is permitted and governed by the Shari'a, but like Western states, even governments that have adopted Islamic law prohibit it today. Similarly, Ann Elizabeth Mayer notes that *jabr*, or forced marriage, is permitted by the Shari'a but was eliminated in the 1981 Universal Islamic Declaration of Human Rights. Article 19.i of that document, prepared under the auspices of the Islamic Council (itself affiliated with the conservative Muslim World League), provides that no one should be married against his or her own will.[14]

Within circles of Islamic scholars, the debate over *huquq al-insan* is fairly constrained, but in the arena of politics, possibilities multiply, and "essential" elements of Islam that transcend local custom are more difficult to identify. While every government of Muslims is theoretically obligated to implement the law of Islam,[15] and although some twenty-five countries label themselves Islamic, only a handful, in fact, claim to apply the Shari'a. Writing prior to the Iranian revolution, Michael Hudson noted:

> Today Saudi Arabia is the only major country where there is extensive practical application of the Shari'a, although in many other countries the Shari'a and the Muslim judges (*qadis*) govern matters of personal status. But there can be no doubt of the long-term historical trend; and in most countries the central state with its European-inspired law codes inexorably extends its authority, circumscribing the Shari'a in its traditional urban and settled strongholds and replacing tribal customary law predominant in the wilder regions of desert and mountain.[16]

If the *'ulama* (Muslim clerics) find it difficult to reconcile positive constitutional law, and particularly its human rights provisions, with the Shari'a, governing elites in the twentieth century have not shown the same difficulty. Even if they are increasingly careful to consult with clerics on policy matters,[17] several Arabo-Muslim states have of their own volition taken liberal positions with regard to international human rights law. The two principal human rights covenants have been ratified or acceded to by Afghanistan, Algeria, Egypt, Iran, Iraq, Jordan, Lebanon, Libya, Morocco, Sudan, Syria, and Tunisia. As an interesting measure of comparison, the United States, with whose legal tradition at least the ICCPR is more consonant, ratified that treaty only in 1992.

Beyond both government and theology lies society, with growing numbers of committed Islamists but an important secular segment as well. The prominent role of Islam in society and the entwining of theology and politics makes secularism publicly taboo (and thus more difficult to discern). A secular orientation in some circles is anathema, heresy that is not pronounced lightly. Secular Arabs may be overlooked because they speak guardedly of their personal beliefs, but their voices, too, must register in an account of the diverse thought of the Arabo-Muslim world. The words of one Tunisian woman, angry at the Tunisian League of Human Rights' internal compromise on the role of Islam, illustrates secular thinking that does not conform to deductive principles of Islamic thought: "Why should

I have to bow to Islam before I can assert my own rights as a human being?"[18] Without the anger, Reza Afshari expresses a similar sentiment:

> In defense of the human rights of millions of educated, secular, and modern Middle Easterners, I urge rejection of the dichotomy created between tradition and modern, between authentic and inauthentic Muslims. . . . I am aware that "human" in human rights has ceased to be the "other," it has become "me," and the experience of my life shared by thousands of men and women who have broken intellectually and emotionally with the past.[19]

The Middle East accommodates considerable diversity even within the religious tradition of Islam, and the fact of diversity takes intellectual precedence over any ideal of unity. As translated ideologically, unity does not represent a common denominator but instead substitutes a single line of thought for all others. Human rights activists contest such representation, as they dispute any claim of exclusionary rights to the legitimate interpretation of text and tradition. Cultural integrity, or essentialism, is as elusive in the Arabo-Muslim world as it is in any other of the world's many cultures. By its nature, culture is dynamic, and within the evolutionary political culture of the contemporary Middle East, adhesion to international human rights standards is one emerging element that deserves recognition. In the words of one Egyptian scholar, "The pressure for democratization, respect and expansion of human rights go hand in hand. The sentiment and voice of each reinforces the other. Together, these developments seem to be the basis of a new, though embryonic, Arab consensus."[20] The several dozen human rights groups in the Arab world have recognized the importance of universality for their efforts to limit arbitrary administration of power.

INTERNATIONAL CONNECTIONS

Human rights groups in nondemocratic societies are offered assistance in their efforts by their international counterparts and, to some extent, by the policy arms of democratic foreign governments. The impact of such support is not, of course, unequivocal. Excessive "support," especially when from politically unwelcome quarters, turns into "intervention" and can be used to discredit or isolate domestic groups. On the other hand, outside support can both strengthen local groups and effectively shield them from government reprisal. North African human rights groups have noticeably profited from outside support, but the story is not without complexity. It is examined closely in Chapter 10, but a number of elements that transcend the North African particulars may be set out here.

Several external factors affect the work of indigenous human rights groups, but none is more important than the development of a large and vocal worldwide human rights movement since the early 1970s. Both the geographic and intellectual footings of the international human rights movement are firmly planted in the West, but the vehicle of universality discussed above has allowed it to spread and take root even in classes and cultures that maintain a critical posture vis-à-vis the Western tradition. This movement is one element in what James Rosenau has labeled the *multicentric world*, a world comprising relatively equal actors, which today functions alongside and interacts with the Westphalian system of sovereign states. Within today's "global universe," states are constrained by responsibilities to protect state interests, but in the nonhierarchically structured world, a host of actors—ethnic groups, corporations, political parties, religious groups, peace groups—freely undertake international policy initiatives untroubled by concerns about sovereignty.[21] In assuming the role of human rights activists, individuals conceive of themselves as members of a global civil society. Their actions may involve or bypass the nation-state as a particular situation warrants.

The origins of the international human rights movement can be traced to Europe in the 1920s and the establishment of an International Federation of Human Rights Leagues (FIDH) to promote human rights ideals and combat abuses. In 1927 the Paris-based organization first proposed a world declaration of human rights, and although World War II interrupted its activities, the passage of the UDHR in 1948 gave it new purpose. Its sixty-five affiliates, including most of the North African groups,[22] work exclusively on issues in their own countries, but for more than twenty years the central organization has dispatched delegations to monitor elections, to investigate instances of abuse, and to observe political trials.

The FIDH's mission was complemented in 1961 by the creation a grass-roots organization that called itself Amnesty International (AI). Individuals from around the world joined "adoption groups" to work on behalf of individuals in other countries; because of practical concerns and a desire to foster international solidarity, the organization's rules prohibited them from addressing human rights abuses in their home countries. From London, AI ran campaigns and conducted research, and its reports early on won respect for their reliability and impartiality. The strength derived from an extensive membership base is more often overlooked, but better than any other indicator, it signals an internationally shared concern about human rights. The organization, which began in 1961 as a narrow group of European lawyers and public figures, now boasts a network of more than one million activists in 150 countries. From 1978 to 1993, the number of its building-block local groups increased from 2,000 to 8,000.[23]

AI's grassroots orientation, its charge to consider violations worldwide, and a restrictive mandate have enhanced its credibility, but have also limited its effectiveness in other regards. Over the past two decades, an entire constellation of groups has emerged—particularly in Europe and the United States—to fill the lacuna. An international register lists more than 1,700 organizations worldwide concerned in some measure with the international protection of human rights.[24] Some groups adopt the grassroots approach but concentrate their energies on a single country or region. Others organize concerned professionals—notably doctors and lawyers—to respond to urgent situations. Still others, including the International Commission of Jurists and the U.S.-based Watch Committees, send out investigative missions and issue reports, which often treat an array of human rights concerns broader than those addressed by AI. In addition to functionally specific human rights groups, numerous professional associations have in recent years created human rights committees or networks that take up cases of concern to their memberships, often by virtue of shared profession or religious belief.

Nearly all groups appeal to their members, or their readers, to make the voice of protest heard by offending governments.[25] The human rights foot soldiers marshaled into action by such organizations have made it their business to take note of and call the world's attention to government actions that contravene the spirit of the UDHR and the letter of its attendant ICCPR. It is difficult to measure their impact on human rights practices, although testimonies from former political prisoners over the past two decades suggest that governments are not impervious even to relatively insignificant citizen action—especially when the citizens in question are those of influential nations. Amnesty International frequently claims, via prisoner testimony, that the sheer volume of appeals can make a difference; in some countries protest letters are measured in centimeters.

For indigenous human rights groups, the international movement makes an important contextual contribution along what might be called an "exposure" dimension. Governments may vary in their relative immunity to international pressures, but no government seeks to advertise its human rights failings. In many cases, egregious abuses violate not only international standards, but domestic law as well. In the mid 1980s, a full third of the world's countries regularly and consistently tortured political detainees, despite the existence in many instances of domestic laws expressly forbidding the practice and threatening punishment for those who engaged in it.[26] In all cases, costs attach to a demonstrated record of human rights abuses, and only the extent and acceptability of those costs are in question. A human rights cause célèbre at very least puts a government at risk of international embarrassment; in some instances, well-publicized cases have inspired the imposition of more painful economic and political sanctions.

The international press serves as the primary vehicle through which human rights abuses by governments have been most publicly exposed, and there has been a noticeable increase in human rights reporting over the past decade. It is now commonplace in both the United States and Europe for major newspapers to run summary accounts of reports issued by international human rights watchdog groups with established credibility. The willingness of the press to print such stories must in some measure reflect both the credibility and stature of these organizations, but one must also surmise that the marked increase in such reporting is itself a function of the same public interest that has fed the membership base of international human rights organizations. Human rights stories are news in large part because there is a demonstrated interest among the readership.

The backdrop of direct pressure on governments by international human rights groups and indirect pressure through the dissemination mechanism of the international press has provided important, if intangible, support for domestic groups. International attention shines a spotlight on abuses; because its beams also illuminate domestic groups, governmental reprisal is at least made inconvenient. Local activists are treated as heroes and have in some prominent cases themselves been awarded regular access to the international press.

Attention from the international community provides a degree of moral support that is impossible to measure. Prominent international visitors seek out local activists and thereby elevate their status; links of communication forged with any number of international groups concerned about a particular situation may at times create confusion, but they also serve to reinforce local commitment. Few human rights activists are selfless saints, and attention from abroad may boost the egos of many, as it does the cause. The urgency of an international phone call may be sufficient to revive flagging energy, just as a timely report issued abroad may provide the missing impetus for local action. The importance assigned a situation by known and respected international activists in general fuels concern locally. Support of this nature cannot be quantified, but anecdotal evidence of its importance abounds. Equally immeasurable, but somewhat more tangible, is the assurance activists have that, in the event of trouble, their own cases will receive international attention. Several international human rights groups provide legal services and trial observers, and human rights activists in trouble can today count on full press coverage as well.

Whereas this backdrop of international human rights movement activity may have been negligible in the past, both numbers and information technology have made it much more important today. For indigenous human rights groups, it provides critical moral support and a sense of solidarity. More important, it keeps the spotlight trained both on the offenses themselves and on quarters where potential reprisals are likely.

Compounding the direct pressure by citizen groups and indirect pressure from the international press, foreign democratic governments have become more vocal about human rights issues. In a few prominent cases, in addition to less-consequential rhetoric, they have included human rights factors among their foreign policy decision-making criteria. Governmental endorsement of human rights concerns is rarely uncontroversial, for mindful of both domestic audiences and foreign policy issues, sovereignty-bound states are more opportunistic in their appeals than members of a global society who demand adherence to a single set of international standards. Underlying political motives may effectively discount the value of government measures, but even discounted, foreign governments' attention to human rights remains an important element in the array of international forces affecting the performance of domestic human rights groups.

Many governments incorporate reference to the safeguarding and promotion of human rights into their foreign policy rhetoric, but none has been more outspoken than that of the United States. Human rights was fully incorporated into U.S. foreign policy discourse only during the administration of President Jimmy Carter, but concern for human rights is embedded in the much older, if variable, U.S. foreign policy objective of promoting democratic values and democratic forms of government. For much of the twentieth century, democracy—in foreign policy application—has been seen in terms of political competition and political institutions, but there have also been explicit references to human rights. The Truman Doctrine, for example, which paired the goal of promoting democracy with that of maintaining and strengthening noncommunist governments in what was the first clear elaboration of containment policy,[27] included freedom of speech and religion, freedom from political repression, and guarantees of individual liberty among the criteria defining democracy. Although President Carter's decision to make human rights the hallmark of his foreign policy gave the concept new rhetorical life, in the aftermath of the Vietnam War, the U.S. Congress had itself begun to pay legislative attention to human rights in foreign policy. Congress had already in 1974 linked human rights performance to security assistance, and in 1978 it made consideration of rights performance mandatory in the aid allocation process.[28] Furthermore, in 1977 Congress created a Bureau of Human Rights and Humanitarian Affairs within the Department of State, and from 1985 on required all U.S. embassies to send regular reports back to Washington about torture. U.S. embassies now routinely designate an officer responsible for following human rights issues.

Critics frequently charge that the foreign policy commitment to human rights, like the broader goal of promoting democracy, is convenient for great powers and is used selectively. Even in the best of circumstances, such policies represent long-term, visionary goals, which inevitably take a back seat to more immediate foreign policy objectives. Despite the prominence of its rhetorical commitment, the Carter administration was never able to forge a coherent human rights policy, ironing out a workable relationship between the civil and political rights it sought to promote and often conflicting security and economic interests.[29] The Reagan and Bush administrations were not been inclined to try. Recent studies conclude that more general efforts to promote democracy have almost always failed, in large part owing to the conception of the policy itself. As Abraham Lowenthal notes, in the Latin American case, U.S. pro-democracy policies have arisen primarily as a function of U.S. politics—not of Latin American realities. "Enthusiasm for active democracy promotion has ebbed and flowed, and the inconstancy of U.S. policy has tended not only to erode the efficacy of U.S. policy but actually to undermine the conditions for democratic politics."[30]

Historical examples abound, not only of U.S. failure to promote democracy, but of actual detriment to existing democratic or democratizing regimes. Even as Washington has officially favored the installation of democracy, its intelligence branches have engaged in operations that by distorting local political forces have also undermined democratic processes and values.[31] In considering Latin American and southern European reaction to the promotion of democracy by the U.S. and western European governments, Laurence Whitehead concludes that most such efforts have been largely ineffective because in fact—particularly in the U.S. case—democracy runs counter to actual foreign policy objectives. He observes that

> one requirement of any genuine international support for democratization is that local actors must be given sufficient freedom of maneuver to act on their own behalf, and to establish their credentials as authentic groupings,

not "puppets" manipulated by external powers. This involves a self-denying ordinance by those external powers wishing to promote democracy. Such restraint may be particularly hard to achieve in countries where genuine progress toward democracy necessitates some clearcut break with a past pattern of power relations.[32]

Historical analyses reinforce the conclusion that in times of peace, outside forces have at best a secondary influence on democratization.

Attention to the manifest contradictions within democracy-promoting foreign policy can obscure more positive aspects of policies designed specifically to ensure protection of human rights. In the U.S. case at least, it is worth distinguishing between policy statements—reflecting the intent of a given presidential administration—and initiatives undertaken by Congress. Human rights positions adopted by both entities are vulnerable to charges of inconstancy and incoherence, but where the former must always be viewed as a function of state concerns to protect and promote sovereignty, the latter has more latitude to escape those constraints and is markedly more open to the influence of human rights lobbyists. The executive branch retains most responsibility for foreign policy, and with regards to most foreign appropriations, it effectively represents the interests of countries it seeks to favor. Congress, whose primary power is to check or alter—rather than initiate—foreign policy, may position itself to pose uncomfortable questions. David Forsythe's 1988 study of U.S. foreign policy making in the area of human rights documents the inherent contest between Congress and the executive branch and assesses congressional efforts to carry both the Carter and the Reagan administrations beyond their original intents with regards to human rights. The limits to congressional efforts undertaken from 1974 to 1984 are patently clear: despite the passage of three major pieces of legislation linking financial assistance to human rights performance, Congress was not able to assure full oversight of the law. Several human rights certifications required by Congress went unscrutinized; the legislature's own attention both to general human rights concerns and country-specific situations was erratic.

A comparison between paper and performance exposes its shortcomings, but all the same, the impact of congressional activism has not been negligible. Congress's most important influence has often been exercised as a veto. It revalued human rights when it rejected Ernest Lefever as the Reagan administration's nomination for head of the Human Rights Bureau, a man who in public statements had denigrated the importance of the rights that were to be his charge. Likewise, Congress acted to modify President Reagan's conduct of foreign policy on South Africa and a number of Latin American countries. Human rights law, even if its letter was not to be implemented, encouraged both policy makers and policy implementers to consider the linkages between human rights and economic assistance.

> Debate [within the foreign policy establishment] evolved over the form of the human rights policy and its linkage with other policies, not whether to have such a policy. This attitude was a clear change from the Kissinger period when human rights was largely regarded as a domestic issue, from the Carter period when many Foreign Service officers and some bureau heads regarded human rights as part of softheaded naïveté in world politics, and from the early Reagan days when high-ranking officials, including the president himself, wanted to substitute simple anticommunism for human rights concerns. Congress must be assigned credit for establishing and maintaining this redefinition of the U.S. foreign policy agenda from about 1973.[33]

The annual country reports on human rights practices have become the central reference point of official U.S. discourse on human rights. These reports are taken seriously by both the Congress and the national press when they are released each February in conjunction with the administration's proposed foreign aid budget, and the importance assigned them has contributed greatly to legitimating human rights in the U.S. foreign policy establishment. The process by which they came to occupy such a place of prominence points up the interchange between human rights groups and official policy makers and points as well to the means by which governments, despite the historical vagaries of democracy-promoting policies, can lend effective support to democratizing forces in other countries.

Congress first required human rights reports on countries proposed as recipients of U.S. security assistance as an amendment to the Foreign Assistance Act of 1961. Members' concerns were aired in 1973 congressional hearings prompted by Richard Nixon's and Henry Kissinger's regard for power politics and commensurate disregard for moral values.[34] The Kissinger State Department complied with congressional instructions only in a minimal sense. The directive was taken more seriously by Cyrus Vance, who in 1977 oversaw the State Department's first major attempt to collect and assemble relevant information from U.S. embassies around the world. Congress in the meantime had created the Bureau of Human Rights and Humanitarian Affairs within the Department of State and in 1980 its assistant secretary for human rights became responsible for annually compiling a comprehensive report on every member of the United Nations, and not simply on recipients or potential recipients of U.S. security assistance.[35] In the initial years of reporting, the Human Rights Bureau under

Patricia Derian's direction privately invited human rights groups to comment on the reports prior to their release. When Eliot Abrams became head of the bureau in the Reagan administration, the cooperative relationship stopped, and a consortium of private human rights groups began to publish, and distribute widely, their own critiques of the State Department country reports.[36] Following the Lefever nomination debacle, the House Foreign Affairs Subcommittee on Human Rights and International Organizations had in 1981 been wary enough of administration intent to issue its own critique of the State Department reports. It did not hesitate to hold hearings in scrutiny of the annual reports, or problematic sections of them; it became a regular practice to solicit independent testimony from private human rights groups and invite State Department officials to explain the compilation process or justify language.[37] By this process the State Department was forced to take the reports seriously. Even if the reports were never used to deny economic or security assistance, as had been the original legislative intent, veracity in reporting did become established as a legitimate demand of Congress. The reports had been extended to cover nonrecipients of aid—that is, the Soviet bloc countries—at the initiative of congressional conservatives who hoped to redirect bad press,[38] but by the mid 1980s, more attention to adversaries did not mean less for allies. The House Foreign Affairs Committee, with human rights groups, gradually saw to it that the unsightly records of friendly governments could not be whitewashed and forgotten.

With a basic norm of honesty in reporting established, and with the first modest reports eventually expanding to 1,500-page authoritative tomes, both the State Department, in issuing, and the U.S. Congress, in accepting, the annual report were on record as officially acknowledging egregious abuses by governments to whom they lent support. Government representatives on their own perhaps have little incentive to act in particular cases, but the human rights activists among their constituents constitute an increasingly vocal lobby, better informed and better organized than at any time in the past.[39] Human rights groups, focusing on just those cases where U.S. leverage was presumed greatest, asked congressional human rights leaders to put at least their pens where their mouths were. Even if Congress as a body was not willing to restrict aid allocations, individual members were ready to direct human rights inquiries through the State Department, draft their own letters to foreign governments, read statements into the *Congressional Record,* or circulate "Dear Colleague" letters to other members for signature. As holders of the national purse, Congress had implicit power at least to embarrass human rights offenders seeking

U.S. aid. Unlike most domestic programs, foreign aid is an orphan in the American political process; foreign governments frequently rely on paid agents to press their cases in Washington. Members of Congress face little political exposure in lodging protests against abuses, and they potentially gain the support of constituents.

If the U.S. Congress and foreign policy establishment have through these mechanisms accorded significant attention to international human rights abuses in recent years, they are not alone. Recently France under the presidency of François Mitterand has awarded considerable attention to human rights, recalling France's two-century commitment to the rights of man. Danielle Mitterand has lent further weight to that cause by presiding over a watchdog group known as France Libertés. In 1993, European states undertook revisions of the Lomé Convention, adding the weight of the European Community to the growing number of industrialized donor states that now link consideration of human rights issues to aid allocation. Scandinavian countries closely monitor the human rights performance of those to whom they extend development assistance, and Canada formally linked its aid programs to human rights in 1987. Japan, the world's largest donor, has also linked aid to human rights considerations, and at one point temporarily cut off aid to Burma for that reason.[40]

Given the manifest contradiction between lip service to promotion of democratic ideals and actual foreign policy behavior, actions underscoring the importance of respect for human rights may in fact do more to support the development of democracy than any of the more direct attempts to induce it. The cost to an individual politician may be slight, but the impact in an allied country of a human rights inquiry by an elected body or a prominent political leader can be significant. The directly expressed concern of both elected officials and foreign policy functionaries effectively legitimizes the concerns of domestic human rights groups, who in the local context are often politically marginalized.

SURVIVAL STRATEGIES

Action and recruitment strategies adopted by indigenous human rights groups constitute a third element that affects their survival and, by extension, their impact on democratization processes. Human rights groups have frequently escaped measures of repression directed at other political actors, and much of their good fortune can be attributed to choices of tactics and strategy. Whereas broad structural forces contribute to the formation of such groups, the day-to-day political parrying is orchestrated at the microlevel.

Microlevel political behavior has been relatively neglected by students of political upheaval, in part because data are difficult to access, but in part because structural explanations lend themselves more readily to empirical observations and in consequence are more immune to ad hoc explanations. The arguments against approaches that rely heavily on interpretation have been powerful ones, but they exclude researchers from arenas of political transaction that are especially important in understanding efforts at political transformation. Structural factors observable at a distance may delimit parameters of possible political developments under given historical conditions, but at most they constitute the setting, not the action.[41] Structural analyses have advanced our understanding of the causes of regime collapse, but class analysis and other forms of structural analysis provide fewer insights into the processes by which a polity is successfully guided toward democracy.[42]

How is democracy generated? Schoolchildren studying the physical world learn that it requires more energy to set an object in motion than to maintain it in motion. The construction of democracy requires effort and initiative; it involves commitment to values and institutions that may be culturally antithetical. Certainly the context cannot be ignored, but neither may the actions of individuals in key roles. Individuals are engaged in conscious choice, and individuals affect political outcomes. Just as they may act to maintain a status quo that affords them advantages, political elites may apply their energies to effecting change. The consciousness of political action should not be presumed, but neither is it to be precluded.

If the action of individuals is admitted in analysis, so must their impact be. Any situation requiring political decisions may be affected by the behavior of individuals. Even when acting within the bounds of rationality, individuals may alter an outcome by screening out information, or misinterpreting signals, or by simply managing to be in the right place at the right time, as a number of studies of foreign policy behavior have convincingly demonstrated.[43]

The role to be played by individuals is amplified in the relative absence of institutions or procedures that diminish the volume of a single voice. That fact undoubtedly accounts for the relatively greater prominence accorded to the study of individuals and small groups in the foreign policy realm. In situations where political institutions are themselves in question, choices made by elites in or out of power may take on great significance.

Likewise, the importance of political errors is magnified. Political mistakes may become blessings—or they may prove fatal. Errors of judgment contained in a limited context may afford an opportunity to reflect on, and correct, strategy in advance of encounter with subsequent challenges. Political behavior, like all human behavior, lends itself to learning, without guarantees that lessons will be mastered.

In many instances, human rights groups are aware of the impact, or potential impact, of their choices. Debates have been waged, for example, about the political advantage of opening as opposed to restricting membership. Modern communications technology and frequent travel facilitate contact between groups, who regularly share their perceptions of experiences to emulate or avoid. The menu of potential action is in large part influenced by the governing macropolitical situation, but selections from the menu are far from automatic. Engaged in efforts to bring about concrete changes, human rights groups devote considerable effort to planning strategies, conscious of implicit trade-offs and wary of the ramifications of their choices.

North African human rights groups have wrestled with a number of such choices, to be explored at length in subsequent chapters. In general terms, however, the strategy questions they have confronted, and sometimes revisited, may be grouped loosely into three categories. The first concerns an organizations's decisions about long-term goals and strategies. Long-term objectives help situate a group within the field of domestic political actors and necessarily affect its more immediate operations. All of the Maghribi groups have had to consider their role in local politics and their relationship with political parties. Party affiliation offers access to the scarce resource of established political organization but also extends the liability of compromised independence.

It might seem natural, or logical, for groups to set forth their long-term goals and address issues of ideological orientation at the initial stages of organization, but it has in fact been more common for North African human rights groups to attend to such issues only as they arise and threaten to inhibit activity or diminish effectiveness. The Tunisian League of Human Rights waited eight years before drafting a charter to delineate its philosophy and clarify its positions relative to the UDHR.

Tactical questions, a second set of strategy issues, have been of more immediate concern. In the short run, the methods by which human rights groups try to advance their causes have the potential to invite governmental reprisal and place members at risk. Such issues cannot be deferred. In broad terms, groups have had to decide whether to cooperate or confront abusive authority. Is potential harassment too high a price to pay for publicity to abuses? Is a "quiet" approach less alienating, and more effective anyway? How advisable is a public demonstration? Is it preferable to approach government officials with poignant, well-documented cases of abuse, or should public statements address only broad issues—torture, disappearance, judicial abuse—that leave the responsible authorities unidentified. Decisions that would seem straightforward matters of principle when viewed from a distance appear considerably more complex when considered in context. Debates are often extensive and trade-offs painfully clear. That groups within the Maghrib have made opposing tactical choices after carefully weighing arguments in light of the peculiarities of their own political reality points up the risks inherent in a blueprint approach to such decisions.

Questions about recruitment and membership have likewise received considerable attention within human rights groups. North African political associations in the twentieth century have tended to seek broad popular appeal, building a substantial membership base. Human rights groups have largely broken with this tradition, but not without debate. Groups are popularly reproached for their elite flavor, their distance from the masses. Group leaders in particular, however, are often conscious of the political advantages that come with a predominantly elite membership. With a professional membership base, human rights groups may find it easier to secure hearings for their concerns behind the closed doors of government. Social stature and perceived common class interests may also diminish the element of threat to authorities, leaving groups to function with greater liberty. In addition to concerns about the way they are perceived within government circles, human rights leaders have also wrestled with questions of internal cohesion and the possibility of police infiltration. Tensions between a recognized need to demonstrate political independence through a diverse membership base and the threat of organizational fissure or political co-optation are never more than temporarily resolved.

Questions of strategy compose a complex web, and many of the choices are interlocking. Membership restrictions have implications for potential action, as do an organization's publicly espoused goals. The importance of strategy cannot be overemphasized for groups that seek to challenge the established order: keeping out of trouble while essentially causing trouble requires careful choices. There are many slick surfaces to negotiate and numerous potential distractions; even without accounting for resistance on the part of a government in place, opportunities to fail abound. Even the possibility of success depends on careful choice.

CONCLUSION

North African human rights activists have garnered attention well beyond the significance of their numbers, and it is posited in this chapter that their political prominence cannot be attributed to any single factor. Rather, it is the combination of several forces—moral claims, international support, and tactical choices—that has amplified their voices, making them audible in the arena of public politics. I return to this argument, and fuller analysis of their role in politics and political transformation, in Part III of the book.

At this junction, however, it is important to note that human rights activists have not simply been heard: their message has also resonated within the range of North African political discourse. The fact that these human rights groups are situated within the local culture and address local concerns attaches meaning to their work beyond any specific changes in law or practice they might advocate. It also means that they cannot easily distance themselves from local political struggles. The analysis of both their effectiveness and their limitations is thus predicated upon an understanding of the local context, and that is the task addressed in Part II.

PART II

The North African Political Context

Every political situation presents ambiguities that allow alternative interpretations or predictions, and the art of political analysis requires attention to nuances that often leads to subtle choice in emphasis. Forces of change must be weighed against elements of continuity; factors that sustain or threaten dominant cultures and subcultures within a society must be identified and assessed, and the nature of relations between the state and those it would govern must be explored. Some elements in the analysis are inevitably downplayed, while others appear in relief, and when interest extends across several units, as in this study of the Maghrib, there is a further choice about the relative emphasis to be placed on differences and similarities.

States and societies across the Maghrib have much in common, but in preparation for closer examination of the Maghribi human rights groups, Part II of this book must emphasize national differences rather than commonalities. In each of the three national contexts, human rights groups have presented themselves as a voice of civil society; their efforts have been directed at altering the predominant configuration of relations between state and society. Both the goals they have adopted and the particular challenges they face are conditioned by national contexts, which are themselves shaped by historical experience. Morocco's well-anchored monarchy and aristocratic *makhzen* class provide a very different political context than does either deeply scarred Algeria, not yet recovered from the ravages of colonialism, or Tunisia, dominated by a single party and with a long history of external orientation.

To acknowledge the common cultural heritage while accentuating the uniqueness of national context, Part II opens with a discussion of the patriarchal authority relations prevalent across the region. Patriarchal relations have linked microsociety to polities, and patriarchal norms have bound the indigenous society, economy, and polity together into a patrimonial order. (It is the decline of this order, I shall later argue, that has fueled both the human rights and the Islamist movements across the Maghrib.) The shape of that order may vary, however, and subsequent chapters accordingly attend to historical experiences and patrimonial politics in the national context.

My intention in the separate chapters on Tunisia, Algeria, and Morocco is to describe power dynamics and political games in each of the national settings. Human rights groups insert themselves in the game of politics by challenging untrammeled state powers (or the power of individuals at the helm of state), and so the scope of those powers bears examination. Each chapter thus traces the historical rise of the state and centralized government structures and then turns to relations between government and governed. In recounting these histories, I have sought to capture the distinct flavor of each national context, and thus each chapter necessarily emphasizes different aspects of political experience and structures. Across the national histories, though, I have emphasized the decades of the 1950s and 1960s, because the moment of political independence from colonial rule afforded North African societies a unique opportunity to reshape dynamics within the polity. Political struggles in and around nationalist movements tinted the politics of the newly recognized states, and the working rules of political games were gradually put in place during the first decade after independence. Certain elements have, of course, been altered, but the structures that human rights groups began to challenge in the late 1970s were anchored in those first critical years. Part III of the book will locate human rights groups in their contemporary setting. Part II, in the meantime, elaborates the context from which they make strategic choices and lays the groundwork for understanding the role they play in the game of politics.

3 State and Society in the Maghrib

Across the Maghrib, the midcentury dawn of political independence rose on strong sentiments of optimism, moral rightness, and political omnipotence. The humiliation of colonial rule had ended, and independence set a historical marker that oriented observers and participants alike toward creation and change. Independence meant birth, or re-birth: national renewal. Scholars no less than statesmen subscribed to an ideology of programmed change, attributing little importance to patterns of social interaction established over long but less remarkable centuries. With independence, a page had been turned, the slate wiped clean. Progress and change were the leitmotifs of the times.

The promise of independence, unfortunately, proved short-lived. Within the span of a single decade, "progress" lost its magic ring, and across the Maghrib cracks began to appear in the new social edifice. Soon after independence, new divisions developed within Tunisia's Neo-Destour Party over the political role to be assumed by its labor affiliate, the General Union of Tunisian Workers (UGTT). Labor's influence was curtailed, and liberal economic policies were adopted, but admission of their failure in the mid 1960s led the Neo-Destour Party to alter its name to the Socialist Destourian Party (PSD) and adopt a program of socialism. To the west in Morocco, nationalist elites and the monarchy wrangled over a constitution that was finally promulgated in 1962, but whose life was short; in 1965, the king assumed full legislative and executive powers. Economic growth, meanwhile, stagnated. Algeria likewise suffered early political difficulties: the politically divisive rule of Ahmed Ben Bella was overturned in a 1965 coup that dissolved the National Assembly and installed Houari Boumediene as prime minister and minister of defense. Economic experiments with worker self-management were abandoned.

Like the earliest political frameworks, analytical models were forced to shift. Ahistorical models of modernization and social change, formulated during a period of historical rupture, had in time to face the tenacious problems of underdevelopment. Modernization models helped promote mobilization policies pursued by central governments but could not explain stagnating or deteriorating economic performance. With the benefit of hindsight, those models appear naïve, but the modernization and development school that had evolved within the social sciences in the 1950s must be seen as a product of its own time. The new political order issuing from World War II, combined with breathtaking advances in technology, left scholars, especially American scholars, predisposed to see change rather than continuity. Reflecting on the construction of modernization theory in the 1950s, Leonard Binder notes that a defining characteristic of the concept of modern culture was the valuation of change itself. The liberal development theory that prevailed at the time was fundamentally optimistic.[1] To scholars as well as to the policy makers they advised, change looked both desirable and easy. Social engineering seemed not nearly the monumental undertaking it now appears to be.

The emergence of what would become the dependency school in the mid 1960s redirected attention to more sobering historical experience, but historical experience of a particular kind. Beginning with André Gunder Frank's *Development of Underdevelopment*, dependency scholars sought to establish the adverse economic effects of international domination on national development, effects that continued and were renewed by mechanisms that survived the formal dénouement of colonial rule. The dependency view was elaborated in a number of geographical and historical settings. In *The Maghreb in the Modern World*, Samir Amin carried it to the Maghrib, analyzing the impact of the French colonial economy on North African society to frame the central question: can there be true political independence under conditions of economic dependency?[2] The concept of dependency was offered as an alternative to an analytical framework that had attributed the intractable problems of underdevelopment solely to the lack of resources and the disposition of a people, a model that made overarching change seem simple, a matter of will and determination. The dependency school reintroduced the historical dimension, but only insofar as it concerned international influence; it failed to subject local history and patterns to the same scrutiny. Dependency theorists thus provided an important corrective of the modernization model, but still left neglected the salience of patterns established locally. Dependency theory pointed to distortions imposed upon a local economy and the society in which it oper-

ates, without at the same time considering the enduring influence of locally rooted culture. Just as the cultural slate had not been wiped clean with
the arrival of independence, the impact of international forces, however
blustery, did not eradicate local patterns, and especially not those that were
either congruent with or conducive to its ends.

An international context of political and economic dominance has
surely stymied growth and development, exacerbating the problems inevitably faced by societies recovering from the ignominy of colonial rule. Attention has now shifted from problems of resource mobilization, which in
the first decade of development seemed most pressing, to structural difficulties that now seem chronic: food security, terms of trade, indebtedness.
The general prescriptive models popularized in earlier decades have all
come up short against these problems. International socialism, once held
out as a remedy for historical wrongs, has been discredited, as was the
naïve liberal model before it. Throughout the South, the politically engaged are increasingly inclined to hold their own leaders responsible for
enduring problems that in practice translate into widespread corruption, high unemployment, and striking disparities in wealth.[3] Whether or
not they fully account for the rigidities imposed by structures beyond the
control of any given leader or set of leaders, such sentiments underlie opposition movements across the Maghrib. They have fueled the Islamist
movement, as they have inspired the critiques of new liberals who see
democratic governance, with full participation and accountability under
the fair application of the law, as the only hope for satisfactory and equi-
table solutions to chronic difficulties.

Human rights groups have actively tried to reorient political structures
in the Maghrib, and it is important to recognize that the men and women
who direct them are not exogenous actors: they are products of the societies they seek to change, and work from within them. For that reason, if
for no other, it is imperative in studying the rise of such groups to take
stock of the prevailing political culture and to assess the nature of state-
society relations across the region. Attention must temporarily be directed
away from the groups themselves to the historical patterns of state-society
relations and the concepts that help elucidate them.

THE LEGACY OF PATRIARCHY

There have been numerous attempts by Westerners to describe Middle
Eastern culture, of which Maghribi society may be considered a part. Until
recent decades, many such efforts focused on cultural elements that to

Western sensitivities appeared exotic or premodern, and Middle Eastern scholars have understandably taken exception to them. Essentialist portraits of bedouin life or the "Arab mind," for example, gloss over enormous diversity across classes and other social divides and produce distortions that lend themselves to perjorative stereotypes. Edward Said has observed that such studies frequently reflect more about the writers and the audiences to which they appeal than they do about Middle Eastern society.[4]

The limited interest of this book precludes an analysis of Maghribi culture that covers a full range of issues and acknowledges important and abiding differences, yet the arguments I make in subsequent chapters require an understanding of cultural elements that undergird personal and arbitrary governance, which easily lends itself to human rights abuse. Force and the fear it engenders do help explain political behavior, and in Chapters 4–6, I describe the ways in which North African governments have fostered such fear to reduce or eliminate opposition. Fear alone, however, does not explain the tenacity of some political patterns and structures. Contemporary metapolitical struggles in the Maghrib raise questions about the nature of authority relations and prevalent social patterns that reinforce heteronomous attitudes, and human rights groups have been concerned with both the structures of governance and the patterns of authority embedded in society. In this chapter I examine elements of Maghribi society that facilitate the production and reproduction of personal rule.

The notion that most requires attention is that of patriarchy, which though economically outmoded continues to provide structure for social and political relations throughout the Maghrib. In this chapter I discuss the importance of patriarchal norms and structures in the daily lives of North Africans and argue that patterns anchored in the psyche and in microsociety support a political culture of patrimonialism, patronage, and personal rule.[5] At the outset, though, it is important to state several points that for many readers will be obvious. First, patriarchal patterning is far from exclusive to the Maghrib and the Middle East; moreover, within the Middle East its manifestation varies from state to state and among sectors of Arabo-Muslim society. The patterns I describe are not found to the same degree or in identical form across the three national contexts of the Maghrib or in all social strata, and they are but one aspect of social relations. Finally, choosing a verb tense within which to write comfortably about patriarchal structures is difficult, in that it is clear that many of the manifest forms are no longer prevalent, except perhaps in certain rural and relatively isolated milieux. Overuse of the present tense risks reifying stereotypes that, in particular, have not served North African women well.

At the same time, the patriarchal model continues to inform social practice, and full use of the past tense lends more credence to notions of social transformation than is warranted. These codicils notwithstanding, patriarchy both *was*, and in important ways *is*, a central part of North African politics.

North African patriarchy is often described foremost as a familial system of authority and is popularly discussed as a mechanism of male domination. Through the first half of this century, the family, a political entity as well as an economic and social unit, was ruled by the authority of the oldest male—great-grandfather, grandfather, paternal uncle, father, elder brother. All were subject to the authority of those whose rank in the age- and gender-based hierarchy exceeded their own, but the lower ranks in the hierarchy of power were reserved for women. Women were valued for affective qualities associated with their reproductive function, and were accepted in public roles only as they advanced in years and surrendered the reproductive capacity that defined them as female. As the Tunisian sociologist Abdelwahab Boudhiba put it, sons learned that their role was to command, to desire, to dominate; daughters were left to find subtle compensations within their devalued status.[6]

The treatment of patriarchy, or its conceptual cousin, patrilinearity, often focuses on gender relations and more specifically, gender-role disparity. To characterize patriarchy simply as a system of male domination does not, however, capture its full power in social relations. An alternative focus on the role of the individual more generally points up the contemporary political significance of patriarchal patterning in society. In this broader view, patriarchy can be seen as a heteronomous system of authority relations wherein all individuals learn to submit their own personal identity to that of the group—that is, the family. "In the traditional Maghribi family," writes the Algerian psychologist Hussain Bendahman, "the family group is the source and base of all definition of the individual; without the family, the individual would hardly exist. . . . It is by his family that [the individual] is defined, that his place is determined."[7] The functioning of the family as a unit requires that all members—and those most subordinate not the least—recognize the critical importance of the group. Social concerns take precedence over individual needs, giving rise to what has been called the "collective me."[8] The impact of a single member and the importance of personality within the unit is reduced. As Nefissa Zerdoumi notes, family members are perceived as roles before they are seen as persons. In some areas of the Maghrib, by virtue of continuing strong factional affiliation or the salience of an economy of affection, identity is a function of parentage; one is known, not by a name, but by a relationship—son, daughter, cousin of someone.[9]

No one, including adult males, is fully autonomous within the patriarchal system. In historical practice the system was notoriously oppressive for young brides, whose status rank was actively devalued, and who also, by patrilocal custom, relinquished at marriage the affective bonds that had protected them in their paternal homes.[10] In the consideration of overall authority relations, it is equally important to point out that men also suffer under a system that subjects the individual to the group and young to old. By virtue of social practices that daily set different age cohorts on separate paths, a son may escape his father's constant oversight, but many a younger son chafes under his older brother's harsh tutelage.

Even the power and independence of adult men are far from absolute. Adult male independence, first of all, is attenuated by the attachment of a son to his mother, which by force of affection exercises a certain power.[11] Male autonomy may be further reduced by father figures who continue to exert influence well into adulthood. Men as sons are not free from social constraints. Zerdoumi offers the general formula: "A son become adult must never let it appear that he has become the equal of his father. His behavior must be imprinted with reserve, self-control, humility." Finally, to secure respect as a man in patriarchal society, an adult man must impose restraint on himself. If children must be quiet and lower their heads before the man they address as *sidi*, the behavior of the father himself is equally constrained by images of patriarchal authority. A young Tunisian man offers his conception of a father:

> In our society, the father is the person we call head of the family (*rab*). . . .
> We expect the head to be tough. He's the one who carries the club, who carries the club in his hand to make everyone work [together]. . . . Of course, there's the factor of affection, because sometimes it happens that you will see a tear in the eyes of your father. You're surprised, and you say: how is it possible that a tear is falling from the eyes of the man who holds the club?[12]

Considerable attention has been paid to constraints imposed on women in patriarchal societies, but in North African society, the place of men is also a matter of social regard. It has become commonplace to observe that domestic space (the interior) is reserved for women. The exterior world has belonged to men; until recent decades women passed through public space, but they occupied it at the risk of their good reputations. In popular exposition, values have been readily attached to this division—women are *confined* to domestic space, whereas men have been *free* to circulate in public. In social fact, men have also also faced constraints: they have been exiled to the public spaces. They have not had autonomous choice over where they spend their time, for although it is rarely expressed this way, men have not been free to circulate in domestic space.[13] Again, Zerdoumi describes a social reality that the advent of television has only begun to change:

> For the man, the house is the place where he comes to unite with his wife and to eat the food prepared by women. . . . In this house, the man is not completely at ease, rather as though he were not at home. [The house] is the exclusive domain of women and it is not appropriate for a man to relax in their midst.[14]

These social practices mirror an equally important division of psychic space. In popular view, the male-controlled exterior world is a place where reason predominates; it is the realm of the conscious. In the same view, women, who enjoy fewer opportunities to develop the capacity to reason,[15] inhabit the disorderly world of emotions. Emotions—fear, sadness, anguish, pain, uncertainty, worry—are not easily shown by adult men, and when expressed imply a loss of virility. Men keep silent.[16] Patriarchal authority is purchased at the price of emotional needs.

I have already noted that as a pattern of relations that facilitates economic production, patriarchy has outlived its usefulness in the Maghribi context. As a function of the nature of production and the level of technology involved, the patriarch derived much of his power from control of an essentially family-based system of production. It was the patriarch who controlled most property, and thus its product. Governed by the father or grandfather, the patriarchal family was a unit of production and consumption: it was up to its head to arrange deals, manage property, and assign tasks.[17] In today's increasingly urban Maghribi society, much of the active work force is salaried, and even in the bazaar sector, family-based enterprises are decreasing in numbers and economic influence. Moreover, where housing availability permits, economically independent young couples express a clear preference for living as nuclear families.

Patriarchy, all the same, is not devoid of all functionality in the contemporary Maghrib. On the contrary, the patriarchal framework provides the basis for a system of social security, and what is of undoubtedly even greater importance, the emotional comfort of personal identity. Questions of identity are important in any society, but they take on added significance in societies where practices of socialization discourage questioning the established social order and even inferential reasoning. The importance of these issues in contemporary Maghribi culture is poignantly illustrated by the challenge to "think the unthinkable" offered by the political philosopher Mohammed Arkoun to his audience of North African intellectuals at a 1991 conference whose organizing question was "Does the Maghribi individual exist?"[18] To many, the price of surrendered autonomy is small by comparison to the benefits of social and emotional security afforded by the patriarchal framework. Some find the system constraining; others fear its decline and seek by all means to buttress it.

FROM PATRIARCHY TO PATRIMONIALISM

Political scientists developing the concept of political culture in the 1950s and 1960s observed congruence between patterns of authority found in microsociety and the public domain and commonly argued that the authority patterns lent support to political structures.[19] Their failure to account for political change, and general dissatisfaction with the modernization/development school, to which they were linked, led many to disregard insights that remain valuable. I argue in subsequent chapters that the North African human rights groups are in varying degrees working to change the patriarchal model and its hold on their lives, but at present we must examine its power. How is the enormous gap between the patriarchy of microsociety and centralized political authority bridged? In other words, what is the link between patriarchy and patrimonialism?

Culture's power is tempered by many factors, and its role in shaping behavior should not be overestimated. All the same, its role cannot be discounted. In establishing the locus of power and agency in the social unit rather than in the individual, heteronomous patterns of authority produced by patriarchal structures incline individuals to command subordinates and acquiesce to superiors. Resistance, or rupture, may create a way out of intolerable or undesirable situtions, but strategies that require bargaining or negotiation are more difficult, because less supported in common cultural patterns.

Beyond simple patterning, several political practices in the Maghrib help reinforce heteronomous norms and transfer them to political behavior. The political ideology embedded in popular Islam is one important means by which patriarchy is extended beyond the family and legitimized as a prevalent political form. In Morocco, of course, Islam is used to legitimize the monarchy through claimed blood ties to the Prophet that establish its king not only as a secular leader but as Prince of the Faithful. More basically, the very term *islam* means submission. The notion of God's will sets the parameters for human action by laying responsibility for basic social order, including fundamental inequalities, at God's feet. Man may act, but in the greater society as in the basic family unit, only within prescribed bounds. In an analysis of Moroccan practical ideology, Dale Eickelman identifies four concepts corollary to the central notion of God's will, *qudrat Allah*. Reason (*'qal*), an essentially masculine quality, allows men to discern intent in the actions of others, making possible effective social action and thereby reducing the uncertainties inherent in the social world. Likewise, the construction and maintenance of bonds of social obligation mandating reciprocation (*haqq*) serve to limit the arbitrariness of actions by those higher in the status hierarchy. Throughout the Maghrib, notions of propriety or deference (*hshumiya*) instilled in childhood help manage relations of social obligation, and in Morocco, when an intolerable social breach has been made, relations of obligation may be restored by what the Finnish anthropologist Edward Westermarck described as a "conditional curse" and what Eickelman has more generally labeled "compulsion" (*'ar*).[20] These social norms provide guidance for individual manipulation of, and maneuvering through, a social order the parameters of which are already basically set. They orient individuals away from questioning the hierarchical nature of the social order, and away as well from questioning the predisposition toward authoritarian politics.

Less perceptible is the power of symbols to bind a people to a polity and its leaders. M. E. Combs-Schilling, for example, argues that cultural rites steeped in Islamic tradition effectively renew allegiance to the Moroccan monarch, undergirding patriarchal relations and binding smaller social units to the polity. In Morocco, on the Feast of the Great Sacrifice (*'Id al-Kabir*), the observance of ritual blood sacrifice is inaugurated nationwide by the king. In a dramatic ceremony that conforms to a practice instituted by the 'Alawi dynasty in the seventeenth century A.D. (eleventh century A.H.), the king slaughters a ram on his nation's behalf. Simultaneously, in communal ceremonies throughout the country, male elders gathered in public squares perform the same rite, repeated later in their own homes. Combs-Schilling contends that the king's appropriation of this most important Islamic rite effectively pulls society together:

> It is, I submit, the most powerful ritual support of the Moroccan monarchy. It bolsters the king's legitimacy by having him perform the most dramatic action in which humans can engage for the most noble of purposes, the causing of earthly death in order to overcome the limits of earthly life, in order to connect with the divine.[21]

Through such well-articulated and deeply resonating ritual, the cultural system of Moroccan Islam integrates its humblest subjects into the political order.

Leaders without such compelling claims to legitimize their rule, and thus unable to manipulate potent symbols so effectively, resort more frequently to the metaphor of the nation as a family. Hisham Sharabi notes that within the Arab world, even revolutionary regimes have taken up the language of patriarchy, replacing the idea of class and class conflict with the "ideology of national unity and harmonious coexistence between classes under the benevolent rule of the Leader (father, patriarch)."[22] In the Maghrib, Tunisia's Habib Bourguiba appropriated the metaphor, first declaring himself father of the Neo-Destour and subsequently of all Tunisians.[23] Through such language, compatriots are reduced to children, and the way is paved for treating them as such—to be instructed and reproved by exhortation and punished for disloyalty. Where benevolence and patient instruction do not achieve the desired political ends, fear may accomplish the task. As children, today's Maghribi adults learned to quiet themselves and lower their heads before a father known as *sidi,* my lord. With transgressions severely punished, it is little surprise that love and respect for the father are tempered by fear.[24] In a region characterized by what Germaine Tillon has called "republics of cousins," there is much in the discourse and behavior of leaders to suggest that the familial model has been mapped fairly intact onto national political systems.[25]

Pervasive use of the family metaphor facilitates a particularistic view of the polity: through personal rule at the top of the hierarchy and patronage networks across society, public policy is made to serve private interests. Patronage systems cultivate dependence and carry heteronomous relationships beyond the family. They establish the basic requirement of patrimonial systems, the ability of a ruler to maintain authority through the distribution of favors. The clientelist dyad that is the basic unit of a patronage system is a personal, hierarchical relationship that effectively limits autonomy even as it promotes personal interests. In an immediate sense, clientelist connections appear to increase an individual's control over the social environment by permitting some degree of maneuverability. More broadly, however, patronage systems lock less powerful individuals into social mechanisms that, while responding to precise immediate needs, serve to elevate the status of the supplier. When the more powerful make excessive demands on their clients, the latter have recourse only to the weapons of the weak.[26] Patronage persists because it is an effective response mechanism, but it also reinforces ties to a system of dominance that bolsters the power of those who keep the gates. Where the state controls the pool of patronage, the fundamental dependence of ordinary individuals is shifted through political elites onto the state. Government offices serve as meeting rooms; an important dimension of "work" consists of oiling the wheels that make the networks function. Sharabi's indictment of public servants in the Arabic world is perhaps harsh, but it captures attitudes and practices not uncommon among officials in the Maghrib:

> For the typical bureaucrat, for instance, the workplace (one's office) is no more than an extension of the place of sociability and relaxation. There is little qualitative difference between what goes on in the office and what goes on in the salon, living room, or *diwan*. In all these places guests are received and entertained, coffee or tea served, and amiable conversation enjoyed at leisure. This is not just a pattern of local behavior, but an institutionally embodied and socially prevalent practice. Thus bureaucracy—in government, the military, education, business—projects a modernized exterior, but internally its structure is essentially patriarchal, animated by an elaborate system of personal relations, kinship, and patronage.[27]

Against the power and effectiveness of patronage networks, the corpus of recorded law appears almost beside the point. Where systems effectively turn on personal connections, law neither provides protection nor assures justice. The place that might otherwise be accorded to law is instead occupied by a single individual or by an executive council. In extreme form the polity is seen as an extension of the ruler, taking full precedence over rules and changing the power and authority of his office to suit the needs of the moment.[28] By force of the repressive apparatus at its disposal, the state may appear strong, but paradoxically, its frequent recourse to coercion betrays inherent instability.[29] Interpersonally, bonds of patronage may be compelling and the charisma of a personal ruler may inspire national pride. As the glue that holds a polity together, however, patronage and personal rule are seriously deficient, working more to undermine the state than to undergird it. Rather than loyalty to ideals or institutions, patronage systems cultivate loyalty only to the state's largess and leave it vulnerable to mass insurgence in times that are relatively lean.

CONCLUSION

North African scholars justifiably take exception to analysis that fails to account for important social differences that distinguish elites from the masses, intellectuals from the petite bourgeoisie, and urbanites in general from the more picturesque peasants and pastoralists in remote reaches of the region. Furthermore, citizens of each country resist confusion with their Maghribi neighbors. While patriarchal norms prevail across the Maghrib, in the late twentieth century, they affect university-educated Tunisian couples with active professional lives very differently than, for example, villagers in the rural communities of eastern Morocco. For the former, questioning patriarchal norms has become possible, if not entirely facile. Men are caught between the contrary goals of advancing their own interests and supporting their extended families; women complain of a double workday and report the stress of managing family obligations as well as professional responsibilities in a society where men's role within the domicile is minimized.[30] By contrast, the Moroccan peasants I take as example can barely articulate their concerns. For them, patriarchal norms structure the full range of social interactions and remain an unquestioned fixture of the social landscape.

At the microlevel, patriarchal frameworks vary according to particular circumstances within microsociety. In similar fashion, the translation of patriarchy into political structures that promote patronage and personal rule is molded and shaped by the particular national histories of North African polities. Although Maghribi countries generally share a common cultural heritage and for one brief historical moment were united under a single dynasty, historical events and enduring phenomena have shaped them in different if related fashion. Tunisia served as a North African point of entry for Phoenicians, Romans, Arabs, Byzantines, and Turks well before the period of modern French colonialism, and at numerous historical junctures experienced partial processes of cultural assimilation and homogenization. Morocco, furthest to the west and most impervious to outside influence, was effectively colonized for only thirty years. Algeria, by contrast, was declared an extension of the French patrimony. As its physical landscape today readily attests, there are few places there where French colonial culture did not write its name.

Human rights groups that emerged over the decade from 1977 to 1988 grew out of and had to respond to different national contexts. No analysis of the strategies they have pursued, the victories they have won, and the setbacks they have suffered can be divorced without cost from the political context in which they operate. As argued above, patriarchal social structures have helped shape, and continue to influence, contemporary political practice, albeit in somewhat different forms across the region. The heteronomous political culture they promote is inherently antithetical to ideals propounded by rights groups, who nevertheless are constrained to work within its bounds. The pervasiveness of patriarchal structures and the political culture they inform requires that efforts to explain the dynamics of the groups that call them into question be based upon an understanding of the nature of the existing political game and elements that affect its continuing evolution in each of the three national settings. It is to that task that we now turn.

4 Tunisia: Strong State, Strong Society

History spared independent Tunisia the pain of state-building. It did not, however, endow the newly self-governing nation with a well-rooted indigenous political culture of civil society. Under French colonial tutelage, Tunisians had participated in civic organizations as widely divergent as the scouts, the Women's International League for Peace and Freedom, Young Tunisians, the General Confederation of Workers (CGT), and, eventually, the General Union of Tunisian Workers (UGTT), but the political independence of such organizations was not well enough established to resist corporatist pressures exerted by the renewed Tunisian state. Threats to the nationalist movement's survival had amplified its concerns for unity, and with the acquisition of power at independence, long-standing political strategies were not readily set aside. Even so, as political autonomy came within grasp in the mid 1950s and leaders of the Neo-Destour grappled with the question of what would constitute a desirable political framework, a model of competitive democracy did gather some support. By the early 1960s, however, single-party rule was well entrenched, and electoral competition had become unthinkable. For most of his countrymen, moreover, President Habib Bourguiba had become indistinguishable from the state. Indeed, Bourguiba promoted this view. To a journalist's question about Tunisia's political system he reportedly exploded, "What system? I am the system!"[1]

Progressively over Bourguiba's thirty-year rule, those who did not share his views or belong to his party were excluded from effective political participation. The party that initially had promised to school citizens in democratic forms, encouraging rational discussion and constructive criticism,[2] was reduced to a mouthpiece for directives issuing from the presidential palace at Carthage. The legislature was patently ineffective, and local party cells only offered Tunisian men a chance to sound off harmlessly. Over time, more and more Tunisians became disaffected with the regime and the socioeconomic measures it pressed; by the mid 1980s, a sizable segment of the population felt that Tunisian policies bore little relationship to Tunisian culture, and that the state served only a well-connected few. Tunisian society revealed its own strength in the form of a clandestine Islamist political movement, which managed to flourish despite concerted policies of repression.

Bourguiba's thirty-first and final year in power was a reign of chaos and terror marked by erratic cabinet shuffling and the arrest and detention of thousands of Islamists. When in November 1987 Prime Minister Zine el Abidine Ben Ali orchestrated a coup that with little effort toppled the aging and enfeebled Bourguiba, Tunisians heaved a collective sigh of relief. The coup was publicly justified by Article 57 of the Constitution, which provided for transfer of state powers to the prime minister in the event of the president's incapacity, and a statement to that effect by seven of the country's leading physicians (including Bourguiba's own) was paraded at home and abroad. The rhetorical importance accorded to the legality of the transition did more than enhance perceptions of the new regime's legitimacy. It raised popular hopes that the impartiality of law might replace the vagaries of personal rule.

Few of those hopes have been fully met. Liberalizing legal measures proposed by Ben Ali's new government and adopted by a revitalized legislature in 1988 were followed just three years later by a new campaign of repression directed at the Islamists, who had still not been admitted to the formal political arena, but who nevertheless stubbornly refused to go away. The political game established at independence remained largely intact, and the dynamics of state-society relations in contemporary Tunisia continue to be shaped by patterns that evolved in the early years after independence. During that time the central state apparatus anchored itself firmly, and subsequent efforts to chip away at its powers have met with only limited success. The Tunisian state remains the strongest in North Africa, but the vicissitudes of personal rule have weakened its ability to meet political challenges, and the discordant voice of society has grown stronger. Before we turn to the implicit contest, the state itself, and the dynamics by which it came to serve patrimonial interests, must be examined more closely.

THE ORIGINS OF A STRONG STATE

The Tunisian state was born well before abrogation of the treaties of 1881–83 recognizing the French protectorate allowed it to govern independent of colonial oversight. Following six centuries of military dominion by a succession of Arab and Berber dynasties, the preliminary work of state-building had been launched in the thirteenth century with the rise of the Hafsid dynasty. The Morocco-based al-Murabitin (Almoravids) had in the twelfth century A.D. successfully united the entire Maghrib, but in 1227 A.D. the descendants of a local governor, ʿAbd al-Wahid ibn Abi Hafs, successfully claimed dominion over the territory known as Ifriqiya (Africa). In the early years of their rule, the Hafsids encouraged Andalusian Muslims fleeing Spain to resettle in the territory. They put the refugees' renowned craftsmanship and technical skills to good use in extensive public works projects that revitalized the city of Tunis. New fortifications were erected, the first consulates were established, and the university attached to the Zaytuna mosque acquired a reputation throughout the Islamic world as an important center of instruction in Maliki jurisprudence. Successive generations of Hafsid rulers relied on Arab nomads to consolidate their political hold and rewarded their service with land grants (*iqtas*) to tribal leaders. The more stable economic base provided by the grants strengthened the Arabs' social position and allowed their influence to grow. Arab tribal shaykhs came to represent the Tunis government, Arabic emerged as the dominant language, and cultural distinctions that divided Arabs and autochthonous Berbers gradually faded. By the time of the dynasty's collapse in 1534, the eastern part of Ifriqiya had become Tunisia—the land of Tunis—and its people Tunisians.[3]

More than 150 years elapsed before the Ottoman Turks, who succeeded the Hafsids, began to mold the emergent nation into a bona fide state. Early Ottoman rulers were locked in internal political struggles that spared little attention for state-building. Only when administrative leaders (*beys*) established firm control over rival military commanders (*deys*) in the early eighteenth century did the Ottoman occupiers actively set about integrating Turkish rule and Tunisian society. The beys further Arabized the bureaucracy and incorporated local religious leaders into decision-making structures. International commerce remained pivotal to the economy, although domestic production for export replaced corsair activity as a principal source of revenue. When an economic downturn toward the end of the eighteenth century dangerously inflated international debt and threatened to expose the Tunisian state to European designs, the Hussainid beys tried to strengthen their position through internal reforms. Ahmad Pasha (1837–55) took the process furthest, inducting Tunisian conscripts into his army, and investing local notables in the administration through the practice of tax farming.[4] Beylical resolve to escape European domination inspired measures that despite disrupting the prosperity of Tunisian society had the effect of shaping the Ottoman garrison into a Tunisian state.

In the end, beylical efforts to maintain independence were not successful. Economic investments did not yield sufficient returns; increased taxes led to uprisings in the countryside; and political reforms, including a brief constitutional experiment and the creation of an appointed legislative body, failed to engage the elite adequately.[5] By 1869, Tunisia was effectively in European financial receivership, a poor position from which to stave off imperial designs. From 1873 to 1877, Muhammad al-Sadiq Bey's prime minister, Khayr al-Din Pasha, undertook fiscal, educational, and governmental reforms to avert a European takeover; it was only a matter of time, though, before the French, installed in Algeria since 1830, found the requisite excuse to move their troops eastward. A protectorate formally created in 1883 established the French resident general and what would soon become a substantial French bureaucracy as the effective governors of Tunisia. All the same, to encourage popular compliance with their regime, the new French masters left local structures intact (including the beylical throne), and over the next seventy years, the colonial power saw clear interest in strengthening the state. French colonists were the direct beneficiaries of efforts to develop the political and economic infrastructure, but Tunisia at independence would as a result inherit a territorial state with a relatively elaborate administration. Colonial policies extended the state's effective control beyond urban centers and eventually replaced kinship networks with territorial links as the basis of governance.

The first French effort was to organize a standing army, financial exigencies having obliged the bey to reduce the number of his troops in 1863. The French took a census in 1883 and under the provisions of an 1860 law that had fallen into disuse began drafting conscripts soon thereafter. The draft assured the French-run state's monopoly of force and at the same time allowed the state to extend its presence to the hinterland. Although residents of Tunis and sons of notables could be exempted from service, military recruitment was systematized; upon discharge, military pensions and other benefits assured reintegration of soldiers into civil society.[6] Social control was otherwise assured by the extension of beylical administrative offices and by the creation of technical services within the state bureaucracy. Administrative duties that once had fallen to tribal leaders were by the turn of the century assigned on the basis of territorial districts. Public infrastructure and social services were overseen by offices within the Prime Ministry and under complete control of the French; they further oriented Tunisians toward the impersonal state and away from kinship ties.

Lisa Anderson notes that administrative reform, in addition to further-
ing social control, played a critical role in the process of colonial land acquisition. As part of their work to delimit administrative boundaries, colonial
administrators also began establishing title to land in efforts to clarify and
expand the real estate market.[7] Basic elements of the Tunisian customary
land-tenure system were overturned when colonial policies redefined *mulk*
lands (fully alienable private property), restricted pasturage rights, and
oversaw the sale of domain lands previously distributed as revocable land
grants. Only clearly identified communal lands (*arsh*) and inalienable
lands (*habus*), set aside in trust for the benefit of religious foundations or
as the indivisible property of private families, continued to enjoy limited
protection.[8] In the process of expanding the supply of alienable property
available to settlers, French policies also destroyed established patterns of
transhumant pastoralism and led to the gradual replacement of the traditional sharecropping contract with seasonal wage labor. Both village solidarity and tribal social structures were consequently undermined, and the
authority of central political forces was reinforced.[9]

By the time Tunisia was granted independence in 1956, a process of
political development spread over seven centuries had equipped the monarchy with all the elements of a modern state. A centralized administration
levied taxes and its representatives were well integrated throughout the
territory. Colonial interests had also seen to it that the central government
established its right to monopolize force, recruiting and regulating police
powers. Both the policies and the institutions of the protectorate had, however, been oriented to the needs of the colonial power. It was left to the
newly independent government, reborn as a republic in 1957, to take the
reins of state institutions and political mechanisms and redirect them to
serve the interests and respond to the demands of the Tunisian people.

CO-OPTING THE STATE:
THE POLITICS OF PERSONAL RULE

It was only in a technical sense that the French transferred the reins of
state to Lamine Bey in 1955. Bourgeois merchants, artisans, community
leaders, and certain 'ulama—most of them from Tunis—had formed the
Destour (Constitution) party in the 1920s to call for modest political reforms. By the end of that decade, they had been joined by a class of young
professionals, many of them from the coastal Sahel region and most of
them educated in France, who were interested in more radical reforms. In
1934 the young professionals broke away from the Destour (subsequently

identified as the Vieux, or Old, Destour) to head a nationalist party, the Neo-Destour, that would call for increasing Tunisia's autonomy and ultimately secure independence. The lawyer and journalist Habib Bourguiba was recognized as the Neo-Destour's leader, although responsibility for the movement was shared within an expansive circle of associates and Bourguiba himself spent many of the years between 1934 and 1955 as a prisoner of the French. For more than two years a nationalist militia (*fellagha*) waged a guerrilla war of raids and selective attacks against French colonists, and despite pressures from equally militant settlers, France wearied of the struggle. The French prime minister, Pierre Mendès-France, opened negotiations in July 1954, and from house arrest in France, Bourguiba served as chief adviser to the Tunisian negotiators. Recognizing the critical role he played, the French released him to participate more fully in the final, most sensitive stages of the talks.

Even before arrangements for the transfer of power were complete, the nationalist movement under Bourguiba's aegis began to appropriate institutions that had served the colonial power and the Ottoman beys before them. It helped that while the ex-prisoner Bourguiba was fêted as a visiting statesman in France, the ruling bey was thoroughly ignored. Unlike his predecessor, Moncef Bey, whose avowed nationalism had won him popular appreciation rarely enjoyed by a bey, Lamine Bey had been a more or less willing tool of the French since his installation in 1943. By the mid 1950s, even that power base had eroded. With accords for internal autonomy concluded, in 1955 the shift of real power was apparent to all, and the bey increasingly found himself bowing to pressures from the Neo-Destour.[10] At their behest, he promulgated a series of decrees that sealed his own fate by vesting the right and power to choose the nature of future governance in a "Constituent Assembly."

What followed is well known. Newly enfranchised Tunisians elected a Constituent Assembly in March 1956 and with great fanfare acclaimed Bourguiba as their president. With the Neo-Destour's blessing a few weeks later, Bourguiba accepted the bey's invitation to form a government and assumed the office of prime minister. In July the following year, the assembly voted unanimously to depose the monarch, declaring Tunisia a republic. Habib Bourguiba was designated temporary head of state, a position solidified in 1959 when by provisions of the new Constitution, he was formally elected president. Already by that time, however, Bourguiba had come to embody the state. His hold on power, reinforced by a 1974 decision to name him president for life, remained strong up through his forcible removal from office in 1987.

However familiar, the chronicle of the transition from protectorate to republic bears reexamination. It was in this period that the rules that would govern state-society relations were drafted and the format of independent Tunisia's political game were established. A close look at the transition sheds light on the process by which the political system came to be dominated by a single individual and at the same time redirects attention to those shut out of power. Some of those opposed to Bourguiba were eliminated, and others were integrated into modern Tunisian society. Still others retreated to nurse their wounds, without surrendering the animosity they bore Habib Bouguiba and the Neo-Destour. This first political battle established basic divisions within Tunisian politics, which in turn inform contemporary social movements and will help clarify the political role eventually played by the Tunisian League of Human Rights.

Both to set the immediate stage and to anticipate enduring social divisions, it is important to establish that in 1955, Bourguiba's hold on the nationalist movement was not uncontested. Through Bourguiba's intermittent years in prison or exile, the Neo-Destour had developed alternative leadership structures. From nearly the time of its formal inception in 1934, Salah Ben Youssef, a politically astute young lawyer from the island of Djerba, played a pivotal role in the shadow party. A French policy of repression in 1938 generally succeeded in dismantling the Neo-Destour, and after Bourguiba exchanged police surveillance for exile to Cairo in 1945, it was Ben Youssef who, together with Mongi Slim, reassembled the party structure.[11] Ben Youssef's ties to Djerban merchants helped him build the Tunisian Union of Crafts and Commerce (UTAC) and the General Union of Tunisian Farmers (UGAT); by 1947 he had become the party's real "patron."[12] He collaborated closely with Bourguiba until 1954, but by the late 1940s a personal rivalry between the two nationalist leaders was already apparent. In 1948 they worked out a compromise that was approved despite procedural objections by delegates to the party congress: Ben Youssef would remain the Neo-Destour's secretary-general, and Bourguiba would become its president. With competition from three vice presidents, Bourguiba—still in Cairo—was marginalized within the party. Fears of being altogether excluded appear to have motivated Bourguiba's return to Tunisia in September 1949,[13] and through the spring of 1950 he made concerted efforts to consolidate his own support. For different reasons, both the weakened bey and the French preferred Bouguiba to Ben Youssef, and Bourguiba finally secured the decisive edge over his rival by making himself indispensable in negotiations for internal autonomy.[14]

In retrospect it is apparent that the political contest between Habib

Bourguiba and Ben Youssef had been largely decided by late 1955, but widespread criticism of the autonomy protocols signed in June provided Ben Youssef with fuel for his final drive to control the nationalist movement. It also heightened Bouguiba's insecurity. Historical accounts have stressed Ben Youssef's opportunism and his ultimate defeat,[15] but the resonance of his Arab nationalism and Islamic rhetoric among large segments of the population is equally noteworthy. More than ten thousand people came to a meeting called by Ben Youssef on October 15, 1955, to protest his ouster from the Neo-Destour's political bureau a few days before. Ben Youssef had given a fiery speech denouncing the autonomy accords at the Zaytuna mosque on October 7, and the next day the Neo-Destour's political bureau quietly convened. Bahi Ladgham, who was influential as a party stalwart but also critical of the accords, was absent. Ben Youssef, apparently, was not invited.[16] When party delegates, pressured by their leadership, confirmed Ben Youssef's expulsion at their congress in Sfax a few weeks later, twenty thousand Tunisians rallied to his support at the Géo André Stadium in Tunis and chanted slogans invoking a *jihad* against the French.[17] About one-third of the Neo-Destour cells had been seen as pro-Youssef prior to the Sfax congress,[18] and particularly in Youssefist strongholds in the south and in Tunis, the rupture within the party was not easily mended. In response to Ben Youssef's appeal, hundreds of *fellaghas* again resorted to arms, and only intervention by the French in a Tunisia nominally autonomous in its internal affairs staved off civil war in 1956. Even so, the rebellion inspired by Ben Youssef eventually claimed more than twice as many lives as had been lost during the two years of armed struggle against the French sanctioned by the Neo-Destour.[19] Prominent Youssefist dissidents were eventually captured, tried, and in many cases executed. Salah Ben Youssef, who had escaped to Libya in January 1956, was himself assassinated in 1963. The Neo-Destour emerged intact from the internecine struggle between two gifted leaders, but apparent disloyalties were not forgotten, or forgiven, as policies were hammered out in the new republic.

The Ben Youssef affair signifies the emergence of an important social fissure, but the orchestration of his ouster also points to an emerging practice of procedural manipulations that signaled the beginnings of personal rule. Already in 1949, party members had met formally to complain about Bourguiba's proclivity to issue orders that bypassed the party hierarchy.[20] The highly irregular vote to expel Ben Youssef was only the first such move by a regime that came to rely on extraformal mechanisms to achieve political ends. Such actions would mark the period of transition and generally characterize periods of difficulty faced by the republic over the next thirty years. Political norms that undergirded a patrimonial view of the state developed in four distinct aspects of the political process. Electoral rules helped fuse party and state, reinforcing the family metaphor and the authority of the "father" at the structure's apex, discussed in Chapter 3. Both the legislature and the courts were stripped of their independence, and as they were curbed, checks on presidential power were removed. Finally, the state developed police powers to serve in extremis. Even with Ben Ali's new government in 1987, the working rules that had been crafted three decades before would prove difficult to dislodge.

Electoral Rules

Tunisia prior to 1956 did not have a history of electoral process. Members of the legislative body established by the short-lived 1861 Constitution were appointed directly by the bey. Within the Neo-Destour, electoral procedures had generally been informal and consensual, despite sophisticated by-laws. The electoral procedures established shortly after the internal autonomy accords had been concluded anchored themselves well, however, and came firmly to establish who would be allowed to play the political game. In January 1956, Bourguiba personally—and with little prior consultation—pressured the bey to promulgate an electoral law setting up a system of straight majority list voting intended to produce a strong government. Voters within a district would effectively choose among lists of candidates assembled by different parties or independents without the possibility of *panachage*, combining candidates from the various lists. The system not only guaranteed Neo-Destour domination; from the start, the winner-take-all rules also eliminated even symbolic representation by party opponents and independents. The measure displeased many both on the basis of its content and for the manner in which it had been decided. Those in the opposition—including communists, remnants of the Vieux Destour, and most important, Youssefists—had argued for a proportional allocation of Assembly seats based on the distribution of votes across the lists, as had independents and many within the Neo-Destour itself. Neo-Destour leaders, for their part, were disturbed that Bourguiba had bypassed them to work out an essentially private deal with the bey.

As elections neared, the Neo-Destour formulated a national front that incorporated its affiliates as interest groups within the party. Candidate lists were drawn up by party chiefs after consultation with leaders of the UGTT, UTAC, and UNAT. Despite the odds, the Communist Party ran lists in two of the eighteen electoral districts, as did a group of independents in one district. In most circumscriptions, opponents of the Neo-Destour could only express their discontent by nonparticipation—which they did in Tunis and the Youssefist stronghold of Djerba.[21]

When municipal elections were held a year later, both independent lists and *panachage* were permitted. Once again the Neo-Destour swept the elections, but in this round victory was not so complete. Officially sanctioned slates were contested in several municipal districts, often by individuals who simply wanted to unseat a local clique. In three districts independents won a straight majority, but their victory was short-lived. To mitigate political and administrative confusion, the central government soon replaced the independent councils.[22] At neither grassroots nor higher levels was the party prepared to accept pluralism.

Opposition parties would soon be altogether outlawed. In the early 1980s, they were allowed a cautious return, but the Neo-Destour (by then known as the Destourian Socialist Party, or PSD) still proved unwilling to share power. The results of the nominally contested legislative elections of 1984 were flagrantly falsified, and the PSD's stranglehold on the legislature, and the greater political system, was maintained.

Ben Ali's overthrow of Bourguiba did not in any way alter this aspect of the political game. Despite great fanfare about pluralism and the proliferation of parties in the first two years of his rule, the 1989 legislative elections delivered a blow to all who had hoped for significant change. Electoral reforms promulgated in 1988 essentially maintained the system intact: candidates were to be elected by district slates, and all candidates were required to obtain a signature indicating exclusive support (*parrainage*) from seventy-five local voters. Small parties found it difficult even to field a slate of candidates, and where such hurdles were cleared, the winner-take-all rules of straight-list voting virtually excluded opposition. Thus while Islamists running as independents in some districts garnered as much as 30 percent of the popular vote, once again all seats were claimed by the Destourian Party, renamed the Democratic Constitutional Rally (RCD) in 1988.

Widespread disaffection with a new political game that yielded results identical to the old led to a second set of reforms in 1993. Within a National Assembly expanded by 22 seats, 144 deputies would be elected on the basis of a straight majority list from 25 district-level slates—thus preserving the winner-take-all aspects of the election. The 19 remaining seats would be distributed among parties that did not win a clear majority, in proportion to their share of the popular vote. In this way, the Tunisian Parliament in March 1994 was opened to opposition parties: the MDS seated ten deputies; the Ettajdid Movement (formerly the Tunisian Communist Party) won four deputies; the Union of Democratic Unionists (UDU), three; and the Party of Popular Unity (PUP), two.

For most of independent Tunisia's history, political leaders have not been able to conceive of opposition and contest as a positive process; "opponents" have effectively been excluded or incorporated into centralized political structures. Doubting the capacity of the new governmental edifice to withstand centrifugal pressures, early leaders did not allow the discourse of divergent interests, competition, and conflict to develop within independent Tunisia. That heritage was carried forward, and the result at the level of electoral procedure has been a fixed game. Of the 1956 electoral outcome, the pro-Youssefist daily *As Sabah* commented with bitterness: "The results were those known by everyone, in Paris and in Tunis, weeks in advance. This campaign was an artifice."[23] The same could be written, with little more commentary, of every election over the following thirty-three years. The elections of March 1994 opened the door to parliamentary pluralism, but as will be discussed below, they did not give access to the largest segment of Tunisian oppositionists. Moreover, the legal requirement that a presidential candidate have the *parrainage* of deputies or mayors effectively precluded competition for the presidency.

Tunisia's electoral barriers did more than exclude opponents of the regime and limit the choice of president and the composition of parliament: by limiting competition over several decades, they promoted fusion of party and state. Reforms enacted in 1958 made party structures parallel with new administrative offices, and in the process they also abolished the most representative, and the most politically independent, structures within the Destour Party. By the end of the 1950s, administrative and party structures were both subjected to hierarchical control, and Bourguiba, as president and head of state, dominated both. The absence of electoral competition assured his ability to control all the political players, which he did with shrewd insight into personality and position. Those who failed to follow his prescriptions were simply removed from office, perhaps to be reintegrated into the higher echelons as time passed and circumstances altered.[24] At the top level, players were rarely left in one place long enough to build up a personally loyal clientele, although from 1968 to the end of their marriage in 1986, Wassila Bourguiba exercised increasing influence. Many top officials owed primary loyalty to her, to the extent that Sophie Bessis and Souhayr Belhassen suggest that she was in fact, if not in title, Tunisia's vice president. Bourguiba sought and heeded her advice, but there were times when concern about Wassila's growing influence itself motivated reshuffling.[25] In a political game of musical chairs, cabinet members who managed to develop independent followings were soon transferred to new posts, and new clienteles. Alternatively, a budding rival's own lieutenants were removed from positions of power or politically discredited. The party's political bureau was not as easily controlled as the cabinet, but by frequently shuffling the cabinet, Bourguiba also weakened the political bureau. Bureau members who lost important government portfolios also lost their clients, and no one was allowed to forget that power bases were constructed at Bourguiba's pleasure and discretion.

Despite the fact that Ben Ali arrived in office raising high the standard of reform, the system of governance that Clement Moore dubbed "presidential monarchy" has largely survived the transition. Early analyses praised the new president for his apparent willingness to delegate responsibility to technically competent cabinet members and predicted a greater sharing of power. Several years into his rule, however, little appears to have been changed. As a military officer, Ben Ali had been prohibited from belonging to a party, and his footing within the PSD was far from secure. Like his predecessor, he soon took decisive measures to anchor himself within the party structures and thereby reduce the party's importance as a potentially independent political actor. Some 80 percent of the 2,500 delegates to the party's 1988 Congress of Healing were newcomers, and Ben Ali personally selected 122 of the central committee's 200 members even before the congress convened. Moreover, Ben Ali accepted the party's presidency, while at the same time the seat traditionally reserved for the party's secretary-general was quietly removed from the presidential cabinet.

Within the administration, cabinet shuffles continued. Ben Ali consulted regularly with his ministers, who were indeed expected to master their portfolios, but as time went by he appeared to rely more and more heavily on an informal coterie of advisers and involved family members in the affairs of state. Executive decisions are generally attributed to Ben Ali; the name of his prime minister is rarely heard.[26]

Limiting the Legislature

The legislature established by the 1959 Constitution might theoretically have limited presidential powers, but a series of formal and informal decisions made from 1956 to 1959 ensured that that body would play a limited role in Tunisian politics. The right to a legislature that could limit the erstwhile untrammeled powers of the bey had been one of the principal elements in the nationalist program, and the story of how that goal came to be abandoned is integrally related to the rooting of patrimonial politics in independent Tunisia. Although prior to independence there was some talk of establishing a republic, the nationalist movement was formally committed to retaining the monarchy, with powers limited by a constitution. For the first full year of the Constituent Assembly's deliberations, a constitutional monarchy was the model on which most projections of the new government rested. In late spring, a subtle shift in rhetoric appeared, and by early summer, Bourguiba was regularly and vociferously attacking the bey and the beylical throne. In July the Neo-Destour's political bureau laid plans to depose the monarch. On July 25 the party orchestrated a full day of assembly speeches denouncing royal shortcomings, culminating in Bourguiba's own two-hour tirade declaiming the lassitudes and treason of the Hussein dynasty. The decision followed swiftly: deputies voted to depose Lamine Bey and unanimously declared a republic. Nearly as quickly, they acclaimed Bourguiba as temporary president. As acting head of state, Bourguiba claimed all of the bey's executive and legislative powers. He replaced the bey's council of ministers with a cabinet responsible only to himself and nipped in the bud any dynamic legislative role envisioned by the Constituent Assembly. The assembly was steered away from debates and voting on government policies to the more restrictive role of constitution making, and under Bourguiba's guidance the first draft of that document was revised to limit the role of an eventual legislature. Early drafts of the Constitution envisioned a legislature in permanent session and endowed with the exclusive right to legislate. Investigative committees would furthermore have empowered the legislature to require explanations of the executive. The text finally approved in 1959 decidedly shifted power to the presidency. The legislature retained some ability to draft laws, but by constitutional mandate the president's legislative projects were assigned priority. The proposed "legislative committees" were dropped in the final draft, and the assembly's own regular sessions were to be limited to six months. For his part, the president acquired commensurate powers to legislate by decree when the assembly was not in session.

Moore describes at length the role played by the legislature in its early years. Because deputies to the National Assembly represented all the various interest groups incorporated into the Destourian family, party discipline was not automatically assured. Nevertheless, most measures received near-unanimous support, and some of the most heated debates concerned form and procedure rather than content. One early contest, for example, was over deputies' refusal to ratify ten decrees as a package rather than as separate measures.[27] In subsequent years the legislature reviewed some matters more carefully, but its role remained an advisory one. Virtually no legislation proposed by the presidency was rejected, and virtually no measures were initiated by the lawmakers themselves.

The legislature has historically offered no check on the presidency; indeed, by its default the executive has been strengthened. As prime minister—even before acceding to the new republic's presidency—Bourguiba began to wield the bey's old powers. His most celebrated and far-reaching pieces of legislation were all enacted by decree. Within weeks of assuming the prime ministry, he had taken steps toward bringing religion under the state's control, abolishing the politically compromised administrative structure that oversaw *habus* lands. By the time the monarchy was formally overthrown in July 1957, Tunisia's new ruler had abolished religious courts, under a liberal Code of Personal Status women had been granted the franchise as well as extensive rights in family law, and the practice of *habus* was altogether abolished. In 1958, the religious establishment sustained another serious blow when the university attached to the Zaytuna mosque was absorbed into the secular university system, leaving most of its 500 faculty members and 16,000 students without a clearly defined place in the educational system.

To be sure, Bourguiba consulted with his principal allies on legislative initiatives, especially those likely to be controversial. A master of political maneuver, he usually managed to secure at least the acquiescence of subordinates, and in some prominent instances he delayed promulgating a controversial edict until, through carefully cultivated debts of loyalty, he had assured the support of pivotal figures. It is doubtful whether many of the legal provisions held out by liberals today as *acquis* (literally, "gains") would have ever been realized without reliance on such tactics. Nevertheless, they came at the price of potential checks on the power vested in the presidency. The implicit social contract held no guarantees of shared power, a working rule that has not been altered since 1956.

During Bourguiba's rule, the National Assembly was less a place of political confrontation than a forum for the president to address the nation,[28] and under Ben Ali that basic pattern has not been altered. A flurry of reform legislation was enacted during the first two years of the new government, but the legislature's own role was minimal. Ad hoc commissions were appointed to draft legislation, which were submitted to the legislature for consideration only after basic approval by the government. In subsequent years, government ministers have regularly briefed the legislature and entertained questions, particularly in times of crisis, but the top-down flow of information and initiative has been restored. Only the annual budget consideration provokes extensive review and discussion, but even there the parliamentary function has been primarily one of review. Moreover, tight party control over the legislative process has assured not simply passage but unanimity on important measures. Thus as discussed in Chapter 9, a 1992 revision of the law of association that critically affected the functioning of the Tunisian League of Human Rights was approved unanimously despite extensive discussions in the halls of the legislature and much popular protest. Parliament has been largely peripheral to the political process, and in consequence, many deputies treat their responsibilities lightly: in 1990 the passage of several measures was held up for lack of a quorum.[29]

Police Powers

Policies inaugurated by Bourguiba promoted modernism and progress, but the fact that they also effectively punished those who had resisted was a political reality not lost on observers. What could not be accomplished directly by decree or through the promise of an extensive patronage system was achieved by coercion. Shortly after the 1955 rupture between Bourguiba and Ben Youssef, the Neo-Destour created an anti-Youssefist militia known as "committees of vigilance," relying on them and UGTT dockworkers to assure security at the party's Sfax congress.[30] In addition to the 1963 murder of Ben Youssef, popularly believed to have been carried out on his orders, Bourguiba is reported to have considered at least one assassination during the twenty years of his fight for independence.[31]

Two police units were created shortly after independence to separately maintain control over urban and rural areas, but in 1967 after incidents that followed the Arab-Israeli Six-Day War, these were brought together under a single Office of National Security, housed in the Ministry of the Interior. The National Guard (gendarmerie) continues to serve security purposes, particularly with regard to counterinsurgency, but its responsibilities more prominently include the patrolling of the country's highways and emergency response functions. The National Security Force (Sûreté national, or SN), on the other hand, is primarily charged with maintaining public order. As it was originally configured, the SN was a decentralized organization, and its units were responsible to the governorates to which they were assigned. By the mid 1980s, the locus of their control had shifted, and the chain of command traced more directly back to the SN director, who at the time was General Zine el-Abidine Ben Ali.[32]

Ben Ali had previously served as SN chief from 1977 to 1980, but was reassigned as ambassador to Poland as punishment for having failed to abort a January 1980 attack by Libyan-trained Tunisian commandos in the southern town of Gafsa. In 1984, following riots that spread across the country to protest price hikes in basic commodities, he was reappointed to his old post. By 1986, he had additionally acquired control of the National Guard and the ministerial post itself. As the final campaign of repression under Bourguiba's rule gathered steam, no one intervened in the chain of command between the general director of the national police force and the president himself.[33]

Bourguiba had limited the mandate of earlier interior ministers, most of whom in addition served only a few years, and over the years, Ben Ali was allowed to accumulate more power than any single individual. (Within the greater political framework, the potential threat posed by a politically neutral officer appeared limited.) As director of the SN, Ben Ali oversaw not only the recognized national security police, but also two auxiliary forces concerned with riot control and intelligence. Each of these two specially trained forces, the Public Order Brigade and the plainclothes Office of Territorial Security, have participated in the arrest and detention of political opponents. Many have claimed they were tortured while held in the SN cells in the Ministry of the Interior.[34]

A Dependent Judiciary

A cast of legality was lent to fundamentally authoritarian political postures through the courts. It had been the clear intent of the Constitutent Assembly to create a judiciary that was both independent and critical of the executive branch, balancing powers within the state. The 1959 Constitution provided for a council of state to arbitrate disputes between individuals and the administration, and in particular "those cases where the Administration is accused of exceeding its authority,"[35] but it never materialized. In fact, the judiciary had been compromised well before the Constitution was promulgated.

Tunisia's first political trial, brought before a specially created High Court, opened even before the end of 1956. Tunisia's independent government first experienced the inconvenience of established legal procedure when confronted with the question of how to bring Youssefist rebels to intended justice. Virulent verbal attacks on Youssefists throughout 1956 left little doubt about the outcome sought and Bourguiba's unwillingness to tolerate adverse judgments from the courts. A significant problem was posed, however, in that the first Tunisian minister of justice from the Neo-Destour had been none other than Salah Ben Youssef.[36] In consequence, the loyalty of the judiciary to Bourguiba could not be assured. The thorny problem was resolved by creating a special court and staffing it with new judges—most of whom had no legal experience, and one of whom was illiterate.[37] In two mass trials, the court convicted 113 Youssefists charged with plotting against state security, sentencing several of them to death.

In 1957, the Law of Ill-Gotten Gains and the Law of National Indignity extended the High Court's charge to include any person accused of having "collaborated" with the regime. The laws were applied broadly—to civil servants who had profited from their public offices, to the beylical family, to participants in regional and municipal councils, to anyone who had worked in the protectorate's security, press, or information services, and to anyone who had "directly or indirectly" aided protectorate authorities. Convictions were won with little regard for legal procedures and no possibility of appeal. By the time the Constitution was ratified, Tunisia had been purged of its old elite classes; the bey was destitute not only of legal powers but of money.

In subsequent years, as the target of repression shifted from "collaborators" to students and professors, Ba'thists, workers and trade unionists, and eventually Islamists, political trials were heard before military tribunals or a court of state security created in 1968. In time, many of the nonviolent political crimes prosecuted by the state came to be of an increasingly personal nature. In ten of the twenty-four mass trials held from 1973 to 1981, the defendants were charged with "defaming the head of state" or "attacking the dignity of the head of state." In 1979 two defendants were sent to prison for writing slogans on a statue of the president of the republic.[38]

When Ben Ali assumed office in 1987, his decision to abolish the state security court brought him much positive press. Strictly speaking, however, the state has retained judicial tools that escape close scrutiny. Military tribunals, which in certain grave instances may be used to try civilians, have generally held their proceedings in secret.[39] Civil courts, too, in prominent instances have failed to meet international standards of fair trial. In 1989 the secretary-general of the Popular Unity Party accused vigilante groups associated with the police of vandalizing property belonging to his party's leaders and was in turn charged with defaming the head of state. At the trial, his attorney presented evidence of police collaboration and was herself arrested and incarcerated for spreading false news, inciting unrest, and defaming the security forces.[40] That story bears striking resemblance to a 1961 case in which a distinguished attorney was sentenced to three months of farm prison and suspended from the bar for having made a derogatory comment about a municipality on his way out of the courtroom.[41]

One after another, political choices made in the period immediately following independence all served to undermine civil society and the rule of law. In and of themselves, few of the decisions were political anomalies or reprehensible, but in concert they acted to promote the effects of personal rule. Writing of Bourguiba's first year in office, Bessis and Belhassen observe:

> Bourguiba [was] more than president of the [beylical cabinet]. Even while the Constituent Assembly was discussing the creation of a constitutional monarchy in Tunisia, he appeared more and more the exclusive source of power and legitimacy. . . . His tours of the interior of the country were surrounded with ceremony, which soon became immutable: the [streets of] cities and villages he crossed were lined with little girls in fancy clothes welcoming him with bouquets of flowers. He was beginning to be a "father."[42]

Political improvisations set precedents, and precedents in turn evolved into patterns. Although at his own arrival in power, Ben Ali could depend on none of the charisma, the nationalist history, or even the party ties that had undergirded Bourguiba's reign, the political game had acquired a force of its own. Instead of personal attributes, Ben Ali has relied on his extensive connections with the vast security network to assure control and stability, even as he promotes the notion of democracy, and the institutions that might reduce presidential power remain underdeveloped.

THE MEANING OF OPPOSITION

Under Bourguiba's leadership, the Neo-Destour's commitment to "total unity through total organization"[43] left little room for pluralistic expression. Not everyone, obviously, accepted this formula. Some within the Neo-Destour had hoped quite openly that Ben Youssef would succeed in creating a second party, if only to introduce a measure of political competition. Even with the eventual elimination of Ben Youssef and the suppression of his followers, there might have been a viable opposition party in the early years of Tunisian independence. No sooner than had the ink dried on the Tunisia's formal declaration of independence than a significant division developed within the ranks of the nationalist movement. Throughout the independence struggle, trade unionists had worked closely with the Neo-Destour, and the UGTT leader Ferhat Hached had shared many of Bourguiba's political convictions. Hached was assassinated by a French resistance organization in 1952, however, and his successor, Ahmad Ben Salah, sought political autonomy for the union. Neo-Destour leaders encouraged a scission within the UGTT to protect nationalist unity and successfully isolated Ben Salah. After independence the party threw its weight behind a splinter group led by Habib Achour, and when the remnant UGTT had largely replaced Ben Salah and his supporters within its own leadership ranks, the two groups were rejoined. The new UGTT leadership was granted a certain liberty of action, in exchange for which it accepted a political role subordinate to the party. The vigorous trade union movement, which in the mid 1950s had boasted 150,000 members, amounting to half of the formal work force, was politically moribund just a decade later. Not only had workers' benefits declined relative to the cost of living but their political clout had been harnessed.[44]

In the meantime, Ben Salah's star had risen again. When early policies of economic liberalism were declared a failure in 1961, he was returned from erstwhile disgrace to head up economic planning. As director of a superministry, he embarked Tunisia on a program of cooperatization that proved as disastrous in political terms as it was disappointing in economic ones. In 1969, following popular protest, Ben Salah was fired, and this time he was tried for treason as well. His forced departure from Tunisian politics offered a new lease of life to Achour and the UGTT, which again began to press a political agenda. After 1970, strikes took place with increasing frequency, particularly in the 1974–77 period as the economic situation deteriorated. A new cabinet formed in December 1977 toughened the government's stance toward the union and inspired plans for Tunisia's first general strike since independence. Tensions were fueled in January by the arrest of a regional UGTT official critical of prevailing politics and by Achour's resignation from the PSD's Political Bureau. In the mêlée that ensued, more than 1,000 union members—including Achour and other prominent leaders—were arrested.

Shortly before the 1981 legislative elections, the rift between the party and the union, and between Bourguiba and Achour, was temporarily patched up. Achour was released from prison, and by a narrow vote the UGTT agreed to run on a PSD ticket in the elections. The price tag of the new "unity," however, was rivalry and fractiousness within the UGTT. In Achour's absence, the union had elected a new secretary-general, more left-leaning than Achour, and Achour's return proved divisive. Problems were only exacerbated by the discomfort of the twenty-seven UGTT candidates elected to the National Assembly and under pressure to support governmental programs to which their union was opposed.

It was an announced increase in the price of bread rather than direct labor conflict that inspired widespread political violence in January 1984. Within weeks, however, the UGTT was at war with the government, and the issue was Ben Ali's reappointment to head the SN; unionists considered him responsible for the bloodshed of 1978.[45] Soon thereafter a new national union, the National Union of Tunisian Workers (UNTT) was given official blessing. Through 1984 and 1985, in the midst of a series of strikes and some talk of forming an independent labor party, several UGTT leaders were arrested for inciting to strike, distributing tracts, and attending illegal meetings.[46] Achour was placed under house arrest in December 1985 and was eventually tried and convicted of charges of fraud and collusion with Libya; in ill health, he was again removed to house arrest in 1987, and finally released in 1988. In the meantime, repression had succeeded in reducing the UGTT's potential threat sufficiently to make the UNTT politically superfluous and even inconvenient for corporatist purposes: it was dismantled in 1987. The UGTT at the same time was restored to its former prominence, but not to its former independence or power.[47] Privatization efforts since the mid 1980s have further eroded its clout, since the union has generally been shut out of the private sector.

Opposition within the party itself surfaced in 1971. Ben Salah's 1969 dismissal was accompanied by presidential promises of political as well as economic liberalization, but when these failed to materialize, liberals within the party made their unhappiness known. A PSD congress, held at Monastir in November 1971, uncharacteristically took matters into its own hands, passing resolutions on party organization and presidential succession that emphasized electoral processes, even as they heaped praise on Bourguiba. Most resolutions required further action—by Bourguiba and by the national legislature—for implementation, but one decision had immediate impact. In elections for the PSD central committee, delegates gave the greatest number of votes to Bahi Ladgham and to the most outspoken "liberal," Ahmed Mestiri; Bourguiba's favorite, Hedi Nouira, came in fifth. Within ten days, Bourguiba had found cause to dismiss Mestiri from the central committee, and it was only a matter of time before he was excluded from the party and the legislature as well. It took three more years to close up all the openings created by the 1971 Congress. When the PSD next convened in 1974, the mood of liberalism had fully dissipated. Although a handful of prominent party members protested the "undemocratic conditions" under which the assembly would meet, Bourguiba vehemently rejected the idea of political pluralism. The dissident liberals, including three former ministers, were expelled from the party. The national motto was changed from "Liberty, Order, Justice" to "Order, Liberty, Justice," and Bourguiba's presidential tenure was extended indefinitely.[48]

After their ouster from the PSD, the "liberal group" associated with

Ahmed Mestiri continued to meet and discuss political reform efforts (one of which eventually would evolve into the Tunisian League of Human Rights). As early as 1976 the group began to call themselves social democrats, but seven years passed before they were formally recognized as a party, the Movement of Socialist Democrats (MDS). Electoral fraud was rampant in elections for which they stood in both 1981 (prior to being recognized)[49] and 1985, and by the time a fairer contest was arranged in 1989, the momentum of popular politics had already passed to the Islamists. As a party, the MDS welcomed the Ben Ali transition and the opportunities it held out for opening up the political system, but Ben Ali's rhetoric of reform had immediate repercussions on the MDS. Many prominent democratic socialists who had for years been forced to the political sidelines simplified their lives by joining (or reaffiliating themselves with) the ruling party, which now seemed to promise genuine liberalization. Several defectors quickly rose to prominence in the revitalized Destourian Party, now the RCD, but their departure weakened the MDS and a poor showing in the 1989 elections only deepened divisions. Ahmed Mestiri resigned the leadership in 1990, and when the MDS was unable to achieve internal agreement on its stance vis-à-vis the government in 1992, many of its oldest and staunchest supporters parted company with it.[50]

Other political parties have not fared better. The 1983 decision to legalize opposition parties reopened the playing field to them, at least in theory, but the political circumscription of civil society assured by the ruling party stymied their growth and development from the outset. In addition to the MDS, the Tunisian opposition includes three other recognized political parties,[51] but all must operate in the long shadow of the RCD and none constitutes a significant counterweight. The inclusion of all major opposition groups in publicized debates about the new National Pact in 1988 generated enthusiastic response and raised hopes that pluralistic expression would be allowed, but those hopes were dashed by elections that left the RCD's legislative monopoly intact. Bourguiba and the Neo-Destour had passed on, but the new era looked very much like the old.

STRENGTHENING SOCIETY:
THE SILENT FIND A VOICE

Building on the Tunisian state's secure foundation, Habib Bourguiba had shaped a political system that through the structure of a single legitimized party allowed the development and incorporation of diverse interest groups even as it cultivated personal loyalty to him. Patronage oiled the many cogs in the political machine.[52] In the years following independence, Tunisia was a "mobilization regime": society was actively courted to participate in political affairs through the medium of the party.[53] No serious dissent was brooked within the party, however, and the system inevitably excluded some from its fold.

Just what happened to the voiceless, and the sons of those so deprived, is a topic of some neglect in the study of Tunisian politics. Bourguiba's regime promoted the sons of the coastal Sahel region, some of whom married daughters of the displaced Tunis elite.[54] Djerbans turned their attention to commerce. But the displaced graduates of the Zaytuna university and many former Youssefists continued to remain aloof from, and even hostile to, Bourguiba and the PSD. Neither patronage nor developmental infrastructure extended to the children of the country's southern reaches, who became the "new social periphery."[55]

During the 1970s, many of the forgotten were discovering, and articulating, an antimodern political doctrine that, in revaluing Islamic tenets denigrated by Bourguiba, established a political alternative to the status quo and simultaneously accorded them a new dignity as political actors.[56] By 1981, Islamism had coalesced to the extent that the Ittijah al-Islami (more commonly known as the Mouvement de la tendance islamique, or MTI) called a press conference and declared its intent to seek recognition as a political party. Within months, most of its leaders were serving 2- to 10-year prison terms for belonging to an unauthorized organization and having defamed the head of state.

Government attempts over the next several years to undermine support for the Islamists were ineffectual. A program of mosque-building was appreciated by a population whose religious devotion had apparently increased, but simultaneous efforts to discredit the MTI simply didn't work. On the contrary, the continued imprisonment of MTI leaders provoked international pressures in addition to domestic discontent. With Bourguiba's appointment of Ben Ali as minister of interior in 1986, a new initiative of conciliation was launched. Rachid Ghannouchi, Abdelfatah Mourou, and other MTI leaders were amnestied, and talks with government officials raised popular hopes that the movement would be officially recognized as a political party. Those hopes were dashed, and authorities made a second effort to quash the MTI. In early 1987, a concentrated effort was made to round up all those vocally critical of the government. Unionists and human rights leaders were arraigned, but the Islamists were by far the principal target. Through spring 1987, several hundred were arrested, and in August 1987, ninety leaders charged with capital offenses were brought before the state security court. Recognized leaders of the MTI were spared the death penalty, but until it was foiled by the November 1987 coup, Bourguiba's intent to have them retried seemed sure to carry the country to the edge of a political precipice.

Political amnesty, legal liberalization, and the inclusion of the MTI in the negotiation of the national pact temporarily applied balm to political wounds, but the patch did not hold. To comply with new laws requiring full separation of politics from religion, the MTI changed its name to Hizb al-Nahda, the Renaissance Party, and once again made application for recognition as a political party. Despite the fact that legal status was once again denied, in the 1989 legislative elections, Islamists showed themselves to be the only viable political opposition. Running as independents, they managed to secure 14.5 percent of the overall vote, and nearly a third of the popular vote in Ben Arous, the working-class suburb of Tunis that has been home to Ghannouchi and many other urban immigrants from the south.

The election won them more repression rather than the legislative seats they had sought. In 1989, Ghannouchi elected for self-imposed exile; al-Nahda's publication el-Fajr was shut down after less than a year in operation. Islamists were arrested in large numbers during the Gulf War, and as discussed in Chapter 9, an isolated incident of violence followed by the discovery of an alleged plot was used to justify extending the campaign of repression in spring 1991. From 1990 to 1992, over 8,000 individuals were arrested, and for a third time the government sought to decapitate the Islamist organization. In July and August 1992, 279 al-Nahda members were tried before military tribunals; leaders in the government's custody were sentenced to life in prison.[57]

The extent of the measures undertaken by the government, and their persistent application for more than ten years, testify sufficiently to the strength of the Islamist movement. Whether the government has now truly succeeded in convincing the broader public of the imminent danger posed by Islamism is not yet clear. What is clear is that the basic division between the state, as represented by its executive and a coterie of party elites, and a substantial segment of society has not been addressed. Originally drawing support from segments of the population once receptive to Salah Ben Youssef, the Islamist movement had by 1992 left few Tunisian families untouched. Students have been the most visible—and to some degree the most vocal—supporters, but those arrested in 1991 and 1992 included civil servants, teachers, and professionals from virtually every corner of the country. Economic and political discontent gave shape to the movement in the 1970s, but it has been steadily fed by a deeper malaise that leaves many feeling culturally unanchored.[58] The voice that gave it expression has at least in the short run been muffled, but the malaise itself has not yet disappeared.

CONCLUSION

By the mid 1970s, relations between state and society in Tunisia had arrived at an impasse out of which, despite several hopeful starts, they have yet to find their way. Mobilization policies that in the first decade of independent rule had generated enthusiasm among a good number of Tunisians as well as among diplomatic and academic observers were ringing hollow, and the state found it difficult to capture the hearts of increasing numbers of citizens. Neither the economic liberalism of the 1970s, the tepid approval of limited political pluralism in the 1980s, nor the dramatic change of leadership in 1987 fundamentally altered the situation. Opposition parties are marginalized, and the National Pact that generated widespread enthusiasm in the initial months of Ben Ali's presidency is now largely forgotten. At root of the dilemma is and a hierarchy of power that, although kept permeable by patronage and the extensive party network, has nevertheless remained fairly small. The price tag of patronage is political conformity, and many gifted and highly skilled Tunisians who have accepted a place within the existing political framework profess personal discomfort. There is simply no other effective avenue of participation, and the alternative, which some accept, is exclusion and alienation.

For as much as a quarter of the population, the alternative has not seemed a choice. Many of those who describe themselves as Islamists had by 1990 come to live beyond the reaches of the state—that is, in apparent disregard of the government's rules and legislation. Banning Hizb al-Nahda meant little, and a shadow *majlis* (Islamic parliament) supplied alternative, if elementary, governance. If the recent arrests, intimidation, and imprisonment of the Islamist leadership have in fact dismantled an organization alternative to the state in Tunisia, it is still not clear that noncoercive means exist to integrate the alienated periphery into the sphere of the state. Possibilities of negotiation that envision political compromise have repeatedly been rejected by the regime in favor of strategies that would revive corporatist structures or, alternatively, strengthen civil—secular—society.

Corporatist strategies are bankrupt. The existence of corporatist structures has often been offered as evidence of a strong state, but as Joel Migdal has noted, state agencies themselves may be kept weak enough to serve only the interests of those at the top.[59] Bourguiba was a master of the politics of survival, which kept rivals in check, and although both rhetoric and the particular pools of support have changed, the political game itself has not been dramatically altered. Ben Ali has derived his own power more from control of the security forces and the specter of an Islamic state than from popular choice.

The promotion of civil society is a slogan that has in effect yielded little. Ben Ali's government was not willing to make any political compromises that would allow the Islamists, the only opposition with a substantially different program and a sizable base of support, into the legitimized political arena. A legislature that might have included a handful of Islamists remains dominated by the party continuously in power since 1956, and neither the legislature nor the party have managed to balance executive powers. Political institutions in Tunisia have not been allowed to develop on their own and spread their roots in society. The state, which was strong at independence, has remained strong, but society has strengthened alongside it, and not necessarily within the parameters of state control.

5 State versus Society in Algeria

In contrast to Tunisia, the Algerian state had a difficult birth. Precolonial Algerian society accommodated peoples of diverse languages and lifestyles, who interacted regularly but nevertheless lived as separate communities. Neither geographic features nor social patterns were conducive to the establishment of centralized authority. Dispersed social and political units did not easily come together as a nation, and they did not readily subject themselves to the governance of a state. Most of the precolonial governors for their part were weak or uninterested in the hinterlands, and efforts to centralize power that did emerge in the early nineteenth century were truncated by the arrival of French troops. Colonial forces eventually altered that status quo, but the centralized rule they imposed corroded local social structures and unified the Algerian people only in opposition to foreign domination.

Thirty years of independent rule have not been able to erase a long history of social division. Politics remains the purview of a few, and the state is held hostage to rivalry among its leaders. Competition among the elite has plagued the Algerian polity since independence, interfering with collective processes of public policy formulation and impeding resolution of pressing political problems. Few links connect state and society, and the combination of coercion and good economic fortune that for many years masked a harsh reality that has of late become difficult to disguise. The Algerian state does not effectively serve Algerian society, and that reality owes much to a long history of social division.

A HERITAGE OF SOCIAL DIVISION

Precolonial Algeria was not united as a nation, and eighteenth-century efforts to establish centralized structures of governance were unsuccessful.

The process of political centralization, which resulted in a strong state in Tunisia, began late and ended early in Algeria. For several reasons, developments that began to shape embryonic states in other parts of North Africa did not yield the same results there. In the first place, geographic position and territorial expanse made political control difficult to establish. The progressive decline of the Maghrib-wide Almohad empire in the thirteenth century did create opportunities for local governance, but these were not exploited in territorial Algeria to the extent they had been in the land to the east. With Almohad collapse, portions of western Algeria came under control of a collaborating tribe, and a local Berber dynasty, the Zayanids, was established. During their brief rule, basic structures of regional governance were put in place, and as the Hafsids had done in Tunis, the Zayanids invited Andalusian refugees to dress the city of Tlemcen as a capital. The Zayanids had to fend off Moroccan sultans' claims to Tlemcen, however, and unlike the Hafsids in Ifriqiya, they were unable to establish clear control over outlying areas. In consequence, Algerian society retained its heterogeneous character. Territorial Algeria, in fact, hosted several separate societies: the Berber (*amazigh*) populations of Kabylia, the Aurès, and the Mzab (each of which had different traditions); desert Tuaregs; Arabic-speaking bedouins; Arabic-speaking city dwellers; and urban Jews. Ethnic differences would eventually serve as a rationale for divide-and-rule policies adopted by the French, but historically these groups were distinguished more by their relative autonomy and isolation than by cultural antagonisms.

The Zayanids successfully defended themselves against Moroccan sultans and occasionally challenged rule in the western reaches of the Hafsid domain, but centripetal forces in Tlemcen afforded little protection against Spanish assault on the Mediterranean coast. By the early sixteenth century, Spain held a series of strategically located garrison ports, including Algiers. The inhabitants of that city chafed under Spanish exactions, and with their blessings, two Muslim corsair brothers, Aruj and Khayr al-Din Barbarossa, wrested Algiers from Spain. Gradually the corsairs extended their claims to Tlemcen and sites along the shore, but continuing Spanish interest and local disinclination to accept domination from whatever source rendered their hold on Algiers itself more tenuous. Upon the death of Aruj in 1518, Khayr al-Din sought the help of the Sublime Porte in Istanbul to anchor his rule and placed his territories under the protection of the Ottoman sultan.

Janissary troops who assured Ottoman hegemony did help lay the foundation of a state in Algiers, but Ottoman sovereignty ended before that work was completed. The Turks initially ruled through a *beylerbey* (governor general), but fiscal difficulties gradually obliged the Porte to cede political control to its military commanders. They in turn worked out an arrangement to share power with the ship captains who supplied the treasury and in the process began to craft the institutions of a state. A divan, or council, that was dominated by Janissaries but included local dignitaries named a *dey* to govern, and by the early nineteenth century the rudimentary structures of monarchy were in place. The divan came progressively to depend upon a more diverse oligarchy, and in 1816 Ali Khodja Dey removed the state treasury from Janissary control. He also named his own successor.[1]

The Ottomans made less significant contributions to nation-building. The occupants of Algiers were oriented to the Mediterranean, and for two centuries most of the Arab and Berber populations of the interior escaped their direct control. Inland territories were divided into three districts, each ruled by a bey, but centralized and bureaucratic governance remained minimal. The caids, or governors, who oversaw routine political and administrative matters were of Turkish descent, but their own power was derived from that of indigenous chieftains. To the extent that Turkish bureaucrats sought a peaceful existence, their strategy of governance reinforced the power of local leaders, who presided over the distribution of lands, collected taxes, maintained security,[2] and in general imposed their will on the population in their charge.[3]

Algiers did not direct its attention to the hinterland until the beginning of the nineteenth century. Expansion of European control in the Mediterranean had seriously eroded the economic basis of the Ottoman province, and neither piracy nor commerce could continue to supply the city-state's needs. In search of revenues, the ruling Turks turned their attention to the Algerian interior. Taxes were levied on produce and livestock; the Turkish bureaucracy sold offices, imposed fines, and farmed out *makhzen* (Ottoman) lands. Rigorous implementation of such fiscal measures quickly created contradictions, however. Local chiefs whose support was critical for successful implementation of the policies found themselves injured, and in consequence made themselves available to lead local populations in revolt.[4]

It was in this context that the French monarchy, under pretext of diplomatic insult and anxious to divert attention from domestic woes, attacked Algiers in 1830.[5] It met little resistance: the vastly outnumbered Janissaries were unaccustomed to actual fighting, and much of the rest of the Algerian population was unconnected to the city-state of Algiers. The French had launched the assault without planning for long-term occupation,[6] but in due course the limited occupied territories were declared a colony, and French troops spread along the littoral and inland. As they went, they established a legal and administrative apparatus capable of supporting a French settler population.

The dey capitulated, but outside of Algiers, resistance was more effective. In Constantine, Ahmad Bey drew on his close association with local notables to block French expansion until 1837.[7] In the province of Oran, a respected descendent of a maraboutic family, Abd-al-Qadir, was locally chosen to direct resistance. By drawing on pervasive antipathy for the Turks and by actively cultivating the sympathy and support of other religious reformists, he consolidated pastoral tribes into a local power base and eventually controlled two-thirds of Algeria.[8] Abd-al-Qadir's emergent state was tacitly acknowledged by the French in two successive treaties of mutual recognition, which ultimately, however, proved untenable: in 1839 the two forces entered into open conflict. When their first assaults were repulsed and efforts to undermine the emir's political organization by corrupting his lieutenants failed, the French opened a campaign of terror in the countryside and augmented their military strength to bring down Tlemcen and other strongholds of resistance. In 1847, Abd-al-Qadir was forced to acknowledge defeat.

Although other resistance continued to 1871, Abd-al-Qadir's defeat removed the most significant obstacle faced by the French. The final outcome notwithstanding, the emir's struggle sets an important marker in Algerian political history. Apart from its sheer heroism, the fifteen-year fight against French colonizing efforts represented a significant attempt to create an autonomous Algerian state. The emir had succeeded in unifying pastoral communities from well beyond his original geographic base of Oran province into a sort of tribal confederacy. Despite his ultimate defeat, Abd-al-Qadir is credited with having devised workable solutions to problems associated with building an army and imposing taxes, problems that had gone unsolved by the Zayanids and that continued to trouble his contemporaries in better established polities to the east and west.[9]

The campaign mounted by Abd-al-Qadir was met harshly by the French. To combat the forces he led and eventually to quell other, more isolated resistance movements, General Thomas Robert Bugeaud was permitted to wage war that had a devastating impact on the embryonic Algerian state and on society as well. In a strategy intended to eradicate opposition by disrupting all economic activity, fields were scorched, villages were razed, and local leaders eliminated. By 1870 the Muslim population had been reduced to two million, roughly two-thirds its size in 1830. The surviving population was progressively pushed inward beyond the coastal plain that offered the country's best agricultural lands, and social structures were systematically destroyed. Through outright confiscation or legal chicanery, the French laid claim to Ottoman domains and *habus* properties, as well as many tribal and freeheld properties. By Napoleon III's rise to power in 1848, they had acquired significant portions of Algeria's most fertile lands. In 1848 Algeria was declared a legal extension of French territory, and a law of 1863 began a process that over time converted all property (including communally held lands) into private and marketable real estate. This French *sénatus-consulte* of 1863, presented to some constituencies as protection for the property rights of native Algerians, effectively accelerated the process of colonization and began to shred the system of economic rights and privileges that had woven together the social fabric of tribal society.

French colonization, meanwhile, continued apace, spurred by a policy of populating Algeria with Europeans, which also permitted France to resettle its own dissidents and, later, refugees from the Franco-Prussian war. The number of European settlers, which had already reached 250,000 around 1870, doubled within the next decade. Their growing numbers, a fervent belief in the French civilizing mission, and clear advantages that were enshrined in law and enforced militarily firmly established the dominance of the *colons* and the colonial regime. Social bifurcation was sealed in 1865 by the introduction of a measure that made Algerians responsible under French law without providing them with its full protection. To counterbalance the obvious inequity, Algerian Muslims were granted the right to seek French nationality. That provision, though, had its own catch. The measure required Muslims to renounce personal status under Shari'a, and in consequence the citizenship option was almost universally rejected by Algerian Muslims. On balance, the law's perverse effect was that by their own choice, Muslims endorsed their disenfranchisement.

Colonialization was as complete, and as brutal, in Algeria as it ever was anywhere. Policies were constructed to wreak deliberate havoc with established socioeconomic structures and were applied variously across the territory as an expedient for colonial interests. Lands were appropriated with impunity and local social systems were torn apart. Populations along the coastal plains and hills were among the first to be dispossessed of land, and many fellahin and tenant farmers were transformed into wage labor for European settlers.[10] For the convenience of administration and control, the French created small political units (*duwars*) that made nonsense of local patterns of settlement and flagrantly violated the patriarchal social order.

In Kabylia, neighboring villages whose geographic separation had served to demarcate dissimilar origins and histories were commonly grouped into a single *duwar*. In Arab territories, where family groupings could be quite large, lineage groups that had previously functioned as single social units were broken into multiple *duwars*, and small tribal fractions were combined without concern for blood relation or social history.[11] The colonial administration allocated and confiscated tracts of land to reward or punish tribal factions as variously suited its interests, levied fines, and occasionally interfered with market mechanisms to control dissident populations.

After 1871, the fires of resistance gradually flickered out, and the colonial power entrenched itself. The truce came more quickly in some areas than in others. Inhabitants of the coastal plains offered little organized resistance, and the Berbers of Kabylia, tied to their land and their trees, recognized their vulnerability to Bugeaud's campaign of devastation and gave up by the 1870s. Mountain areas, the steppes, and the desert edge continued to offer sporadic resistance, often inspired by the shaykhs of religious brotherhoods, for several more decades. In the end, however, resistance could not be sustained, and even among their erstwhile adversaries, the French found Algerians willing in some measure to represent their interests.

Algerian society found an equilibrium of sorts, but it had come at great cost. The authority of clan councils had been undermined by local assemblies (*jamaʿa*) instituted in the new *duwars;* brotherhoods that had provided a lateral structure capable of connecting disparate social groups had in many instances ended up at odds with local leadership imposed or endorsed by the colonial administration, and swelling, unemployed urban populations attested to pervasive socioeconomic dislocation. Pierre Bourdieu summarizes the social devastation:

> An impersonal and abstract monetary value is replacing the former values of prestige and honor. . . . The cleverest . . . make use of legal techniques to accumulate a fortune or to acquire great domains; the great lords, loath to adapt themselves to these new conditions, preserve a mere facade of wealth by mortgaging their lands, a fact which has contributed to the relative overthrow of the traditional hierarchies; finally, there are those who remain faithful to the soil and continue to work as in the past, but with a much keener awareness of their wretched condition. . . . The emigration of the uprooted, poverty-stricken proletariat to the towns and cities, the destruction of the economic unity of the family, the weakening of the ancient solidarities and of the restraints which had been imposed by the group and which had protected the agrarian order, the rise of the individual and of economic individu-

alism which shattered the community framework, were all so many breaches in the coherent fabric of the social structures.[12]

The process of social fragmentation begun in 1830 would be completed in the 1950s, when in concerted efforts to destroy the bases of new insurrection, the colonial administration began systematically to uproot, divide, and relocate families and communities promoting the dissidence. From 1954 to 1958, approximately one of every two Algerian peasants was forcibly transplanted, cut off from home and land, and a way of life that had in substantial measure withstood earlier assault was now more finally ruptured.[13]

It is difficult to imagine policies more socially and economically disruptive than those advanced by the colonial regime in Algeria, but it is important all the same not to lose sight of the fact that in 1830, the Algerian territory was home to neither a nation nor a viable state. Prior to the arrival of the French, the people and territory of Algeria were defined as much by what they were not as by what they were. The efforts of Ottoman rulers in Algiers and Constantine to reinforce centralized rule came too late—or the French arrived too early. Efforts that might have carried nation- and state-building forward were cut short.[14]

As it was, French policies only exacerbated, albeit severely, long apparent tendencies and prevented any coalescence of forces that might have integrated indigenous peoples into a society organized at the national level. The nationalist movement that did emerge in the 1930s began to create a sense of "Algerianness" but proved incapable of transcending more than temporarily the numerous fissures that divided society. In 1936, the Algerian leader Ferhat Abbas despaired of "building on the wind":

> Had I discovered the Algerian nation, I would be a nationalist. . . . However, I will not die for the Algerian nation, because it does not exist. I have not found it. I have examined History, I questioned the living and the dead, I visited cemeteries; nobody spoke to me about it. . . . One cannot build on the wind.[15]

Nationalists subsequently developed a rhetoric of national unity, but that ideal notwithstanding, it was division rather than unity that characterized Algerian society, and even the revolution did not effect transformation of that aspect of political life. By the time the nationalist movement had won independence in 1962, the social cohesion of Algerian society had been compromised to the core, and distrust was the modus operandi of politics. The Algerian nationalists' failure to overcome their heritage of social division provides the historical context for problems that have plagued the state since independence, and thus requires closer attention.

THE NATIONALIST MOVEMENT

Out of the wreckage of colonization, an Algerian nationalist movement gradually began to assume form after the turn of the century. Unlike Tunisia—where through an evolutionary process one single and cohesive group split off from and essentially replaced its forebear and left Tunisians with a reasonably unified nationalist movement—the Algerian movement from its birth was torn in different directions. One early Algerian group, identified by William Quandt as the "Liberals" for their moderate and inherently reformist positions, sought only assimilation[16]; the Algerian Association of the 'Ulama represented the interest of Algerian religious elites; and the radical Algerian National Star (ENA) made an outright call for independence. As Elbaki Hermassi notes, despite many attempts, these three separate strands were never successfully united in a single, recognizable national leadership.[17]

The nationalist movement in every guise met fierce resistance from colonial interests. For the *pieds noirs* of Algeria and initially for the French National Assembly as well, Algeria's basic relation to the French polity was not negotiable. Alone of French colonies, Algeria had been established as an extension of the metropolis, and any call for independence constituted political heresy, especially in the ears of those who had transplanted themselves to the overseas territory. The intransigence of French settlers in the face of even modest demands left moderate nationalists in untenable positions. Over the decade leading up to 1945, the influence of those who had called for assimilation or reform diminished within the nationalist movement. Independence was eventually endorsed by all as the only acceptable end, and revolution seemed the only way to achieve it.

Nationalist convictions notwithstanding, the path to the creation of the National Liberation Front (FLN) was tortuous. Through the entire fight for independence, the nationalist movement headed by the FLN never became more than an amalgam of disparate interests, personal and collective, united by the single intent to remove the colonial yoke. While in Tunisia the nationalist contest boiled down to a struggle between the Vieux- and Neo-Destour, the Algerian struggle from 1936 to 1954 involved at least ten separately identifiable groups,[18] some of which over time were banned, some abandoned, and others superseded and absorbed. The lineage of the FLN itself involves many twists and turns. The FLN was created late in

1954 by an ad hoc group that out of impatience with more conventional political strategies had forged plans to launch an armed revolution. Politically, it was not the direct descendant of any political party—and indeed, its founders sought to redirect momentum away from parties. Intellectually and organizationally, however, the FLN's heritage may be traced back to Messali Hadj's ENA, though "Messalists" were ultimately the only nationalists who refused to join the Front.

After being banned by the French in 1936, the ENA had had two subsequent incarnations as the Algerian People's Party (PPA) and the Movement for the Triumph of Democratic Liberties (MTLD). One offshoot of the MTLD was the Special Organization (OS). Disbanded by the French in 1950, several of its members later regrouped as the Revolutionary Committee of Unity and Action (CRUA) and met clandestinely over the summer of 1954 to plot a course of action. On November 1, 1954, the CRUA issued the historic manifesto creating the FLN, and launched a national insurgency, not entirely successfully, with coordinated attacks on colonial installations throughout the country. For their role in planning and sustaining the armed revolt, nine CRUA leaders came to be known as the *chefs historiques* of the Algerian revolution. Five of them were named commanders of interior military zones, or *wilayas,* from which the eight-year guerrilla war was waged.[19]

The FLN in 1954 was immediately opened to all Algerian nationalists. Despite its failure to inspire a mass uprising, it did rally nearly all those who had been politically engaged in the quest for independence. As its name implies, however, it was not a political party but a broad coalition of all forces bent on routing the colonial power. Even Algerian communists, whose association with their French counterparts had made them slow to embrace the nationalist cause, were welcomed. Ironically, only the most loyal followers of Messali Hadj resisted incorporation into the FLN, and within a month they had in fact organized their own rival Algerian National Movement (MNA). The ensuing internecine struggle claimed thousands of lives, involving treachery on both sides. It remains a shadowy chapter of the Algerian war.[20]

The founders of the FLN were men of action. Partly in reaction to their political predecessors' failure to reap results, they explicitly deferred questions of ideology and organization until after the rebellion they charted had gained sufficient momentum. In a pattern that would become familiar in independent Algeria, no single party was allowed to accumulate excessive power, and each zone leader was accorded full autonomy in his own region. FLN leaders outside the country, charged with collecting arms and money, likewise acted on their own. Only as the FLN grew did the need for coordination and a coherent platform become apparent, but even so, the fear of personal dominance remained strong. When several dozen FLN "delegates" met in the Soummam Valley in 1956 to hammer out guiding principles, they vested the revolution's ultimate authority in a seventeen-member committee, the National Committee of the Algerian Revolution (CNRA), that reflected the balance of forces within the FLN. A provisional government (the Provisional Government of the Algerian Republic, GPRA) was formed two years later. Without—in theory—undermining the CNRA's role, it was intended to counterbalance the CNRA's growing military strength.[21] The prohibition against concentrated power made it difficult at times to determine just where executive prerogatives lay.

FLN leadership was not cohesive, and the rhetorical claims about service to the Algerian people notwithstanding, the Front had no identifiable constituency. It was not a political party, and it never developed an organizational infrastructure that catered to the Algerian masses. The *wilaya* commands provided the primary linkage to the people, and by their military function, the FLN remained an organization of limited access. Its leaders were guerrilla fighters, *mujahidin*. Most had had little formal education, and few had experience in political leadership. Their energies went into fighting the French and one another rather than into winning over the Algerian masses.

Divisions within the FLN appeared early on, but serious problems developed only after the Evian accords granting Algeria independence from France were signed. The power struggle that erupted in 1962 pitted interior *wilaya* forces against the National Liberation Army (ALN), which since 1958 had been confined to positions beyond the Algerian border, and divided the GPRA, five of whose members had spent long years in French prisons nurturing mutual enmity. As it first emerged, the primary struggle was over the structure and control of independent Algeria's military command, but by late May issues of rule-making and legitimate governance had also arisen. Meeting in Tripoli, the CNRA easily united behind an ideologically coherent program of social and economic policy derived from socialist principles, but it adjourned the meeting without resolving critical questions about interim structures of governance. The GPRA, headed by Ben Youcef Ben Khedda, insisted that it remained the FLN's legitimate representative, while a new "Political Bureau" headed by Ahmed Ben Bella made the equivocable claim that it had the support of the CNRA.[22] The FLN lacked institutional means of resolving the dispute, bringing Algerian politics to an impasse. Civil war in August was averted only by a last-minute political agreement struck by the two feuding leaders; order was thereafter assured by the long shadow of ALN troops advancing toward Algiers and offering support to Ben Bella.

The 1962 fissure within the FLN is well documented, but accounts are inevitably lengthy and entangled.[23] Players resigned from their positions, were reinstated, and sometimes changed sides. Indeed, "sides" are at times difficult to identify. Issues and ideologies fail to differentiate either actors or their espoused positions, leading to a common conclusion that divisions were a function of personal ambitions and rivalries rather than ideological commitments. Algerian politics at independence was an unregulated contest for power among elites who as a class were defined only by the role they had played in the war for independence. The independent Algerian regime identified itself as socialist, but ideology was a secondary concern. As Quandt notes, within the nationalist movement, elites had not successfully devised processes to reconcile opposing demands; conflicts within the FLN were commonly resolved by ceding autonomy to dissenting groups.[24]

Immobility was the obvious price of this strategy, and Algeria in 1962 could not afford that solution. Just as the stubborn independence of Messalists in 1954 was attacked by the newly formed FLN, the 1962 crisis was framed in all-or-nothing terms. Players on both sides pursued short-term strategies, pressing advantages as openings appeared rather than seeking compromise solutions that might have been longer-lived. Neither could incontestably hold up popular or institutional legitimacy to support its claim to govern, and so it was left to the army—with demonstrable force—to confer power and authority upon one of the contenders and legitimize its claim to shape the new political game. This it did on August 27 by inviting the Political Bureau to take the necessary measures to reestablish a "definitive peace" across the entire territory, and especially Algiers.[25] By early September, ALN forces had secured control of dissident *wilayas,* including Algiers, and with army support, Ben Bella could make a credible claim to power. Independent Algeria's first political crisis was at least temporarily solved.

Underlying problems, however, went unaddressed. The Political Bureau made no apologies for tampering with previously agreed electoral procedures, and many of its opponents were systematically excluded from the National Constituent Assembly formed in September. That collegial body proved fractious and ineffective and within a year had been overshadowed by President Ben Bella, who in the interim had taken several steps to concentrate power in his own hands. In 1963 Ben Bella assumed control of the FLN, which had expanded its membership but remained a party of the new political "elite." By presidential decree, all other parties were banned, and former opponents were selectively arrested.

Out of independent Algeria's first internecine conflict, patterns and problems can be isolated that have in various shapes over the past thirty years continued to subvert public policy and inhibit the development of political institutions. Leadership has commonly vacillated between extremes of anarchic collegial rule and authoritarian personalism. It is a paradox of Algerian political culture that the most politically acceptable form of governance is in the long run unworkable, and workable styles are not politically acceptable. Egalitarianism is fiercely defended as the political form of choice, but in practice collegial rule has not been able to assure the most basic function of politics, that of allocating values and deciding public policy. The political culture assigns high value to an ideal of unity that in fact is rarely manifest, and lip service to unity has had the perverse effect of rendering the political process incapable of accommodating dissenting views. Where consensus cannot be reached, subgroup autonomy substitutes for political choice, allowing power centers to multiply and leaving broad policy matters unresolved. Where autonomy will not suffice to appease dissent, ruled and rulers alike have frequently resorted to measures as extreme as assassination.

Egalitarian principles may be celebrated in rhetoric, but in practice collegial rule has served primarily to deprive the ambitious of a solid power base. In collegial form, political processes have fostered neither bargaining among the elite nor the formation of clear interest groups, and political differences have inevitably degenerated into power contests between constantly shifting factions. As the historian Ibn-Khaldun had observed six centuries earlier, resolution of such struggles depends upon the emergence of a leader who through the judicious use of available resources incorporates others into a larger and more disciplined unit. Algerian political culture, however, resists the emergence of a *za'im*. Efforts to forge group cohesion (*'asibiya*) regularly bring charges of personalism—abhorred as much as egalitarianism is admired. Unwritten rules prohibit one political leader from towering above the rest, and vigorous defense of the equality principle spurs political elites to contest his rule. Coalitions are inherently unstable, and the personal ruler commonly resorts to repressive force to maintain power. The Algerian "republic of cousins" has not found it easy to choose a leader and fix the terms of his office. Rulers have not been subordinated to rules, and the state remains weak.

The paradox of authority expressed in politics at the national level is not without parallel in microlevel social relations. Studies of Algerian society at the time of independence commonly made reference to an ideal-type of patriarchal authority.[26] Obedience and deference were expected within the home, where the patriarch's word was law, and insubordination was not suffered. Autonomous behavior was reserved for adult males, who governed their own families and participated in the political assemblies of the community.

If normative ideals have vaunted the Algerian father's power, in practical reality it has been more seriously, and pervasively, eroded in Algeria than elsewhere in the Maghrib.[27] Colonial policies destroyed economic units and divided families, and relocation schemes made urban migration more socially traumatic than elsewhere in the Maghrib. Sons who migrated to the cities began life without the economic and emotional support of a family, but likewise without its imposing restraints. As though creating a new identity, symbolizing their individuality and independence, nationalists who engaged in the war of liberation commonly assumed *noms de guerre* that effectively superseded their given names and family identities. Houari Boumediene, for example, was born Mohamed Boukharouba; he made himself the namesake of Sidi Bou Mediene, the venerated shaykh of Tlemcen.[28] Colonialism exposed the impotence of Algerian patriarchs, bringing shame on society and its sons, and in the struggle for independence, real fathers were forgotten. The myth of fatherhood, however, retained its power. The nine *chefs historiques*, most of whom were imprisoned during the war and played no direct role in it,[29] symbolically supplied the missing patriarchal leadership, but as they came within grasp of recognized power, their flaws, too, were magnified. Neither individuals nor institutions appeared capable of striking a balance, and in the several times since 1962 that the Algerian polity has edged toward either extreme patrimonialism or political anarchy, Algerians have depended upon the army to play the role of arbiter.

INDEPENDENT ALGERIA: THE ARMY AS POWER BROKER

Political and military support from the ALN's Etat major allowed Ben Bella to ascend to the newly created presidency in 1962, and a coup d'état led by Houari Boumediene ended Ben Bella's rule in 1965. The military's role in these two transitions was key, as it has been in subsequent political crises. Algeria is nominally a republic, whose successive constitutions have envisioned a strong presidency, but in practical reality, presidential initiative has always been subject to military approval. Military leaders have generally preferred not to involve themselves in routine matters of governance, but the decisive role they have played at critical moments underscores the army's overall political importance and the metapolitical function it has repeatedly served.

It is important to examine the role the army has carved for itself before attempting to explain its impact on Algerian politics. Algeria's two longest-ruling heads of state were both ranking army officers, but neither that fact nor the army's part in the transition of 1992 necessarily reflects an interest in direct rule. Military officers have frequently occupied posts of administrative responsibility in Algeria, but the power they have wielded from behind the scenes has arguably been greater. When in office, the military have generally behaved as civilians.

In the absence of well-developed political institutions, the Algerian military at independence helped construct the new state; since that time, it has never surrendered its interest in national politics—nor has it been under pressure to do so. After successfully playing the role of balancer in the 1962 power struggle, the reconfigured National Popular Army (ANP) continued to engage in politics from the sidelines, and Ben Bella's efforts to diminish its influence are generally understood as the principal motive underlying the 1965 coup. Ben Bella had been on the verge of reconciling differences with old foes and seemed poised to dismantle a rival clique, which included Boumediene, minister of defense since 1962. For all of Ben Bella's supposed charisma and popular support, the coup met little resistance, and the deposed president was virulently condemned for personalism and political opportunism. As Jean Leca and Jean-Claude Vatin note, the notion of a "coup" and its political implications resonated abroad to a much greater extent than it did in Algeria, where the change was discussed in terms of the individual leaders.[30]

Boumediene immediately set about reordering administrative structures—without, however, substantially altering policy. Ben Bella had placed selected ministries under his own direct control; Boumediene constructed a more decentralized system, and "personalism" was replaced by collegial rule. The Council of Ministers was assigned responsibility for day-to-day administration and in the early years was nominally accountable to a Council of the Revolution (with which, in any event, there was substantial overlap). The preponderance of the military within the new system did not represent the military's efforts to wrest power from civilians so much as it acknowledged the country's real locus of power. The Council of the Revolution, which supplanted the constitution as the "supreme instance" of the revolution, was comprised primarily of men who had been militarily active during the war,[31] and the new system incorporated ex-*wilaya* commanders politically displaced by Ben Bella, as well as Boumediene loyalists who had also served within the inner circles of the Ben Bella government. Overall, it was an inclusive system designed more to co-opt potential opposition than to promote the military as a body.[32]

Over the years, the disadvantages of collegial rule became evident. Decision-making was inhibited, and conflict among the elite gradually resurfaced. Boumediene responded to an attempted coup in 1967 by curtailing dissent and elite autonomy. The power of the Council of the Revolution was gradually allowed to wane until it was formally superseded by a new constitution in 1976. By that time, Boumediene was ruling through the "Oujda Group"—an informal clique that included key members of the moribund council—and, reflecting the regime's concern with technical competence and economic development, a class of technocrats had taken charge of the country's bureaucratic politics. Boumediene himself had accrued considerable power: in 1978 he was president of the republic, minister of defense, and secretary-general of the FLN. Collegial rule had again given way to personal rule, sanctioned in the interim by a constitution and legitimizing elections. Although Boumediene's government was staffed by military men, in its style, his was essentially a civilian regime not unlike the one he had overthrown.[33]

Boumediene's presidential tenure was cut short by a rare blood disease, which caused his death in late in 1978. His successor, Chadli Bendjedid, could claim neither illustrious origins nor a past of revolutionary glory. The son of peasants from near Annaba, Bendjedid joined the armed resistance in 1955, served with Boumediene at Ghardimaou, and slowly worked his way through the ranks. At the time of Boumediene's death, he was commander of the second military region (Oran) and had for some time served as coordinator of military affairs. Politically, however, he was unknown. Under provisions of the 1976 constitution, 3,290 delegates to a specially convened congress of the FLN were charged with selecting a presidential candidate. High-ranking officials individually supported one or another of several competing factions, but the army's bloc of 640 votes at the 1979 FLN party congress were pivotal in the selection of Chadli Bendjedid. By contrast to other candidates, closely linked to contending cliques, Bendjedid represented only army-national interests and, ironically, was thus viewed as the "independent" candidate.[34] His nomination to the presidency was confirmed by popular vote in February 1979.

Bendjedid's government, like that of his predecessors, was a civilian regime. Bendjedid reoriented public policy away from the heavy industries favored by Boumediene and after 1988 progressively oversaw political liberalization, but in important regards, he did not fundamentally alter the structure of Algerian politics. Over the first years of his rule, the new president gradually purged his government of the men who had been closely associated with Boumediene. Some were fired amidst allegations of corruption and malfeasance; others were successively removed from key positions within government and the party. The military adopted a lower public profile, but its influence did not recede. Army officers who were offered ministerial positions frequently declined them, recognizing that acceptance would entail loss of the fiefdoms they controlled within the military.[35]

In the mid 1980s, several distinct factions vied for influence. One important group teamed Bendjedid's wife, Halima Bourekba, and General Larbi Belkheir, Bendjedid's chief of staff, with generals from the defense ministry and the national guard corps (gendarmerie); a second coalesced around Mustafa Benloucif, who from 1984 to 1986 headed the army's Etat major. A coterie led by Mohamed Cherif Messaadia, an FLN stalwart, found support among the national police (Sûreté national) and army personnel in the Algiers region; another grouped itself loosely around Kasdi Merbah (né Abdellah Khaled), for fifteen years head of the much-feared Military Security. Conspicuous in its absence was the entire presidential cabinet, which, although it executed policy and managed the bureaucracy, did not participate in the state's real power.

Bendjedid himself maintained a low profile, preferring not to impose policy and not to combat rivals openly. Boumediene had projected characteristics typically ascribed to an idealized patriarch—strictness, austerity, and distance. Bendjedid, by contrast, was socially affable and enjoyed material comforts, a populist not overly concerned with discipline or power. Unlike Boumediene, who after 1967 continued to accumulate power, Bendjedid never successfully consolidated his regime. Even before the chaotic events of 1991, observers questioned the existence of an identifiable, governing central authority.[36] Following the resounding defeat of the FLN in December 1991 legislative elections, Bendjedid resigned the presidency in January 1992. The military rule imposed a few days later was in many regards only an extension of the politics of the previous decade.

For two years the army declined to run the state, positioning itself instead behind a collegial body known as the High Council of State (HCE) originally headed by one of the last remaining chefs historiques, Mohamed Boudiaf. For most of the interregnum, Defense Minister Khaled Nezzar was the lone military representative on the council, but behind him rested the formidable weight of an informal directorate representing the entire military.[37] Mohamed Harbi's quip remained pertinent: "Every state has its army. The Algerian army, however, has its state." Under the HCE, the military publicly declared its intention to confine its role to defending Algerian territory and national unity, yet with martial law used to govern and soldiers deployed to patrol the streets, its power was scarcely masked. When the HCE's mandate expired in January 1994, and no civilian could be persuaded to assume the new presidency, General Lamine Zeroual was named head of state.

Although it has expressed an obvious interest in politics, the army has in general been loathe to flex its muscle. Before 1988 it rarely intervened even to restore public order.[38] Its influence in routine politics has depended as much on its independent control of patronage and broad police powers as on the open exercise of force. In both of these regards, the army has to a significant degree assumed functions normally ascribed to the state. In addition to the instruments of force under their control, army officers have benefited from state-assured salaries and an independent, corporate base of wealth. Since independence, for example, the army has controlled a number of formerly French farms and small enterprises seized during the war.[39] Especially at the upper echelons of the officer corps, there is considerable mobility, and material comforts are assured. The army has been perceived and has perceived itself as holding access to the state's most important patronage. Under Boumediene, army officers placed many young technicians in lucrative positions within the state bureaucracy, and for securing favors at the local level, military influence is reputedly more efficacious than party connections.[40] Military officers have commonly used their positions to establish themselves as patrons and power brokers, and rivalry among officers has sometimes produced a political stalemate. Arguably, it was the balance struck between factions in the military that kept Chadli Bendjedid in the presidency so long. At the same time, at critical moments, the military has also demonstrated the rare capacity to act cohesively as an interest group, protecting shared advantages.

Less recognized than the privilege of patronage are the formidable police powers that have been controlled by military and paramilitary forces. Algeria has a long history of reconciling political differences by means that circumvent normal political and judicial processes. One leading nationalist, Abane Ramdane, died under suspicious circumstances in Morocco in 1957; four others were executed in 1959 after a tribunal presided over by Houari Boumediene found them guilty of treason.[41] Algeria's first parliamentarians expressed concern that single-party rule would confuse the activity and authority of the party with that of the state[42] and that the death penalty would be used to rid the new regime of its opponents.[43] In the final years of Ben Bella's rule, discontent within the FLN and the formation of an opposition movement, the Front of Socialist Forces (FFS), resulted in numerous arrests of prominent politicians, including two of the *chefs historiques*. Opposition that formed in the early months of Boumediene's rule met with a similar response. To no one's surprise, Ben Bella was placed under house arrest, but leftist dissidents who had organized an opposition movement were also arrested. Mohamed Khider, the former treasurer of the FLN, who had collected funds to overthrow Ben Bella, was assassinated in Madrid in 1967. Belkacem Krim, who had led the Evian negotiations in 1962 and had since openly criticized successive governments, was brutally murdered in Frankfurt in 1970. Neither murder was ever solved, but both men had been excluded from the party, and their deaths are popularly attributed to government forces.[44]

Control of opposition in Algeria has long been facilitated by a multifaceted security apparatus. The army and special police brigades known as National Security Units (CNS) have typically been used to quell unrest, and in outbreaks of political violence over the past decade, demonstrators have not withheld their venom from these police units. The gendarmerie and the national police visibly represent the state, but the primary responsibility for national security has lain in the hands of the military. Its intelligence agency, the Sécurité militaire (SM), has been feared as much as the CNS have been hated. The SM was established at independence to conduct counterespionage activities, but after the 1965 coup, its mandate was expanded to include surveillance of all political actors and activity, whether in support of the regime or in opposition to it. Few controls were placed upon the SM. Its broad powers facilitated arbitrary arrests, and many of those who fell into its hands were allegedly detained for extended periods and subjected to torture, beyond the reach of the judicial system.[45]

Administrative structures allowed the SM to develop autonomy: its first two directors, Colonel Kasdi Merbah (1962–79) and General Lakhal Ayyat (1979–88), reported only to the president (who after 1965 was also minister of defense).[46] Frequently referred to as the "political police," the SM operated as freely in France as in Algeria, and coteries were formed within its ranks to pursue particularistic agendas. According to Harbi, its networks penetrated government offices, the FLN, and the police, and the SM selected the municipal and regional representatives of these bodies.[47] Influential members of the SM were thought to be critical of Bendjedid, and observers speculated that they had helped instigate each of the main incidents that troubled the Bendjedid regime from 1980 to 1988. After the events of October 1988, critics of the regime charged that the army, through the SM, had abused its powers and was responsible for the torture and ill-treatment of many taken into custody. Bendjedid responded to those charges by initiating a series of reforms intended to limit the scope of the SM's activities. In 1990, after being renamed the General Office of Documentation and Security (DGDS), the Sécurité militaire was formally dissolved. What has happened to its files and its informants remains unclear, but its reputation remains intact.[48]

Under Boumediene the Algerian army ascribed to itself the role of "guardian of the revolution," and it continues to represent itself as an extension of society. Although it eschews public office and other trappings of power, the army's direct control of state patronage and the military security apparatus indisputably establishes it as the polity's éminence grise. Reforms introduced by Bendjedid have not in actuality diminished its influence. When Bendjedid relinquished the military portfolio in 1990, the new minister of defense, General Nezzar, agreed to build a professional army with limited political prerogatives, and Nezzar and his top generals resigned their positions of leadership within the FLN. The army maintained its own publication, however, which continued to comment on Algerian politics through the elections of 1991, and its role in the transition of January 1992 was hardly disguised.

If the army's interventions since 1988 have helped stabilize explosive situations, its other activities have had a less salubrious effect on Algerian politics. Machinations behind the scenes have continuously undermined political institutions and thwarted processes open to public scrutiny. The performance of cabinet ministers has commonly been gauged by their success in not offending the military, and public policy has in consequence been held hostage to military dictates. No structures envision, much less ensure, popular accountability of public officials, and the principal beneficiaries of state capitalism have been the *nomenklatura* themselves. Those who might have objected were pacified with patronage or, alternatively, silenced by intimidation or more drastic measures. Until 1989 there was little opportunity for viable political opposition to develop.

OPPOSITION

For most of independent Algeria's history, opposition has been largely confined to groups that had splintered off from the FLN. Mohamed Boudiaf formed the first of these groups only days before the newly elected Constituent Assembly asked Ben Bella to form a government. The Party of the Socialist Revolution (PRS) drew on socialist theories and jargon of the day for its rhetoric, and the program it originally advanced was largely indistinguishable from positions officially endorsed by the FLN at Tripoli. The PRS defined itself in opposition to the FLN, quite simply, and directed its most acerbic commentary at Ben Bella and the party it accused of betraying the revolution. Verbal attacks eventually brought harsh reprisals: Boudiaf was arrested in June 1963 and spent the next few months in prison.

While Boudiaf was in jail, a second opposition movement was launched, this time by Hocine Ait Ahmed. Like the PRS, the new Front of Socialist Forces (FFS) declared itself an avant-garde organization and called for the rehabilitation of the compromised revolution. Those who joined Ait Ahmed, many of them Berbers from Kabylia, were bristling at their exclusion from debates on the constitution.[49] Ait Ahmad himself was apparently miffed at not having been offered the Foreign Affairs Ministry in the Ben Bella government.[50] Tensions between the government and the new FFS quickly escalated, and by the end of 1963, army troops had been called into Kabylia to quell the dissidence. Conveniently, an attack by Morocco on the southern border town of Tindouf offered itself as a rallying cry for national unity and provided a plausible rationale for some FFS leaders to reunite with the FLN. Ait Ahmad and followers who continued to hope against the odds for the regime's overthrow renewed their assault, however, and from April 1964 to July 1965 a civil insurrection flared intermittently. FFS guerrillas assassinated local FLN officials, and again the army was called in. In October 1965, Ait Ahmad was arrested,[51] and over the next few months more than three thousand people were imprisoned or transferred to detention camps as the army carried out mopping-up operations. Many were tortured.[52]

In the midst of this uprising, the army staged its coup, but the Boumediene regime was no more receptive to opposition than Ben Bella's had been. Ait Ahmed escaped from prison and took up residence in France; Boudiaf exiled himself to Morocco. Both men continued to wage a rhetorical war from abroad, within the sizable expatriate community of Algerian workers in France, but changes in the political terrain at home coupled with a campaign of repression curtailed their activities and their effectiveness. In 1968 the FFS entered a long hibernation, and several smaller opposition groups that were created shortly after Boumediene's takeover disappeared altogether.[53] The PRS began a slow decline in the mid 1970s, and well before the final edition of its monthly newsletter El Jarida appeared in 1984, the party had ceased to have any practical impact on Algerian politics. Apart from the FLN, only the Avant-Garde Socialist Party (PAGS), whose radical-left program served certain interests of Boumediene's regime (and those of the party strongman Mohamed Salah Yahiaoui), was allowed to operate as a political organization. The PAGS owed its origins to old Algerian Communist Party members who from within the FLN initially sought to distance themselves from Boumediene. It did not really become an "opposition" movement until Chadli Bendjedid dismissed his political rival and PAGS patron Yahiaoui from his position of leadership within the FLN.

The failure of Algerian opposition movements to survive and develop is attributable only in part to the repression waged against them by successive regimes. Even abroad, opposition groups operated clandestinely, and leaders did not typically cultivate a relationship with their membership. Overall, they showed little interest in responding to the immediate needs of their constituents or articulating their demands. Neither the PRS nor the FFS managed to produce a coherent platform and, of greater importance, neither was able to build a viable organizational structure. The FFS, in fact, did not try. Ait Ahmed's initial alliance with Colonel Mohand Oul Hadj, head of the army's 7th region (Kabylia), and with Colonel Si Sadek (né Dehiles Slimane), head of the Kabylia *wilaya* during the war for independence, facilitated recruitment of *maquis* for the insurgency, and his mostly Berber supporters were encouraged to fight their political battles within the framework of existing organizations.[54] Early documents endorsed the principles of consultation and rotation of leadership, but these were never enacted. From 1964 to 1967, funds collected by Mohamed Khider to overthrow Ben Bella subsidized opposition groups abroad, including the FFS, and Ait Ahmed himself retained tight control over his supporters.[55]

The PRS did elaborate a formal organization, but hierarchical rigidity rendered it as much a liability as an asset to the party. Recruiting principally from among students and workers in France, through two party militants in Paris, the PRS maintained close contact with Boudiaf in Morocco. With little tolerance for dissent, Boudiaf's aides directed activities and ensured adherence to the party line, which after 1968 began in vague terms to promotelong-term social transformation, to be wrought gradually by a mass-based workers' party.[56] In 1968 Algerian students from Grenoble openly challenged the demagogues in Paris and for their troubles were subjected to a tribunal and expelled from the party. Thereafter, the PRS saw a continuous attrition of its membership.[57] Its staunchest supporters had been routed for demanding debate, and peripheral members (immigrant workers who at any rate had found it difficult to digest the party verbiage) drifted away. As Ramdane Redjala observes, although opponents of the regime decried the lack of "democracy" within the FLN, the PRS and the FFS were in practice both also highly autocratic.[58] Neither Ait Ahmed nor Boudiaf and his lieutenants were prepared to run a party they did not fully control. With little practical hope of changing the regime in power, and no patronage to distribute, such parties could not be expected to thrive.

If the opposition was as unconcerned as the FLN about building party structures, it also suffered from competition among the elite and the divisiveness seemingly endemic in Algerian politics. Relations within and between various opposition movements were as complex and tangled as those of the nationalist movement prior to the creation of the FLN. Coalitions were troubled by rivalry and betrayal, and strong positions elaborated one day were easily reversed the next in favor of a new alliance. Ait Ahmed's collaboration with Mohand Oul Hadj did not hold, and neither did two loose coalitions linking the FFS and the PRS. Boumediene's proposal in 1975 to elaborate a new national charter opened up the possibility of various groups within the fragmented opposition finding common cause, but their failure to do so served instead to underscore basic divisiveness. Alarmed that the proposed charter might serve to legitimize political monopoly, four politicians who had largely retired from the political scene— Ferhat Abbas, Ben Youcef Ben Khedda, Mohamed Kheireddine, and Hocine Lahouel—circulated an appeal for a new Constituent Assembly. Their call was initially met enthusiastically by both Boudiaf and Ait Ahmed and the groups they led, but despite several meetings in Paris and Morocco, the opponents of the regime were unable to endorse a common program. Redjala assesses their failed efforts with some bitterness: "Incapable of transcending their intrigues, their petty little calculations, and their personal conflicts, these opponents once more sacrificed the general interest in favor of the particular interests of their coterie."[59] Behind the mask of ideological purity held up so easily in the 1970s, personal concerns continued to dominate political debates.

The much-heralded "opening" of the Algerian political system from 1989 on did little to change that basic reality. A wave of political violence in 1988 spawned a new constitution in 1989 and a decision later that year to permit multipartyism. By late 1991, nearly fifty parties were registered with government authorities. Most had been hastily assembled, and some were led by politicians only recently identified with the FLN.[60] An initiative in early 1991 to create a united front in opposition to both the FLN and the Islamists succumbed to age-old political antagonisms. More established groups fared no better. The FFS had been reawakened in the late 1970s and had gathered some momentum as a clandestine organization with the rise in Kabylia of a Berber cultural movement in the early 1980s. It continued to grow after Ait Ahmed's return to Algeria in 1989, but its appeal remained largely regional. A Movement for Democracy in Algeria (MDA) founded by the deposed Ben Bella among Algerian workers in France likewise failed to generate substantial interest in Algeria.

"Opposition," in fact, is a term with little meaning. If Algerians indict the FLN for personalism, there is scant reason to be more forgiving of those who over the years have opposed it. Whether the choice was Mohamed Boudiaf and the PRS, Ait Ahmed and the FFS, or, later, Ben Bella and the MDA, in the popular view the question has simply been a matter of one set of peeved politicians wishing to substitute themselves for those in power. Those who ruled seemed unable to address the country's pressing problems, and until 1989 the opposition offered no real alternative. The emergence of an Islamist movement in the early 1980s gave Algerians an organized political vehicle through which to express their discontent and vote for change for the first time since independence.

ISLAMISM

The contest for power that engaged the army, the FLN, and opponents of the regime from the outset occurred primarily within elite circles, and over time that contest became further and further distanced from the needs and concerns of society. The *wilaya* system that organized guerrilla fighters during the war had provided some linkage between nationalist leaders and society, but at its dissolution no new bridge was fashioned between party and people. Within urban settings, the national labor union might have played such a role, but as a price for its remaining neutral—and independent—in the 1962 political contest, the FLN replaced its leadership. The gulf between the political elite and society at large began to grow, but it was masked by the new state's ability to absorb virtually all its educated cadres into a burgeoning bureaucracy, and by the sizable stock of property available for redistribution. To political competitors locked in highly personal competition, society seemed an encumbrance, extraneous to the real centers of politics and power, and the price for ignoring it appeared minimal.

Meanwhile, all was not well in Algerian society. The 1970s worldwide boom in hydrocarbons had disguised structural weaknesses in the economy, but as export revenues tumbled in the mid 1980s, Algerians began to experience steep hikes in the prices of consumer goods and shortages of such staples as potatoes, coffee, sugar, and eggs. The population had expanded, from 9 million in 1962 to 22 million in 1986, and neither housing nor public infrastructure had kept pace. By 1985, 60 percent of Algeria's population was under 22 years of age, and although the upper divisions of the national education system enrolled six times as many students as had been accommodated in 1965,[61] few graduates found jobs. French remained the language of commerce, and those schooled only in Arabic suffered most in the keen competition for jobs.

Proposed changes in the structure of secondary school exit exams—imposing yet another obstacle to success—set off riots in Constantine in 1986 and revealed the first signs of a deep social fissure. *Lycéens* were joined by university students with grievances of their own, and by the youthful unemployed, who had little else to occupy their time. With rare discipline, rioters directed their anger at the state and its symbols, ripping down pictures of Bendjedid and attacking government enterprises and party offices with careful discrimination. Two years later, these scenes repeated themselves, this time in the capital city. Demonstrations that followed an anonymously organized call for a general strike quickly degenerated into riots and plundering. In the mêlée that gripped Algiers for seven days, as many as a thousand people died, and an estimated $250 million of damage was done to property, most of it belonging to the government.[62] In both instances, the selective nature of the targets, and the undisguised willingness of many onlookers to extend critical aid to the protesters sent what could only have been a chilling message to those in power.

Until 1988 ordinary Algerians had found only anomic expression for their alienation and discontent, but the political liberalization that followed the revolt of October 1988 opened up new avenues of expression. The rapid expansion of the Islamic Salvation Front (FIS), constituted only in February 1989, and its subsequent electoral victories reflected above all Algerians' deep-seated disaffection with political elites in general and with the FLN in particular. The gulf between state and society had never been greater, or manifested itself so clearly.

By the time of the 1988 riots, an Islamist presence had been established for some time in Algeria, particularly on university campuses, where bearded young men in *gandurahs* were popularly known as "Muslim brothers," and their female counterparts, wearing the *hijab*, as "sisters." Islamists had first appeared in Algeria at the end of the 1970s, and through

1982, they made their presence known by organizing informal mosques and handing out tracts that variously called for university reform, prohibition of alcohol, and "systematic Islamization" of Algerian institutions. In late 1982, a violent clash between Islamists and Berber students over the composition of an election committee at the University of Algiers left one student dead and raised the stakes for the government. Twenty-one leading Islamists were arrested, and two weeks later, an organized demonstration drew a crowd of five thousand to protest the arrests.[63] Islamists remained in prison without trial for nearly two years, but by 1985 a truce of sorts had been arranged. The Islamists were released, the state renewed its commitment to religion and religious symbols, and in return the Islamists ceased to denounce the government.[64]

Like other Algerian political groupings, the Islamist movement was subject to division. The principal Islamist presence was noted on university campuses through the mid 1980s, and it eschewed violence, but other groups had fewer compunctions. The most notorious of them was the Algerian Armed Islamic Movement led by Mustapha Bouyali. In 1982 Bouyali's band attacked a police school outside of Algiers and absconded with a cache of pistols and ammunition. Bouyali retreated to a mountain hideout, where to the consternation and embarrassment of government officials, he eluded capture for several years. He was finally killed by government forces in a January 1987 ambush.[65]

In the late 1980s, Islamist students had grouped themselves informally around two popular preachers, Ahmed Sahnoun and Mahfoudh Nahnah, but prior to the October revolt, there was no formally structured and politically oriented Islamist organization in Algeria. The Islamist presence in the October demonstrations was unmistakable, however, and Sahnoun and Nahnah, along with a young imam from the Bab al-Oued mosque, Ali Belhadj, met with Chadli early in the week. They repeatedly called for calm, and many were impressed with the demonstration of Islamist solidarity when on the final day of the uprising, several thousand moved silently and resolutely into the open fire of army troops.[66]

Perhaps it was the possibilities suggested by the uprising itself and the responsiveness of young Islamists to impromptu but effective leadership that inspired Abbas Madani, a specialist in education and professor of sociology at the University of Algiers, to announce the creation of the Islamic Salvation Front (FIS). Sahnoun and Nahnah thought the plan ill-advised, but Madani, who decades earlier had been active in the MTLD, the OS, and CRUA, openly sought political engagement.[67] Under his leadership and that of Ali Belhadj, the as-yet-unsanctioned FIS organized quickly.

Within six months, it was able to demonstrate impressive organizational strength. It outperformed the state in distributing relief to victims of an earthquake, and thousands regularly participated in the demonstrations it organized. Throughout the country, in mosques funded by private sources and therefore free to operate without government intervention, its preachers castigated the country's leadership and delivered fiery exhortations against cultural decadence. Banners at public rallies decried social injustice and a crisis of faith. The Islamist message resonated among the unemployed and alienated, for whom austerity and privation were not a matter of choice, but as elsewhere in the Maghrib, it also reached students in technical fields, who in another epoch might have expected to fare better within the economic system.

The FIS received official recognition in September 1989—despite a constitutional provision prohibiting parties with religious affiliation. Its popularity grew, even to the point where a quarter of the deputies in the National Assembly privately expressed some attraction to new party![68] In June 1990, the FIS swept Algeria's first contested municipal elections, wresting control of all major metropolitan areas from the FLN. A year later, it again prepared to face off at the polls, this time for legislative elections. The FLN now took greater precautions, drafting an electoral law blatantly prejudiced against the FIS. The entire city of Algiers, an FIS stronghold, was accorded only as many deputies as the much smaller Kabyle city of Tizi-Ouzou, which was hostile to Islamism and Arabization. In response to this prejudicial measure, the FIS launched a strike, which again forced Bendjedid to rely on the army to restore order. This time a state of siege was declared, and again the cabinet was reshuffled.

Throughout this period, the Islamists were not immune to the fissiparous tendencies of Algerian political culture. Mahfoud Nahnah, and the leaders of two other small groups announced the merger of their separate organizations in January and declared the intent of their new party, Hamas (the Islamic Society Movement), to participate in the upcoming elections.[69] Shaykh Sahnoun continued to direct the League of the Islamic Way, and several smaller groups operated clandestinely.[70] Not all of the competition was friendly: in December 1990, Islamists in Médéa opposed to Shaykh Nahnah pelted him with the shoes his own supporters had left at the entrance of the mosque where he was preaching.

When soldiers arrested Madani, Belhadj, and five other FIS leaders in June 1991, it seemed likely that government efforts to decapitate the movement would succeed. Over the ensuing months, FIS activists were locked in their own internecine struggle, unable to replace their leaders.

Through mid December 1991, even their participation in the legislative elections remained in question. Some had speculated that the high level of technical training among its cadres would enhance the FIS's ability to govern,[71] but by 1991 several municipal governments were in shambles and the FIS's performance much criticized.[72] It was despite such criticisms and despite its internal disarray that the FIS swept the first round of legislative elections in 1991, winning 188 out of 430 seats by a clear majority. Its victory was above all a rejection of the FLN, but it also signified the extent to which the political class had lost touch with the people. Even if it could offer no coherent, pragmatic program to address the ills that manifestly troubled Algerian society, it stood alone in at least acknowledging them. Society's problems, like its voice, had been marginalized, and at the polls society expressed its anger and alienation.

CONCLUSION

Algeria's experiment in democracy ended abruptly in January 1992. Elections were nullified, and within a month, the FIS was outlawed and thousands of known or suspected supporters were transported to camps in the Sahara. Many doubted whether, after his long political exile, Boudiaf would have much influence within the collegial HCE, but he surprised some observers with efforts to bridge the gap between the political leadership and the Algerian people and with his apparent intent to restrain the military. However laudable, though, his efforts came too late and availed little. Volatile segments of society had been provoked, and sporadic bursts of political violence sparked across Algeria like brush fires. General Nezzar escaped an attempted assassination in February 1992, but Boudiaf was not so fortunate. Since his death in July 1992, terror has reigned more or less continuously. Small bands of Islamists openly enjoined the violence, and in the streets of Algiers there was speculation that many with more direct access to power were taking advantage of the general chaos to settle old and unrelated scores. Thousands of arrests were made, and new judicial councils created to expedite trials began handing down death sentences with chilling regularity. Violence continued, however, and fear rose to a new pitch in late 1993 with one Islamist group's warning that all foreigners remaining in Algeria would be responsible for "their own sudden death."[73] By the end of 1993, several thousand people—including prominent writers and academics as well as the former SM chief and prime minister Kasdi Merbah—had been lost to the terror.

The Algerian state is at risk. For thirty years, it appeared to dominate all aspects of civic life, and its power seemed incontestable, but as the adage would have it, appearances sometimes deceive. At close regard, Algerian leaders at the helm of state protected their image of strength by avoiding controversial policy areas. They deferred to the military and hid behind a cadre of technocrats. The country's natural endowment was used to co-opt critics, to pay for mistakes and lost opportunities, and to line various pockets. The illusion of state strength was created out of society's own weakness. Relatively speaking, the state was strong because Algerian society had been thoroughly sundered by the colonial experience and the war to end it. On the rare occasions when society managed to muster force, the state's only weapon was violence of its own. Most protest movements quickly succumbed to state force, but despite their own multiple divisions, the Islamists present a new challenge. As a result, the state's future is uncertain. In January 1994 General Zeroual was named interim president and charged with returning the country to the rule of its constitution, but there were few signs that the struggle for control would abate. Political elites remained divided about the desirability of dialogue with Islamists engaged in armed struggle, and in exile, FIS leaders proclaimed their own provisional government. The only clear truth to emerge from Algeria's second civil war is the incapacity of the old political class to govern society and run the state.

6 Morocco: God and King

Morocco is a monarchy, and all the complexities and contradictions that color relations between its ruled and ruler are embedded in that simple assertion. Morocco's monarch is not merely king: he rules over one of the world's oldest monarchies as a *sharif*, descendant of the Prophet, and as Prince of the Faithful, *amir al-mu'minin*. Although political parties mediate competition among elites and a constitution ostensibly defines the parameters of legitimate political play, Morocco in the late twentieth century remains in the tutelage of patrimonial principles. The king towers over the political system, and his role must be understood before we can examine either the activities or the impact of human rights groups. The king defines the players and the play; he sets the tone of political discourse. Any analysis of Moroccan state-society relations must thus commence with the monarchy.

THE MONARCHY

The Moroccan monarchy appears to many a quixotic political anachronism. Efforts to explain its staying power in terms of the intrinsic weakness and fragmentation of the opposition or in terms of the charisma and good luck (*baraka*) of individual monarchs have their merits, but they are not fully persuasive. The opposition has indeed been fractious, but it is arguably better developed in Morocco than in other Maghrib states. For their part, the most recent monarchs have proven resilient and canny, but along the way not every occupant of the throne has been so gifted or so fortunate. Elsewhere the tendency toward personal rule commonly undermines political institutions,[1] yet in Morocco the monarchy itself has been relatively immune to attack. Even in the abstract there is little noteworthy support for republican rule, and while critics may attack individual policies or—cautiously—the monarch himself, the legitimacy of the monarchy as an institution is rarely subject to open questioning.

What the Moroccan king possesses that other Maghribi heads of state lack, and what the Moroccan opposition alone must face, is the weight of an institution gradually constructed over twelve centuries and now deeply anchored in the political culture and psyche of the Moroccan people. It is not a social contract so much as a psychological contract that binds the people to the monarchy; richly symbolic rituals have sealed the relationship and in their regular reenactment continuously renew it.[2] Historical processes have made the sharifian principle—the popular belief that Morocco's legitimate ruler is and should be a descendant of the Prophet Muhammad—the cornerstone of the political system. Rituals associated with the monarchy helped establish the king as a patriarch, attributing his rights of governance to divine origin. Because the rituals successfully incorporate all strata of society, they likewise manage to integrate both ruled and ruler symbolically into a single community of faith. Ritual enactments reconnect Moroccans to their forebears and to the divine, and the monarchy emerges from them as the centerpiece of the Moroccan polity. More mundane practices of politics can by consequence only revolve around it.

The sharifian principle was elaborated over several centuries, but the Sa'di dynasty (1548–1641) was the first to have grasped the legitimizing power of blood descent. From 1069, Moroccan territory had been controlled by a succession of Berber dynasties whose cultural and political achievements made of Morocco an important seat of power in the world of their time.[3] Rulers presided over a centralized state apparatus that effectively organized military force and permitted expansion. Marrakesh and Fez were transformed into imperial cities. A vast network of bankers and merchants traded gold, sugar, salt, and slaves, and Fez was renowned in the Islamic world as a center of learning.

Early in the fifteenth century, the dual assault of bubonic plague and rising European power caused centralized rule to collapse. About the same time, however, the fortuitous discovery of a tomb purported to be that of Idris II, Morocco's first true sovereign directly descended from the Prophet, introduced a potent new political force. Religious zeal flourished in the 1600s—partly in reaction to the Spanish Reconquista and Portuguese invasions—and sharifs popularly symbolized the ideal of Moroccan unity.[4] From the south, Sa'diyan sharifs were able to build a religio-political movement that by 1554 allowed them to control both Marrakesh and Fez and unify the Moroccan territory.

Powerful as it was, blood descent was not the only source of political legitimacy in uncertain times, and to an aspiring dynast, devout Sufi shaykhs and the *tariqas* (brotherhoods) they headed posed the greatest threat. The Sa'di ruler Ahmad al-Mansur (The Victorious) understood that political reality, and he understood as well that contemporary questions about the Sa'dis' own claim to the bloodline increased his vulnerability.[5] He governed ruthlessly and levied heavy taxes to support the splendor of his court, but he took great care to develop the symbolic linkages between the Prophet and his contemporary heir. The first Islamic millennium was marked during Al-Mansur's reign and afforded abundant opportunities to strengthen those linkages. Most important, a celebration of the Prophet's birthday that had been developed in the eastern Islamic world during the twelfth century was adapted for the Moroccan monarchy. A fabulous ceremony opened with a candlelight procession that was followed by Arabic recitations and a sumptuous feast at the sultan's palace. In the course of festivities, crowds were admitted to the palace by social rank in a manner that clearly established social order and set the Prophet's descendant at its head.[6]

Al-Mansur's death in 1603 created a power vacuum that was filled for several decades by Berber Sufis from the Dala'iyya *zawiya* in the Middle Atlas. The eventual transition from the decentralized rule of the Sufis to the 'Alawi dynasty that reigns in Morocco today brought with it the foundation of the modern state and domination over the 'ulama in Fez. There is some dispute among scholars about the circumstances that led the sharif Mawlay Rashid to arrive from the south, unseat the Dala'iyya and reestablish dynastic rule. M. E. Combs-Schillings suggests that seventeenth-century Moroccans awaited messianic deliverance and found it in the 'Alawis.[7] Other accounts are more equivocal. According to Jacques Berque, the notables of Fez respected the Dala'iyya for their religious piety and were critical of Mawlay Rashid.[8] More important, though, they prized their autonomy. Fez resisted Dala'iyya entry in 1641, and similarly, the city surrendered to Mawlay Rashid's ambitions in 1668 only after a protracted struggle.[9]

Berque argues that rather than any religious respect they commanded, it was military might combined with their initial distance from the power center of Fez that finally allowed the 'Alawis to establish their rule.[10] The bloodline was insufficient: Al-Mansur had left sons with sharifian claims, but they compromised the dynasty with internecine conflict and concessions to Spain; likewise, descendants of the original Idrissid rulers were unable to establish control. The sharifian principle established eligibility, but the fundamental basis of the 'Alawi dynasty—from its inception to the present—was its distance from both the masses and political elites. Once in power, the 'Alawi dynasty expanded the kingdom's domain and laid in place the foundations of a modern state. Dissident tribes in its outreaches, the *bled al-siba*, acknowledged the political authority of the sharif monarch even if they still refused to pay taxes or comply with requests they judged unreasonable. During the reign of the greatly feared and equally admired Mawlay Ismail (1672–1727), privateering supplied wealth to rebuild the kingdom, and a professional army of black slaves imposed order even on lands beyond Fez and the central plain. No fewer than seventy-six fortresses were built to guarantee security of the *bled al-makhzen*, land in the government's firm control.[11]

The territory was secure, but the throne less so. Primogeniture was not recognized, and the 'ulama in Fez held formidable religious and judicial authority. The 'Alawi dynasty, like the Sa'dis that preceded it, needed to insert itself into the actual practice of religion to curtail the power of rivals and undergird its claim of divine right to rule (*qutb al zam'an*). The dynasty continued and expanded ritual performances, but most important was a change that put the Great Sacrifice, the most important of Islam's canonical rituals, at the service of the Moroccan monarchy. The ritual as observed throughout the Islamic world involves the sacrifice of a ram and, when possible, a pilgrimage to Mecca. Its observance gives social form to the notion of *umma* (community of believers) and links it to God and eternity. Beginning in the second half of the seventeenth century, Moroccan monarchs publicly slew a ram on behalf of the nation, and in so doing added another layer of meaning. As Combs-Schilling observes, in creating the ritual, the Prophet Muhammad had inserted himself into the mythic event of Ibrahim's sacrifice; in carving out a role for itself in the sacred ritual, the Moroccan monarchy represented itself as the intervening link between the Prophet and the *umma*.[12]

The rituals associated with both the Prophet's birthday and the Great Sacrifice effectively bound the masses to the monarchy, and it would appear that they were introduced for that explicit purpose. They also have the effect, no less important, of setting the monarchy apart from the people and reinforcing the distance that allowed monarchs to establish and maintain their rule. Incorporated into the practice of the Moroccan monarchy more than three centuries ago, rituals that entwine the monarchy with Islam have remained largely in place through the fortunes that have followed, and they are performed today by King Hassan II. Even colonial rule, which stripped the Moroccan throne of governing power, did not rob the rituals of their own potency. When Mawlay Hafiz was forced to sign the capitulation papers in 1912, he also destroyed the scarlet canopy and the sedan-chair that had been emblems of the 'Alawi dynasty, but he continued to perform the Great Sacrifice on behalf of the nation.[13]

Through deeply resonating rituals, the sharifian principle has imbued the Moroccan monarchy with a potency that extends beyond any given occupant of its throne. The French learned this lesson the hard way. In 1927 they handpicked the sultan's successor, choosing his youngest son to maximize their own control, but to their dismay Mohammed V grew into the role that had been constructed for Moroccan monarchs over the previous three centuries. Colonial rhetoric was turned against the French by the young sultan, who used the religious power that yet remained attached to the monarchy to endorse the cause of political independence. When in 1953 the French exercised exceedingly bad judgment and deposed the sultan on the very eve of the Great Sacrifice, the wheels that turned Moroccan society ground to a halt. So potent a symbol of the nation was Mohammed V that, in stark contrast to other contemporary independence movements, the national cause was framed in terms of his return and the renewal of a traditional institution.[14] In 1955, Mohammed V was restored to the throne, and Morocco was granted independence—the last of the Maghribi countries to be colonized and the first to free itself of colonial rule.

The power of the Moroccan monarchy's symbols helped it survive colonial rule and harness the energies of the nationalist movement. The dynamics of political life today involve the high drama of court rituals less centrally, but those rituals nonetheless specify the relationship between ruled and ruler and form a backdrop against which even the most ordinary political event must be viewed. They create a context for political activity that at times overshadows the political play itself, and the power they lend to a reigning monarch cannot be discounted. The country's mass media ensure that Moroccans do not forget that their ruler is a king, and on celebrated occasions throughout the year they are reminded that their king is *amir al-mu'minin*. Neither the sharifian principle nor the powerful rituals prevent political contest, but they do impose parameters on the political game and affect the relationship between the king and the country's political class.

THE KING AND HIS MEN

When Mohammed V was permitted to return from exile in 1955 and the French ceded their claim to Morocco, the weight of history was on the sharifian monarch's side. For tactical reasons, the nationalist movement that emerged in the 1930s had not adopted republican rhetoric, and the dependence of both the French and the nationalists on the sultan to advance their interests shaped a framework by which, at independence, Mohammed V could reclaim control over the political system. Yet the process was not automatic. There was no significant dispute over the legitimacy of the monarchy, or the monarch, but the nature of the relationship between sultan (or king, in the new parlance preferred by Mohammed V) and subjects was nevertheless open to renegotiation. The monarchy had been restored, but its terms had not been set, the various roles to be played by the nationalists had not been clearly delineated, and there was no consensus about the effective balance of power between political forces. Apart from the principle of sharifian descent, there were no generally accepted rules of succession, which opened speculation about legitimate rule; the spread of nationalism and Wilsonian principles of self-determination also provoked questions about the role and powers of the monarch.

For close to twenty years—until the emergence of the Western Saharan issue in the mid 1970s—kings and political parties were locked in a contest for control of the political agenda.[15] Although from the outset both Mohammed V and his successor Hassan II enjoyed certain advantages, the outcome of early political battles about the determination and prioritization of issues to be addressed by public policy was far from certain. The sultan and the nationalists had found common cause in the struggle for independence, but as the only viable political party in Morocco through 1959, the Istiqlal Party also aspired to control the country's political processes, and although internal contests prevented it and its offshoots from imposing their will on the throne, their collective influence was sufficient to deny both Mohammed V and Hassan II control over the political debate about important social and economic issues for nearly two decades.

During that time, the working rules of the modern monarchy were gradually crafted, leaving the king in clear control of the political game. Mohammed V had spoken lengthily about constitutional monarchy prior to independence, but enactment was delayed. Demands within nationalist circles for a constituent assembly like that elected in Tunisia were ignored, and instead a National Consultative Assembly was created, its members being appointed by royal decree. The first in a series of constitutions was finally drafted by loyal monarchists in 1960, but the process of approval and enactment was interrupted by Mohammed V's death in 1961. His eldest son and successor, Hassan II, finally promulgated a constitution in 1962, which reinforced the monarchy by establishing the inviolability of the person of the king and the successionary principle of primogeniture.

Simultaneously, it capped the strength of any given political grouping by prohibiting the development of a single-party system.

Through the life of this constitution and three successive ones, parties and the Palace have struggled over control of the political process, although as outlined below, the early contests clearly gave the upper hand to the 'Alawi monarch. Parliament and parties have since become well established on the Moroccan landscape—leading some to claim that Morocco is an effective multiparty democracy[16]—but the king remains free to bypass these institutions and pursue his ends through alternative means.

Parties, Government, and Parliament

Under its constitution, Morocco has a pluralistic, competitive party system, and successive slates of government ministers have represented a variety of party affiliations. The functioning of government and the vigor of parties are not, however, to be confused with political power. Over the years, that prize has fallen to the king alone. How then do the democratic institutions of parliament and political parties fit into the patrimonial framework of Moroccan politics?[17]

Parties are numerous, but their role is limited. In the first place, there is a tendency toward fragmentation and multiplication that keeps parties weak—and serves the Palace. In the years following independence, the Palace actively encouraged the creation and development of parties that might carve away some of the Istiqlal Party's support, and the initial government appointed by Mohammed V gave disproportionate representation to smaller, less significant groupings to offset the Istiqlal Party's influence. Even by 1960, the field was cluttered. In 1959 the Istiqlal Party split, and followers of 'Abdullah Ibrahim formed the National Union of Popular Forces (UNFP). The UNFP was an urban mass party, promoting a program of social and economic reform and recruiting supporters from among workers, urban migrants, bureaucrats, and students. It would itself experience a schism in 1974, but until then it remained an important political force. In the meantime, it was joined in the political arena by several royalist groupings with various degrees of political organization. The longest-lived of these has been the Popular Movement (MP), a party based in the countryside, which promoted aspects of Berber culture but above all proclaimed unconditional support for the monarchy. Other, smaller groups—such as the inchoate Liberal Independents, first known simply as the "Friends of Rachid Mouline"—eventually disappeared.

The proliferation of new parties continued well beyond the constitutional monarchy's formative years, fed by sentiments of political rivalry and the Palace's own interest in balancing power. (Table 1 traces the somewhat discontinuous and fissiparous evolution of Moroccan political parties.) In 1974, for example, divisions within the UNFP gave birth to a new Socialist Union of Popular Forces (USFP) and promised to weaken the political left. When the USFP began to gain popular favor, though, its new strength was balanced in formal instances by the pro-Palace National Rally of Independents (RNI), founded in 1978 by none other than the king's brother-in-law. Before long the RNI's own internal divisions and quarrels with the Palace over political spoils made it less than reliable as a source of support, and yet another party stepped into the breach. The Constitutional Union (UC), created by Prime Minister Maati Bouabid in 1983 and made up largely of young professionals, consolidated the parliamentary majority in 1984.

To mitigate the isolating effects of their size, small parties have frequently formed electoral coalitions. In 1984 five parties ran together as the Kutla (Democratic Bloc), and in preparation for the 1993 legislative elections they again joined forces.[18] Of the thirteen parties that participated in the 1993 legislative elections, all but the fragmentary UNFP and the Constitutional and Democratic Popular Movement (MPDC), a small splinter group that broke away from the MP in the late 1970s, won seats in the new parliament. A de facto royalist coalition consists of parties commonly allocated government ministries and is referred to as the Wifaq (Entente).

If parties are prone to fragmentation, they are also subject to political tutelage and even repression. The USFP, for example, might eventually have had a significant effect, but its vigorous early growth was severely checked by government repression and in elections generally acknowledged as fraudulent. Such experiences were common on the left—and are discussed at greater length later in this chapter. Other parties have generally been spared repression, but they are not altogether independent of the Palace. The MP's founder, Mahjoubi Aherdane, for example, fell out with the Palace, and with many within his movement, in 1985. Although he retained his seat in parliament, relations deteriorated with others in the MP to the point where in 1990, twenty-one members announced their intent to hold a party congress to establish a new leadership. It was a nod from the royal councilor Reda Guedira that empowered the *fronde* to reorganize the party and exclude Aherdane.[19]

The impact of political parties is limited, not simply by deficiencies in their own strength, whether inherent or imposed by the Palace, but also by the relative weakness of the two bodies in which they may find expression,

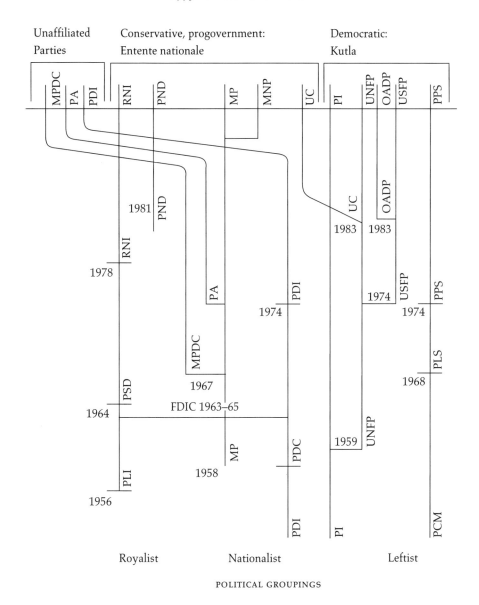

Figure 1. Evolution of Moroccan Political Parties, 1956–1993

Table 1. Principal Moroccan Political Parties, 1956–1993

FDIC/Front pour la défense des institutions constitutionnelles Front for the Defense of Constitutional Institutions	A monarchist electoral coalition created in 1963, comprised of the PDC, the Liberal Independents, the MP, and several independent political figures. It was dissolved in 1965.
MNP/Mouvement national populaire National Popular Movement	Founded in 1990 by the former leader of the MP, Mahjoubi Aherdane.
MP/Mouvement populaire Popular Movement	Rural-based party appealing to Berber ethnicity. Created in 1959 by Majoubi Aherdan.
MPDC/Mouvement populaire démocratique et constitutionnel Democratic and Constitutional Popular Movement	Created after a 1967 split in the MP by Dr. Abdelkrim Khatib.
OADP/Organisation pour l'action démocratique et populaire Organization of Democratic and Popular Action	A leftist party founded in 1983 by former members of the unauthorized March 23 Movement.
PA/Parti d'action Action Party	A small party organized in 1974 by Berber intellectuals.
PCM/Parti communiste marocain Moroccan Communist Party	Formed prior to independence; formally banned in 1959.
PDC/Parti démocratique constitutionnel Democratic Constitutional Party	Founded in 1959 by the original leaders of the PDI after a split in that party. It dissolved when the PDI was reconstituted in 1974.
PDI/Parti démocratique et de l'indépendance Democratic Party of Independence (Party of Choura and Independence)	Originally a small splinter of the nationalist movement, the PDI operated briefly during the first few years after independence. It was reorganized in 1974 and first participated in elections in 1974.
PI/Istiqlal Independence Party	Morocco's oldest party, founded in 1944 by nationalist political elite. The Istiqlal Party dominated the political scene during the first three years of independence.
PLI/Parti des libéraux indépendents Liberal Independents' Party	A small party originally centered around two influential friends of the Palace, Rachid Mouline and Reda Guedira.

Table 1. Principal Moroccan Political Parties, 1956–1993 *(continued)*

PLS/Parti de libération et socialisme Liberation and Socialism Party	A short-lived successor to the Moroccan Communist Party.
PND/Parti national démocratique National Democratic Party	A royalist party founded in 1981 by 59 former RNI deputies in the Chamber of Representatives.
PPS/Parti du progrès et du socialisme Party of Progress and Socialism	Formed in 1968 to replace the banned Moroccan Communist Party and legally recognized in 1974.
PSD/Parti socialiste démocrate Socialist Democrat Party	Short-lived faction within the FDIC intended to counterbalance Aherdan and the MP.
RNI/Rassemblement national des indépendants National Rally for Independence [National Assembly of Independents]	Originated as a parliamentary group in 1977. Initially branded the "King's Party" by left-wing critics; internal disagreements and disagreements with the Palace eventually resulted in its designation as the "official" opposition.
UC/Union constitutionnelle Constitutional Union	A moderate party emphasizing economic self-sufficiency. Created by Maati Bouabid in 1983 during his tenure as prime minister.
UNFP/Union nationale des forces populaires National Union of Popular Forces	Principal leftist party, 1959–74; thereafter eclipsed by its offshoot, the USFP.
USFP/Union socialiste des forces populaires Socialist Union of Popular Forces	The largest party representing the political left. Organized in 1974 as the result of a split in the UNFP.

parliament and the cabinet. Irrespective of electoral outcomes, the cabinet represents royal interests. The monarchy has secured constitutional recognition of its right to appoint the prime minister, and like his father, Hassan II has jealously guarded control over key ministries. He has entrusted sensitive portfolios only to those with known personal loyalty, and although lesser ministries have occasionally been allocated to outlying parties, turnover is frequent and ministers have rarely enjoyed administrative autonomy.[20]

Parties are given more license to construct a national debate in parliament and through their press organs—and they do—but the structure of power relations in Morocco leaves most of their actions without consequence. The Istiqlal Party's early battle for separation of powers was lost, and despite legislative and oversight functions registered in constitutions, all Moroccan parliaments since independence have been conceived of primarily as consultative bodies. Alain Claisse notes that in 1983, when parliament was dissolved at the end of the term without new deputies having been elected, the king empowered himself to assume legislative as well as executive responsibilities. A few months later, following the 1984 legislative election, Hassan II invited the newly elected deputies to fulfill their function as "council" to the sovereign, issuing the patrimonial charge, "You are all my ministers."[21] Parliament may approve legislation, but its members are discouraged from acting independently, and they are without means to restrain monarchical powers.

With such a serious handicap, parliament is generally reduced to a rubber stamp, although it has occasionally used what powers it does have to deprive the Palace of support or contest policy. Such was the case of the first parliament, seated from 1963 to 1965. In the election, a hastily assembled royalist coalition known as the Front for the Defense of Constitutional Institutions (FDIC) had won a plurality of seats, but it failed to establish a clear majority. Moreover, Palace supporters were set back psychologically by the strong showing of the UNFP, which halfheartedly decided to run only two weeks before the election. The cabinet appointed by the king favored FDIC leaders, but neither the FDIC nor the opposing Istiqlal Party and UNFP were in a position to make the system work. It didn't. "From the outset of parliamentary life it appeared that the king wished to make a mockery of the experiment, and it is only fair to note that all concerned aided him admirably in its task," John Waterbury observed. "The opposition parties resorted to debilitating tactics designed in general to embarrass the government. The latter reciprocated with systematic hostility."[22] Between 1963 and 1965, parliament passed only two laws.

Unfortunately for the parties that sought an oppositional role, deadlock ultimately resulted in parliament's dissolution. When in 1965 general discontent about unemployment and inflation led to riots that shook Casablanca and left several hundred people dead, the Palace sought to make amends to the parties it had contrived to exclude. They held out for fair elections and a government formed on the basis of the parliamentary majority, however, and Hassan II parried by declaring a state of emergency that dissolved parliament and suspended the constitution. From 1965 to 1970, Morocco was governed directly by the king.

However ineffective it was at elaborating a body of law or balancing executive powers, and however annoying it was to the Palace, the king recognized the usefulness of parliament as a bridge to his subjects. Consequently, the question after 1965 was not so much whether to have a parliament as how to fashion a legislative body that would serve royal purposes and under what conditions to install it. Since suspending the original constitution in 1965 the Palace has—with direct input from Hassan II— drafted three successive constitutions. In each iteration, modifications have primarily concerned the number of parliamentary seats and the means by which they would be contested. Ironically, none of the constitutions has restored even the narrow powers known to the first parliament.

Morocco's second constitution (1970) severely limited direct suffrage, and with both the Istiqlal Party and the UNFP opposing the election itself, under its terms the government—that is, the Palace—easily won an overwhelming majority. The victory, however, proved a pyrrhic one. Parties atrophied in the five-year hiatus between legislatures, and institutionalized participation virtually disappeared: 158 of the 240 deputies were elected as independents. The king was isolated and from the vantage of the military appeared to be losing control; two attempted coups in rapid succession pointed up the attendant perils.[23] Only luck and the awesome moral presence of the sharifian monarchy saved Hassan II,[24] and after 1972 he set about reconstructing his regime on less precarious grounds.

Morocco's third constitution (1972) loosened the royal vice grip on participation but it did not reflect a change in Hassan II's fundamental disdain for parliamentary government.[25] In an overture that would mark a basic shift in political dynamics, the Palace in 1973 formulated its own program, introducing economic reforms and initiating a program of substantial state investments.[26] During the first decade of independence, the monarch had frequently taken his cues from the Istiqlal Party or the UNFP, appropriating their political platforms as his own,[27] but now he laid claim to the political agenda. Neither the emergence of new parties nor the reconvening of parliament under new rules altered that reality.

The legislature, though, continued to serve royal purposes, and the timing of elections conducted under the rules of the 1972 constitution accommodated the interests of the Palace more than they conformed to the letter of the law. The enormously successful 1976 Green March to annex the Western Sahara had poignantly reminded Moroccans of their venerable patrimony and the majesty of the dynasty that governed it, and the Palace unabashedly capitalized on the patent spirit of unity that infused even the most critical of the political parties. Without sacrificing any of its own powers, the Palace openly courted opponents. In 1977, thus, the king created a politically all-inclusive Royal Council to prepare for elections, and in similar fashion, he appointed a "unity government" in 1983 to induce widespread participation in the 1984 elections. Neither gesture was of lasting political importance, except to underscore the king's desire to have a functioning, pluralistic legislature—on his own terms.

The fourth constitution was submitted to popular referendum in 1992 following an unusual period of parliamentary activity that directly relates to the human rights issues discussed in Chapter 10. Legislative elections scheduled for 1990 were postponed, ostensibly pending a UN-sponsored referendum on the Western Sahara. In fact, unrest was already brewing on a number of domestic fronts. Austerity measures announced in March sparked protest from labor and provoked parliament. A finance policy proposed to parliament in May evoked substantial ire and led eighty-two members of the USFP, PPS, and the OADP to file a motion of censure. Emboldened by their own initiatives—and by pressures being levied on the human rights front—various members of parliament began to speak publicly about issues as contentious as *habus* laws and women's rights. Members of the Istiqlal Party raised the issue of constitutional reforms, and argued that the current constitution did not permit installation of a real democracy insofar as powers were not separate and human rights not guaranteed. Political tensions increased through fall 1990 with the commitment of Moroccan troops to defend the Saudi palace, and a general strike called in December gave way to rioting and political violence in Fez. In numbers it was at least matched by a February 1991 demonstration in Rabat to protest the Gulf War, and by extension, Morocco's engagement in it. Even the military, closely monitored since the attempted coups, was said to have conveyed its opposition to Morocco's participation in the allied effort. Kutla parties sought to exploit those sentiments and renewed their efforts to woo the electorate. For its part, the Palace recognized the need to recapture popular sentiment, particularly as it faced the eventual disappearance of the Saharan issue, which has served as the only real basis for national unity over the past fifteen years. In March 1992, Hassan II announced plans to renew the constitution and rework the balance between Palace and parliament. In a familiar pattern, the new constitution expanded the number of seats in parliament, and although much fanfare was made of a preambulatory nod to international human rights norms, the Kutla was disappointed with provisions that allowed the monarch to preserve all conventional powers. Elections for the 222 directly chosen seats in June 1993 gave the Kutla parties 99 seats and a stronger showing than had ever been recognized, but their relatively weak showing in contests for the remaining 111 seats chosen indirectly in September once again returned the parliamentary majority to a royalist coalition. In apparent disregard for the provisions of the new constition allowing a prime minister to choose his own cabinet, Hassan II offered an array of ministries to the losing parties. They refused, holding out for application of the new rules, and the game was returned to the status quo ante. Hassan reappointed Mohamed Karim Lamrani to his fourth term as prime minister, and Mawlay Ahmed Alaoui (minister of state without portfolio), Driss Basri (interior), and Abdellatif Filali (foreign affairs) took up their familiar ministerial posts.

The king thus continued to control the political game. Since the mid 1970s, Hassan II has established himself as both the master player and the referee. Contestants have been admitted to the playing field at his discretion and remain so as long as they abide by his rules. He frequently addresses the Moroccan nation as "my children," and that patrimonial phrase has set the tone of politics. For as long as they play by the king's rules— and despite the obvious risks, that posture does vary—all recognized parties are in substantial measure "king's men." That term is conventionally reserved for those who have belonged to the various monarchist coalitions, but in practical reality it has broader application.

The King as Referee

The sociologist Max Weber developed the concept of "sultanism" as a variant of traditional authority that maximizes the arbitrary will of the ruler,[28] and Hassan II of Morocco in many regards epitomizes the ideal type. Parliament and parties lend a certain form to Moroccan politics, but most significant political transactions leave these institutions aside. Real power lies elsewhere.

As a starting point, it is worth noting—however impolitic—that the Palace owns much of Morocco.[29] The king is said to be the country's largest landowner and has a controlling interest in Omnium Nord-Africain (ONA), the Maghrib's largest holding company. Manipulation of its wealth is central to the way the monarch controls the political game. Privately, elites exchange stories of the king's interventions to confiscate property or to award it at royal discretion. "Agrarian reform" implemented in times of crisis, for example, has permitted the Palace to allocate land and secure commensurate political support.[30] As Waterbury remarked in the first decade after independence, patronage and surveillance over commercial activities are the king's two most effective levers of elite control.[31] It is an advantage to the Palace that the Moroccan elite is small; intermarriage within it assures close contact and gives the king access to politically valuable information about his most esteemed subjects. Hassan II has not hesitated to use personal idiosyncrasies and interpersonal rivalries to maintain competition for patronage.[32]

In the lower echelons of the state apparatus, advancement is controlled by bureaucratic mechanisms, but the Palace has maintained its prerogative of filling all high-level posts by royal decree.[33] Such appointments are prized, for in the tradition of the Moroccan *makhzen* (government administration), they open the doors to personal aggrandizement of a sort that might elsewhere be condemned as graft. Palace favorites may be rewarded with control of public enterprises, and public office has facilitated access to such benefits as real estate, import licenses, commercial licenses, and noncompetitive contracts.[34] Even the contractual particulars in the lower echelons are subject to royal intervention and manipulation, so that the entire corpus of government lies open, and vulnerable, to the king's pleasure.

Commercial enterprises and banks in the private sector are also heavily dominated by the royal family, with the result that policies of privatization progressively implemented since 1983 have not reduced the Palace's control. Indeed, the king's influence in the private sector has been strengthened through the recent marriages of his two daughters, which consolidated linkages with both the Casablanca industrialists and the Fez bourgeoisie.[35] The king does not openly flaunt these powers, but in both public and private sectors, he remains in a position to make, or break, individual fortunes.

Government and commercial perquisites actively cultivate a royal clientele and in turn make powerful patrons of the king's own clients. The Moroccan political economy turns on such relations, and the close incorporation of political elites into the system reinforces the monarch's own position. Even the political parties as a whole are beholden to the royal purse. In 1987, each of Morocco's twelve political parties were extended 1.7 million dirhams ($200,000), ostensibly to strengthen their unions and encourage a "free" press.[36] Such largess serves to bind parties, for what is extended may also be withdrawn. When otherwise faithful clients overstep their bounds, they are removed from office, and only when they have been sufficiently chastised may they be reinstated or reintegrated within the elect circle of power. The king alone has such freedom of maneuver, and through it his patriarchal authority and patrimonial control is reinforced.

Where patronage cannot fully ensure royal dominion, the king has himself taken charge, directly or indirectly. Military and security forces in particular come under close surveillance. Matters of internal governance that corresponded to traditional *makhzen* functions were of immediate concern to the Palace in the early years of independence, and the outcome of a political contest between Mohammed V and his Istiqlal Party ministers left the Palace in tacit control of the internal security apparatus. It was overseen first by General Mohammed Oufkir, who for many years was the most feared man in the kingdom. Since 1979 it has been confided to the interior minister, Driss Basri, a security agent who came up through the ranks and was groomed for the position.[37] The Interior Ministry is responsible for a formidable security apparatus, but in addition, its administrative purview has gradually come to include the oversight of other ministries as well as technical areas carved away from other administrative units.[38] Not surprisingly, as the ministry's powers have expanded, so has the Palace's own surveillance. As one measure of control, the king has retained powers to appoint the caids with whom security forces collaborate closely.[39] To protect the monarchy, the security apparatus is fragmented, and rivalrous: as many as four separate security and intelligence agencies report to the Interior Ministry, and the largest of these is also subdivided into four units. For further insurance, the operations of the two most important security units are additionally overseen by the Gendarmerie royale, a division of the armed forces.[40] Checks and balances notwithstanding, Basri is considered by many to be the second most powerful man in the kingdom.

The military is also carefully watched by the king. After the second attempted coup implicated no less a personage than General Oufkir, Hassan II reclaimed direct command of the Defense Ministry and implemented reforms to limit its power and cohesion. In particular, the largely Berber officer corps, intended by Mohammed V to counterbalance the influence of the more politically and economically favored *makhzen* elite, was diversified.[41] Even so, General Ahmed Dlimi, a trusted Berber officer, had by the early 1980s accrued power sufficient to threaten the throne. Dlimi had been assigned command of the royal guard and the secret service, as well as of the politically paramount Saharan forces, and the mysterious circumstances of his death while traveling on a remote mountain road in 1983 raised suspicions of official complicity. After Dlimi's death, the army was placed under the command of the crown prince, Sidi Mohammed, and the Royal Armed Forces are regularly and poignantly reminded of their charge to defend the throne. The officer corps is reviewed with great pomp and pageantry on the anniversary of Hassan II's accession to the throne each year; promotions are enacted, and officers are individually and publicly received to kiss the hand of the monarch in the venerable ceremony of *ba'ya* that reaffirms loyalty and submission to the throne.

Control of the judiciary is less straightforward, but little less effective. Successive constitutions have affirmed separation of powers, but only rarely has the judiciary exercised independence. In fact, the Moroccan monarch has retained powers to appoint all magistrates, and Moroccan judges are no less beholden to the throne than are other state employees. The ability of the judiciary to moderate relations between state and society, as through judicial review, is limited by the tacit understanding that a royal decree, regardless of its subject, supersedes other positive law. As Prince of the Faithful, the king is protected against adverse judgments on his own pronouncements, and the Moroccan Supreme Court has ruled clearly that appeals in court against royal fiat are forbidden.[42] Like many heads of state, the king also possesses powers of clemency, but in Morocco these have been exercised in such a way as to make of the court only an auxiliary to the monarch. Royal pardons are frequently extended to common law offenders on national or religious holidays, but they have also been applied, often arbitrarily, to individuals convicted of political crimes. At a 1972 trial of UNFP leaders, for example, the king pardoned and freed the only physically present defendant sentenced to death, while twenty-seven others with lesser sentences (of ten years or more) were locked away. Likewise, pardons for political prisoners tried en masse in 1977 were meted out intermittently from 1984 to 1991, unrelated either to the charges against them or the length of their sentences. Clemency emphasizes the arbitrary powers of the king and establishes him, rather than the courts, as the supreme dispenser of justice.

Finally, to thwart those who might seek to make of high government office an independent base of power and policy, Moroccan monarchs have relied on personally appointed and personally loyal councils to formulate and even implement policies. Mohammed V initiated the practice of appointing special councils with the creation of the National Constituent Assembly in 1957, and councils were convened by Hassan II in 1965 to replace the dissolved parliament; in 1968 to deliberate the new five-year plan; in 1977 to oversee elections; and in 1990 to address issues of human rights. No corpus of law sanctions the existence and functioning of such councils or of the king's personal advisers, but their influence has often exceeded that of the formally appointed government ministers. In addition to narrowly mandated councils, a royal cabinet functioning parallel to the government often confuses the analysis of power, as does the appointment of influential ministers without portfolio. Guedira has intermittently functioned as grand vizir, privately advising the monarch and overseeing the royal cabinet, and other royalists of undisputed loyalty likewise function as the *makhzen* of an earlier era did. Mawlay Ahmed Alaoui ('Alawi), a minister of state without portfolio, but with links of parentage to the royal family, travels the length and breadth of the kingdom cutting ribbons, patching up small disputes, and generally serving as a bridge between Palace and people; through the daily *Matin du Sahara*, he also acts as publicist for the throne.[43] Such informal mechanisms allow the king to control most formal institutions that might develop or exhibit autonomous thought and behavior vis-à-vis the Palace. Those who accept these parameters and cooperate are, perforce, the king's men. Those who do not, when they do not, are excluded from the legitimate game of politics.

OPPOSITION:
BEYOND THE SANCTIONED BOUNDS

Although both ideological conviction and personal connections have guided the formation of political parties, neither factor effectively identifies "opposition" in Morocco. Opposition is defined not so much by rhetorical content as by a challenge to royal power. The rules that govern the relationship between state and society in Morocco are clear, and the fundamental axiom is that the king is sacrosanct. The Moroccan constitution, newly revised in 1992, is only ancillary to the monarch.[44] The king retains virtually all significant powers: he may promulgate law, appoint a prime minister and dismiss the government, dissolve parliament, suspend the constitution, and bypass parliament with constitutional amendments. It is forbidden by law to publish an article offensive to the king and the royal family, and it is illegal to inquire into royal finances. Criticism and public debate are permitted—and arguably, encouraged—so long as they neither implicitly nor explicitly contest the monarchy, Islam, Morocco's territorial integrity, or the king himself. As a practical consequence, certain subjects are politically taboo. Predictably, the most controversial and politically compelling issues lie beyond the tolerable limits: to advocate self-determination for the peoples of the Western Sahara has been considered treason; open debate about Islamism or limits to monarchical power are similarly ill-advised.

Any breech of the tacit code of consensus constructed around king, God, and country places politicians in the opposition, but subtle changes in the Palace's own positions and accommodations by erstwhile opponents give the system a certain fluidity. Opposition in Morocco is a temporal variable, indicating the state of relations with the monarch rather than a stably occupied position within a political spectrum arrayed along social or economic lines. Politics can make odd bedfellows, and in Morocco what any two groups suffering repression at a given time may share in common is antipathy toward the Palace or some position it favors. A recognized, tolerated party may fall out of favor, and likewise, political pariahs may be invited to participate at the king's discretion. The experiences of the political left and, more recently, Moroccan Islamists provide some empirical content to the notion of opposition in Morocco and very clearly make the point that it is challenging the Palace rather than ideological position that reaps repression in Morocco.

The Political Left

The political left has been the most frequent target of repression in Morocco, although only the particulars of its relationship with the Palace explain what otherwise seem arbitrary and inconsistent reprisals directed its way. In a nutshell, the moderate socialist left, represented by the USFP, maintains a difficult relationship with the Palace, whereas more radical parties of the left are tolerated in their more outspoken criticism of political practices. The Party of Progress and Socialism (PPS), a permutation of the dismantled Moroccan Communist Party, was sanctioned in 1974, and in 1983 the rival Organization of Democratic and Popular Action (OADP), a spur of the outlawed March 23 Movement,[45] also joined the ranks of the recognized left. Once forced to operate clandestinely, both of these smaller groups were ultimately able to claim a seat or two in parliament. By contrast, unsanctioned groupings with policy interests similar to those of the OADP and the PPS continue to suffer harsh repression. Only a combination of size, influence, and political opportunism explains the variation in their experience over time. Forerunners of the PPS such as the Moroccan Communist Party and the Liberation and Socialism Party (PLS), for example, were banned through the 1960s, and Ali Yata, their leader, was imprisoned. Only when the USFP emerged in 1974 was the new—and potentially rival—PPS allowed to form, and with communism appearing an ever decreasing threat, Yata's small party has since enjoyed considerable political freedom.[46] A manifestly militant position on the Sahara has made its followers, like those of the OADP, the "king's leftists."[47]

Even those who enjoy the mantle of legitimacy must not take political liberties for granted. The history of the UNFP and its successor the USFP, as well as the stories of groups obliged to operate clandestinely, is replete with cheap successes, serious defeats, and sobering lessons. Even a partial history illustrates the arbitrary nature of access to the political arena.

Almost from the outset, relations between the monarch and the political left were difficult. In late 1959, Mohammed V unsuccessfully attempted to control the UNFP by according it the prime ministry,[48] and the UNFP's popularity at the polls in June 1963 won it only the monarch's wrath. Before the first parliament was even seated, more than 100 UNFP leaders—including 21 of the 28 newly elected UNFP representatives—were arrested on the pretext that they had plotted against the king. The accusations were not substantiated at the trial, which was quite obviously about political power and its exercise. Only after eleven death sentences were handed down and some time served did the king "retouch his own image of the magnanimous father of the country by pardoning his errant subjects."[49] The death sentences were eventually commuted, and an amnesty in 1965 put an early end to most of the other sentences.

The drama was reenacted several times over the next decade, with some variations. By 1972, Fqih Basri, a charter member of the UNFP, had been sentenced to death no fewer than four times.[50] A dozen political trials involving the UNFP or the left-wing National Union of Moroccan Students (UNEM) and the National Syndicate of Secondary Students (SNL) took place from 1963 to 1976.[51] Even as one wave of repression ended with measures of clemency, another opened. Coincidental with the 1965 amnesty was the disappearance of one of the UNFP's most outspoken and most popular leaders. Medhi Ben Barka was abducted while in France. A French court tried General Oufkir in absentia and found him guilty of complicity in Ben Barka's presumed murder.

The Palace in this period occasionally held out carrots but continued to wield the stick. In 1971, for example, Hassan II reportedly summoned the UNFP leader Abderrahim Bouabid to the palace at Fez, but Bouabid declined: the king's prosecutor in Marrakesh was asking for forty-eight death sentences and he was needed to defend his UNFP colleagues.[52] Efforts at rapprochement were renewed following the 1972 coup attempt, but neither the UNFP nor the Istiqlal Party was willing to participate without guarantees of civil liberties. Soon thereafter, hundreds of UNFP members and supporters were arrested on charges of a plot against the king. Their 1973 trial at Kenitra marked the nadir of UNFP relations with the Palace: the seventy-two defendants acquitted by the court—including thirteen Rabat barristers—were kept in custody for three more years.[53]

Greater tolerance was extended to the left from 1976 to 1981, but it came at the expense of political independence. Spanish retreat from the

Western Sahara in 1976 created an unexpected basis of national unity, and the king's new mastery of the political moment made him more disposed to reconciliation. In the interim, Bouabid's faction within the UNFP had evolved into the USFP and had largely supplanted its forebear. The new party's leadership were early advocates of incorporating the Western Saharan territories, and their enthusiasm for the issue offered a politically valuable tool to the king. The enfants terribles were transformed into emissaries and dispatched on diplomatic missions to promote the cause.[54] National fervor, now in the service of unity—and the monarchy—softened the Palace's view of the USFP, and demands for elections and political amnesty that had previously been rejected were now heard in the Palace. By the end of 1976, most of those sentenced from 1971 to 1976 had been pardoned.

The reprieve, however, was short-lived. The compromised electoral contest of 1977 almost surely underestimated the USFP's popularity, and within the party a vocal minority actively pushed a progressive social program. When riots erupted in Casablanca in 1981 over the precipitous announcement of price hikes for basic commodities, hundreds of USFP members with no apparent connection to the unrest were arrested. The party's leadership subsequently faced capital charges for a memo criticizing the king's Western Sahara policy as too conciliatory.[55] Eventually, a new compromise was worked out with authorities. Rank-and-file members of the USFP's radical wing shuffled in and out of prison throughout the 1980s, but legislative elections in 1984 strengthened the USFP mainstream. As a party, the USFP "found a niche where it could survive near the edges of political consensus."[56] A decade later, after their disappointment with the 1993 legislative elections, the Kutla parties have resolved to use the consultative mechanisms of parliament as a means to press their agenda and institute a process of seeking government accountability, a strategy that seems safer, and likely to be more efficacious, than direct confrontation.[57]

Greater tolerance of the USFP did not necessarily extend to radical leftists who contested the rules of the political game more frontally. Out of the student unrest of the mid 1960s, a political coalition known as the Progressive Front had been assembled. Its several splinter groups included most notably the 23 March Movement and Il'l-Amam, whose leader Abraham Serfaty eventually achieved notoriety as a political prisoner. The Frontistes dared leave the demarcated terra firma. Their Marxist-Leninist rhetoric implicitly called the monarchy into question, and the liberationist position many adopted vis-à-vis the Western Sahara isolated them further. Beginning in 1972, successive waves of arrests, followed by incommunicado, secret detention and a mass trial in 1977 resulted finally in lengthy prison sentences for 173 individuals, including 3 women.

As time passed, Il'l-Amam was identified as the extremist group par excellence, whereas 23 Mars was eventually accorded a significant measure of legitimacy. In 1984 and 1985, seventy-two individuals, most of them members of UNEM or the SNL, were charged with threatening state security in conjunction with efforts to revive the defunct Il'l-Amam and were given long prison sentences. By contrast to the threat presumed to reside in Il'l-Amam, the remnants of the clandestine 23 March Movement were allowed to reconstitute it as the OADP and run in legislative elections. Its formal recognition followed by only five months a published article clearly stating the group's position in favor of Moroccan territorial integrity. The political crimes of secretary-general Mohammed Bensaïd, twice condemned to death in absentia, are long forgotten, and the OADP's widely sung motto, "Law, Constitution, and Respect for Procedure" raises no untoward eyebrows.[58]

Islamism

Political nuances that explain the Palace's differential responses over time and across the range of leftist groups also explain the equivocal treatment of Islamist groups in a land where the king is Prince of the Faithful and defender of the faith. Although the king has explicitly denounced fundamentalism (*intégrisme*), and although Islamists arrested in 1983 and 1984 were given particularly harsh sentences, more recently there have been considerable leniency toward Islamists and rumors that an Islamist party might be allowed to join the table of politics.

For a number of reasons, Islamism was late to take shape as a popular movement in Morocco. At roughly the same time that Tunisian Islamists were finding a voice and attracting significant followings, two different groups evolved in Morocco, but neither the al-Shabiba al-islamiyya (Islamic Youth) led by Abdelkrim Muti nor the al-'Adl wa'l-Ihsan (Justice and Charity) of Abdessalam Yassine have grown to the proportions known by the FIS in Algeria or al-Nahda in Tunisia. Islam is more politically anchored in Morocco than elsewhere in the Maghrib, and from the monarch down, the ruling class is careful to adopt an attitude of decorum and deference toward it. Popular Islamic culture was bypassed by the throne, but never came under official assault as it did in Tunisia and Algeria. Cultural alienation likewise has not reached the same proportions in Morocco as elsewhere in the Maghrib, and Islam has generally not offered the same new possibilities for political expression.

At the same time, events in Iran that resulted in the 1979 overthrow of a likeminded monarch were worrisome in Rabat. Over the summer of 1983, and after the political unrest of January 1984, Moroccan authorities arrested several dozen Islamists who were accused of belonging to an illegal association and intending to distribute tracts of "Iranian inspiration."[59] Those arrested were for the most part secondary school students, and according to two European attorneys observing the trial, the tract supposedly bearing a photograph of Ayatollah Khomeini in fact only had pictures of King Hassan II.[60] Twenty of the seventy-one defendants were tried in absentia, all of whom—including Muti—received sentences of death or life imprisonment. All the defendants present in the courtroom were found guilty of having plotted against the monarchy; twenty-one were given life sentences and six others were sent to Morocco's death row. It was the first time since 1973 that the death penalty had been called for in Morocco for political crimes. Two successive trials in 1985, involving followers of Muti and a former associate, Abdelaziz Enaamani, involved similar charges and returned several life sentences.[61]

From 1985 through the onset of the Gulf conflict in 1990, only the troublesome figure of the former Sufi Brother Yassine ruffled feathers with Islamist doctrine. After publishing a most impertinent open letter to the king in 1974, Yassine had been punished with six years of imprisonment, three of them in a psychiatric hospital. Upon his release in 1980, he began to build Justice and Charity as a formal organization. Although its operation was briefly interrupted by his arrest in 1983, he was released in 1985, and until 1988 he operated more or less freely. Waves of arrests began in 1989 after many of Yassine's numerous visitors refused to cooperate with police surveillance. Justice and Charity was declared illegal, and Yassine was placed under house arrest. Although protests were launched by Moroccan human rights groups, and lawyers associated with such groups provided defense, Yassine's closest associates—the complete executive bureau—were soon thereafter imprisoned, and remained so for two years.

The Justice and Charity movement has supposedly been decapitated and formally dismantled, but in the meantime, the Gulf War and anti-Western sentiments fueled Islamism in Morocco. In early 1991, ten thousand Islamists took to the streets of Rabat, brandishing copies of the Qur'an. Demonstrators refrained from criticizing the king's decision to support the allied forces, but did not censor their pro-Iraqi slogans. By mid-1991, as many as twenty politicized religious groups were thought to be active and recruiting members in Morocco.

Since 1991 several incidents involving Islamists have marked Morocco's political landscape, and the apparent arbitrariness with which they have been handled by the forces of order point up an irony in the Palace's stance vis-à-vis this element of opposition. In July 1991, for example, following an altercation with university security forces, fifteen Islamist students were arrested and charged with a wide range of political offenses.[62] By contrast, there was remarkably little interest in a series of violent assaults perpetrated by radical Islamists in Fez and other cities of the interior, which in at least one instance resulted in the deaths of leftist students.[63]

The Palace has indicated its interest in using Islamism to silence other critics, and in 1991 it made no effort to disguise overtures to Yassine. Two delegations close to the Palace visited him, their mission being to find grounds for an understanding. A declaration of fealty to the monarch, it was speculated, might open the door for the creation of an Islamist party. So long as Islamists were willing to play by the rules that left the monarchy unquestioned, they too might be admitted to the game of politics.[64] Since 1991 the Palace has backed away from its flirtation with Yassine, but its position remains equivocal enough to accommodate either tolerance or repression as best suits royal purposes.

Reprisals and Repression

Despite nominally democratic, pluralistic structures, political repression has been more extensive and more dramatic in Morocco than elsewhere in the Maghrib. The punishment for not abiding by the prescribed rules of the game is exclusion, or, in the extreme, outright expulsion. Regular players who have temporarily contested the game may be punished mildly and temporarily. As noted earlier, it has not been uncommon for high-ranking officials to be dismissed, ostracized, and even imprisoned, then subsequently courted and reintegrated into government. All are invited to play the game of politics, but the playing field is quite limited. In addition to being a player, the king serves as referee, and more egregious offenses to the central precept receive harsher responses. Moroccans advocating self-determination for the Western Sahara in the early years of the Moroccan irredentist campaign were locked away after torture and patently unfair trials. Saharans in the south of Morocco with possible connections to or sympathy for the Western Sahara liberation movement Polisario (Popular Front for the Liberation of Saguia el Hamra and Rio de Oro) were "disappeared."[65]

Occasional releases served to reinforce the object lesson about the king's raw power. Other pointed lessons have been embedded in the arrest of prominent political figures and in sanctions imposed on parties for political transgressions. In 1986, for example, the PPS newspaper *Al Bayane* was suspended for seventy days following an editorial exchange with Guedira. In elaborating the nondebatable elements of the national consensus around God, king, and country, the editors had referred generically to "institutions" instead of "monarchy."[66]

There is frequently a quality of arbitrariness attached to reprisals. In practice, a political action directly challenging the king's judgment or policies may meet reprisal only after some time has passed, and this may appear to be in response to a lesser offense. In 1990 a general strike called by the Democratic Confederation of Workers (CDT) in Fez turned into a riot that claimed forty lives; a luxury hotel owned by the king's family was among the property losses. Hundreds of demonstrators were arrested, but despite their adamant and tendentious call for policy change, in a period where local tensions about the Gulf War ran high, labor leaders were left untouched. Months later, however, through Alaoui's *Matin du Sahara*, a campaign of public criticism was launched against the CDT secretary-general, Noubir Amaoui, which reached a dénouement in April 1992 when Amaoui was given a two-year prison sentence for opinions expressed to the Spanish paper *El Pais*. Delayed and disjointed reprisals throw players off balance even as they underscore the discretionary—and thus enhanced—powers of the monarch.

CONCLUSION

For some time Morocco has been faced with important problems that do not have ready, easy solutions. Like those of Algeria and Tunisia, its population (like Algeria's, almost 26.5 million in 1993) has expanded beyond the economy's ability to absorb it and provide the necessary infrastructure. Casablanca is the most congested city in the Maghrib. Its unemployment rate soars, but cities of the interior fare no better. Riots in Fez in December 1990 were fed by the outrage of recent arrivals to the city who were frustrated in attempts to find decent employment. Although its debt service is slowly being reduced, payment on Morocco's $21.5 billion debt still absorbed more than 28 percent of its export receipts in 1992, and efforts to annex the Western Sahara continue to drain the royal coffers. Willingly or not, the state is responsible for policies that address these issues, but in Morocco it is misleading to speak of the "state" as though it were an entity independent of the monarch. A civil service has functioned continuously since the late seventeenth century, but the monarchy is the linchpin that holds it in place and assures its operation. The effectiveness of parties at articulating popular demands is perhaps limited by their own divisiveness, but is even more restricted by the weight of the monarchy. Neither parties nor the state bureaucracy can operate with any significant measure of independence from the throne, and since 1973 the king has carefully controlled the political agenda. In stipulating that the prime minister be drawn from the majority party, and in requiring parliament to debate and vote on a program initiated by the majority party, the new 1992 constitution held some potential for altering this arrangement. The king's readiness, and ability, to set these provisions aside following the results of the 1992 elections only underscores the point that their effectiveness depends heavily on one man's willingness to have his powers limited by a parliament, parties, and government ministers not of his choosing. In the meantime, the fact that the constitution was prepared by the Palace and submitted to referendum without debate or wide consultation casts doubts upon the king's inclination to relinquish his monopoly of power.

In this chapter I have emphasized the weight of the monarchy in the relations between state and society. Few factors balance the raw power of the throne, and the fact that the king remains the sole mediator between society and the apparatus that governs it leaves the "state" as secure and as fragile as the monarchy itself. The monarchical regime's unwillingness to legitimate popular political expression has periodically resulted in large-scale outbursts of protest and political violence or serious acts of insurgency that point up the precarious nature of political rule. On the other hand, despite the dramatic moments of unrest, the Moroccan regime has proven extraordinarily resilient. In Morocco's patrimonial political system, through the sharifian principle and the rituals that reinforce it, the monarchy supplies the sort of framework of cohesion that is missing in Algerian society. That even in moments of great stress, Moroccan monarchs have successfully appealed to the transcendent basis of their legitimate right to rule and evoke contrition from errant subjects attests to the symbolic power of the throne.

The weight of monarchy may reduce the likelihood of change, but it is important to recognize that even radical change is not precluded in Morocco. The Palace's great strength is also its acute weakness, and the stability of the regime rests entirely on one man and his ability to manipulate the powerful symbols of the monarchy. The heir to the throne is a young man now completely dwarfed by his father, and although the throne itself seemed to transform the mild Mohammed V and the playboy Hassan II into mighty kings, the times and the challenges that confront Morocco today are far more complex than those that Sidi Mohammed's father and grandfather first faced. The Moroccan monarch holds the symbolic potential to unite a nation, but embedded in his role is also the possibility of betraying the nation and reaping its wrath.

PART III
The Politics of Human Rights

It is a premise of this book that neither the strategic choices of nor governmental response to local human rights groups can be understood apart
from a nation's historical and political context. Culture shapes and conditions responses to social and political challenges, even when causal explanation for a problem lies beyond its bounds. With major elements of political culture identified and the parameters of political games as they are
played in each of the three countries laid out, we are now prepared to
address and assess the role of human rights groups. Part III seeks to relate
events and developments involving human rights groups to long-standing
patterns of political interaction in the Maghrib.

To begin, Chapter 7 introduces the nongovernmental human rights organizations as political players in their own right, tracing their origins and
early coalescence. Chapter 8 then examines the objectives the groups have
set out for themselves and relates them to the national context. The focus
of the Tunisian League of Human Rights on legal reform and the legitimacy of political opposition is, for example, directly related to a political
culture of single-party rule and abridgments of legal procedure first sanctioned by the Bourguiba government. The challenge for Moroccan groups
has been to widen political discussion and bring into view the plight of
those who have transgressed the political taboo of God, king, and country.
Algerian groups have faced a more basic challenge of human rights education and the promotion of law as a force in politics. The groups' own dynamics, including strategic choices and tactics, are examined in light, not
simply of their own goals and objectives, but in relation to Islamism, a
second and in many regards rival social movement.

In Chapter 9, the interplay between Maghribi governments and nongovernmental human rights groups is presented as a battle over the control

of political discourse. Although pathways differed, all three governments ultimately established human rights offices within their governments in efforts to gain control over the political rhetoric of human rights. Chapter 10 considers the role of international actors in the North African politics of human rights. Finally, Chapter 11 seeks to assess the lasting contribution of human rights groups to democratization and the structural transformation of Maghribi political systems. In all cases, human rights groups set out to alter prevalent patterns that hampered political participation and impeded efforts to democratize. The goal was a formidable one and the difficulties abundant. In some instances or in certain aspects of their work, groups fell prey to the very dynamics they were trying to change. In others, they have simply not been strong enough to match the counterstrategies of governments in power or stand up to new winds of political change. On the other hand, some reforms have been implemented and the discourse of human rights is now an important element of political culture across the region. In this regard, at least, the efforts of human rights groups have met success.

7 The Emergence of a Maghribi Human Rights Movement

On December 10, 1988, the fortieth anniversary of the Universal Declaration of Human Rights, some four hundred people assembled in Allal al-Fassi Hall outside Rabat to give formal shape to a politically independent human rights group in Morocco. Previous attempts to hold such a meeting had been blocked by the police. First, there had been last-minute questions about the backgrounds of some of the founding members, and when those were cleared, subsequent delays were attributed to inconvenient timing. Organizers of the new Moroccan Organization of Human Rights (OMDH) were thus somewhat apprehensive on the morning of December 10. There had been impassioned debate over the preceding weeks as to whether the organization—which had been meeting informally for more than a year—should press for formal recognition, or if it might not be more efficacious in the long run simply to work quietly behind the scenes.

Participants were relieved when the December 10 meeting opened without disruption. The new human rights organization's troubles were not completely over, but it would be allowed to exist within the national political framework. Over the previous year, many of the organizers had been brought in for questioning by the police; they had been systematically followed, and family members had been harassed. That period now seemed over. The work of a preparatory commission was accepted without revision, and a leadership slate spanning much of Morocco's political spectrum was accepted by acclamation. With the creation of the OMDH, each of the three Maghribi countries could lay claim to a politically independent human rights organization. A Tunisian League of Human Rights had been formed in 1977, and in Algeria two separate leagues emerged in the mid 1980s.

The appearance of indigenous human rights groups in the Maghrib is a political development equivalent to the emergence of nationalist political parties in the early twentieth century. Implicitly or explicitly, they have indicated their intent to reshape the basis of state-society relations established at independence. Subsequent chapters will explore in full the workings of the Maghribi human rights groups across the different national contexts, accounting both for the strategic considerations outlined initially and the particularities of national political contexts. More immediately, the task is to introduce the indigenous human rights groups as significant political players. It is largely through their efforts that talk of human rights has emerged in political discourse throughout the region.

THE TUNISIAN LEAGUE OF HUMAN RIGHTS

Tunisia's League of Human Rights was officially born on May 7, 1977, with formal authorization accorded by the Ministry of the Interior. In fact, its period of gestation had begun several years earlier. After the former interior minister Ahmed Mestiri and a handful of dissidents were expelled from the ruling PSD in the early 1970s, a small group of self-identified "liberals" began to meet privately to discuss means of breathing new life into their proposed program of democratic reform. Among the three principals—Mestiri, Hassib Ben Ammar, and Caid Essebsi—there was a divergence of position. Essebsi hoped eventually to return to the party, Mestiri advocated founding an opposition party, and Ben Ammar wanted to exert pressure through indirect political means. Out of their discussions the Movement of Socialist Democrats (MDS) was born, but so, too, were the proposal for a National Council of Public Liberties and in time the Tunisian League of Human Rights (LTDH).

The formal structures of a political party began to emerge in the mid 1970s, although the MDS was not officially recognized until 1983. One of its standing committees, revolving at first around Ben Ammar, reported regularly on work to advance respect for civil and political liberties. This working group, made up of Ben Ammar, Hammouda Ben Slama, Dali Jazi, Habib Boulares, and Mohammed Moadda, sought primarily to exert liberalizing pressures on the political system. Its focus was on political process; the promotion of human rights served as a vehicle to that end rather than as a cause in its own right. Most of those involved were already men in their forties with a substantial investment in Tunisia's political system. Jazi was a lawyer, Moadda a university professor, and Ben Slama a practicing physician. Boulares, a promising young journalist, had already occupied a ministerial post, as had Ben Ammar. These men sought not to overthrow a system, but to reform and redirect it. Tunisia had already ratified the ICCPR and the ICESCR, and its government claimed to ensure the protection of political liberties. By working within a framework intellectually acceptable to the government while exposing internal contradictions, Tunisian liberals hoped to force the political system open and reserve a place for themselves within it.[1]

The informal committee on public liberties initially took actions of fairly limited scope, but toward 1976 the idea of creating a politically independent human rights organization began to emerge. The concept of human rights, it must be noted, was far from fashionable at the time. As persistent critics of the ruling elites, the leftists who constituted most of the country's intelligentsia might have supplied a logical constituency, but they commonly dismissed human rights as a bourgeois notion and dangerously American.[2] The small committee labored against such intellectual and political prejudice and gradually claimed recruits from among Arab nationalists, Islamists, segments of the left, and, of course, the group of liberals as yet unrecognized as the MDS.

Tunisian law in 1976 required explicit government approval for the public operation of any association, so when the by-laws of a human rights organization had been drafted, making prominent reference to the Constitution, an envoy was sent to discuss the matter at the Ministry of the Interior. The government was caught in an awkward position. It was reluctant to sanction a political group it could not control, but there were no formal grounds upon which to deny the LTDH and its distinguished membership an official *visa* (or certificate). Instead, through a series of delaying tactics it bought time, hoping to weaken the new organization.

When by early 1977 approval had still not been granted, the public liberties committee devised a new strategy to advance their organizational cause. In March, 30 academics, trade unionists, and high-ranking civil servants associated with the banned political group known as the Movement of Popular Unity (MUP) and affiliated with the former minister Ahmed Ben Salah, were arrested for distributing leaflets and circulating a magazine. The public liberties group used this blatant abrogation of political rights as the basis of an appeal to the country's elite to direct a message in support of basic liberties to President Bourguiba. The formal statement bore 168 signatures when submitted to the presidential palace in Carthage, but it touched off a tinderbox of emotions and sparked political imagination; the text continued to circulate and gather signatures for some time. The petition called for a general amnesty for political prisoners but also explicitly criticized the government's failure to authorize the independent human rights organization. Furthermore, it announced plans for a national conference on civil liberties. To promote the conference, Ben Ammar embarked on a tour of Europe and the United States seeking support for the human rights group and inviting scholars and public figures to participate. As June approached, numerous obstacles were planted in the way of the conference, but to reduce embarrassment and adverse publicity, the government granted the League of Human Rights its formal certification on May 7.

The government's pretexts for delaying approval of the LTDH had most prominently involved the sudden emergence of a rival group consisting exclusively of PSD loyalists, and discussions turned on the supposed awkwardness of legitimizing two organizations with virtually identical mandates. The government proposed to merge the two groups, an arrangement unacceptable to the independents. A compromise was eventually reached whereby seven of the party members would be added to the fifteen-person executive committee proposed by the independent LTDH.

In recruiting leadership for the human rights organization, members of the ad hoc public liberties committee had sought individuals who although they had good rapport with the Bourguiba government were also demonstrably capable of exercising independent judgment. They had carefully identified fifteen professionals known both by professional reputation and for their positive relations with those in power. The executive committee they had proposed included doctors, lawyers, and academics. Dr. Saadeddine Zmerli, well respected as a professor of medicine but politically unknown, was chosen largely because of that double qualification to preside over the proposed Tunisian League of Human Rights. In scrutinizing the list subsequently presented by the government, the league's executive committee was able to choose from among the fifteen PSD members those individuals with similarly prestigious professional backgrounds but who likewise promised to show independent judgment. The LTDH thus escaped control of the party and indeed, incorporated into itself party members whose beliefs and principles were largely compatible with those of its broader membership base.

Less than two weeks after its formal inception, the new human rights organization set to work in earnest. The wives of eleven MUP detainees lodged a formal complaint that their husbands had been beaten and tortured while in police detention, and the league quickly established a commission of inquiry to investigate the situation. Within ten days it obtained an audience with the interior minister, Tahar Belkhodja. He refused the LTDH access to the detainees, saying that the cases had been referred to the state security court and were now within its jurisdiction, but the league sent an observer to the trial and contacted the physicians who had examined the defendants. Its report, issued in August, avoided even the impression of an open attack. In carefully chosen language, it raised important questions about the practice of torture and incommunicado detention and strongly protested the obstacles that had been placed in the league's way. The LTDH's intent to pursue such matters was clearly established.

Over the next decade, the Tunisian League of Human Rights launched inquiries into numerous allegations of individual abuse; it regularly observed political trials and often intervened with the minister of the interior in particular cases; it conducted studies of a wide range of issues, including incommunicado detention, torture, prison conditions, and rights of association; and it made numerous public statements about press freedoms, special courts, and unconstitutional legislation, among other things.[3] In the aftermath of a violent clash between unionists and police forces in January 1978, the league was the first of several Tunisian groups to denounce the government's handling of the confrontation itself and the abuses that multiplied in its aftermath. If it did not distinguish itself in 1981 by calling for the release of Islamists sentenced to up to eleven years for having violated the country's law of association, it did address the issue obliquely by devoting its 1981 general meeting to a discussion of the right of association in Tunisia.

The LTDH commissioned its own study of the handling of the "bread riots" that rocked the country in January 1984, which offered the only publicly critical view of the government's conduct. In stern language, the league commission decried the regime's ineptitude in managing the political aspects of its economic policy and laid responsibility for the conditions that had inspired the uprising at the government's own feet. According to the league, price increases had been imposed too summarily, and the police had fired on crowds of demonstrators without adequate warning.

Even when critical, in this communique as in others, the league scrupulously avoided hyperbole and inflammatory language. With great care, it spelled out the procedural steps it had followed and stayed close to the facts. For many opponents of the regime, the language of its criticism was not harsh enough. Risk was implicit in any public criticism, however, and league members were protected only by the unassailability of their reputations. The prestige of their own names called government acts into serious question. The league was the first politically independent organization the Tunisian state had allowed to exist, and its exemplary behavior was a dilemma for the regime. Violating international human rights principles it allegedly supported and repressing the LTDH were equally damnable in the eyes of those the Tunisian government was seeking to impress.

As is often the case, success bore with it the seeds of problems the LTDH would have to resolve. From a membership base of 1,000 in 1982, the league had by 1985 tripled its membership and extended its footing nationwide. Courageous stands against the death penalty following the 1980 commando attack in Gafsa, numerous calls for the release of Islamists imprisoned for acts of conscience, and dispassionate criticism of the government's part in the 1984 riots had won league members respect and admiration in many circles, but the league's own popularity threatened to undermine its effectiveness. What had begun as an experiment closely governed by a fairly intimate band of professionals who shared a common vision of justice had rapidly evolved into a popular movement without a clearly articulated mandate. Wary of the loss of control implied by precipitous expansion, the national bureau had already elected to slow the proliferation of local branches.

An incident at the LTDH's second national congress in March 1985 brought the implicit problems to a head. When the election of a Jewish human rights activist to the league's executive committee brought protests about Zionism from the floor, a lively debate about pluralism and the essence of human rights ensued. The irrelevance of Serge Adda's religious community was quickly established, but so too was the need for a clear statement of the principles for which the league and its members stood. From March to June, a committee therefore elaborated a charter for the LTDH, which was then brought before a specially convened council for approval in July. Although most charter items were adopted nearly verbatim from the Universal Declaration of Human Rights, there was heated debate over the right of Muslim women to marry non-Muslims and the right of a Muslim to change religion. Ultimately, a compromise was crafted on the question of religion, which raised the difficult question of apostasy. The league endorsed liberty to *choose* rather than to *change* religion. Sentiment was evenly divided on the question of marriage, and this issue was put to a vote. The league decided to reject all restrictions on marriage based on race or religion, but only by a single vote. For many members, the controversy underscored the need to maintain their ideological independence.[4]

Although the popular influence of the league continued to grow, the working relationship that, in all decorum, had been cultivated with government officials gradually collapsed. Repressive measures imposed by the government were successively denounced by the league. As the fissure between state and society grew, the league was left alone to call for respect of principles and due process. In early April 1987, the LTDH was saluted in Paris by *Le Monde* as a lone discordant voice in what was otherwise a "concert of self-satisfaction,"[5] but that voice too was muffled just weeks later with the arrest of the LTDH's secretary-general, Khemais Chemmari. Chemmari was eventually acquitted of charges that he had slandered the prime minister, but the sobering incident reminded all in the league of the continuous risk faced by members as they in good conscience executed the tasks mandated by their 1985 charter.

When the coup orchestrated by Prime Minister Ben Ali on November 7 diverted the Tunisian polity from its disastrous path, human rights was advanced as the byword that would help the nation heal. Hundreds of political prisoners benefited from presidential amnesty in the final months of 1987, and important legal reforms were enacted. The league's stock soared; eventually four of its leaders, including two of its founders and its first two presidents, were given ministerial appointments in the new government.

The government's success in persuading LTDH leaders to join its ranks created a crisis of identity within the league. Bylaws clearly prohibited members from being active in the league while holding government office, and the organization's internal regulations were respected. At the league's third national congress in March 1989, Moncef Marzouki, a physician from Sousse and previously an LTDH vice president, was elected the organization's new president. With the transition, the problem was formally resolved. Informally, however, it persisted in the form of uncomfortable questions about the league's relation to those in power. Well into 1989 the league was quiet, its role confused. With the Ben Ali regime loudly proclaiming the cause of human rights, the league had lost its thunder along with its leadership. Many wondered openly if it would simply collapse.

Over the next several years, the voice of the league alternatively rose and faded as a function of its internal dynamics, and at times it was simply lost as the nation's attention was diverted to other matters. For a time in 1992, it disappeared altogether, but as explored in subsequent chapters, it has clearly become a player in Tunisia's political game, and one that the government itself would not entirely like to do without.

THE ALGERIAN LEAGUES OF HUMAN RIGHTS

In Algeria three politically independent human rights groups emerged almost simultaneously in the mid 1980s, and although the field was ultimately narrowed to two, competition persisted. The divisions of ethnicity, ideology, and class that had troubled the Algerian polity at least since independence were evident from the outset, but they did not, however, stifle the desire to open up a political system tightly controlled for more than two decades. Many analyses of political liberalization in Algeria chart the openings from October 1988, but political developments in 1989 and 1990 cannot be disentangled from the Algerian human rights movement and a story that had begun several years earlier.

The impetus for the Algerian human rights movement can be traced to the early 1980s, when popular unrest broke more than a decade of political quiet. Dissonance was expressed first among Berbers in the Kabylian capital, Tizi Ouzou, angered primarily at the government's interdiction of a seminar on old forms of Berber poetry. Authorities judged the seminar as inflammatory in view of policies intended to make Arabic the lone language of national unity. Berbers protested their cultural rights, but tracts distributed at the time also tended to link cultural injustice to economic privation.[6] Unrest over cultural issues grew but was complicated by conflict with Islamists belonging to an as yet inchoate association; political violence sporadically flared in Algiers, Annaba, and Bedjaia from 1981 to 1983. In separate and related incidents, the authorities arrested numerous Berber and Islamic activists. Abdennour Ali Yahia, a lawyer and former government minister active in the defense of Berber activists, was himself arrested in October 1983 and detained without charge for several weeks.

Partly in response to the repression, new interest in civil and cultural rights spread through Kabylia. During 1984, several small conferences on liberty were held in the region, with discussions extending through the night; eventually the idea of creating an association was shaped.[7] Discrete contacts were made within a small but diverse network of individuals thought to be sympathetic to the idea, and in November 1984 a small group of six individuals met in Algiers to discuss the creation of a new league of human rights. In the same fissiparous style that had characterized the nationalist movement fifty years before, three of the six would eventually head up their own small groups. Each represented different segments of Algerian society: Ali Yahia had for a time been minister of agriculture under Ben Bella and had more recently been associated with the Berber culturalist movement; Omar Menouar was identified as a Trotskyite from Algiers; and Miloud Brahimi, although personally aloof from the ruling FLN, belonged to the country's political elite. Each, accordingly, brought a somewhat different vision of the desirable shape of an eventual national human rights organization. As the discussion progressed, Brahimi became persuaded that the proposed organization would be seen as a threat to the state, and he elected not to participate further.[8]

Ali Yahia and Menouar (who, according to Brahimi, initially had the greater following) nonetheless pursued the idea. In a semi-clandestine meeting at an Algiers restaurant in March 1985, they assembled a number of people committed to the concept of human rights and discussed the question of organization. When differences could not be worked out, both groups submitted requests for approval to the government in June. Both met with silence.

In the meantime, Ali Yahia's group had informally set to work defending Berber activists and issuing calls for democratization. By fall 1985, ten of its members were under arrest. Berber activism formed a backdrop to the arrests and revolved around the activities of another recently formed and unauthorized organization, the Association of the Sons of Martyrs. That organization, whose membership largely overlapped with Ali Yahia's League of Human Rights, had been set up to help families of those who had died in the war of independence; the attention it called to the role of Kabylia in the war served to buoy the Berber cultural movement and rankled authorities. About a dozen people were detained in July 1985 for attempting to place their own memorial wreaths during official ceremonies of commemoration.

As president of the newly formed human rights group, Ali Yahia protested the Sons of Martyrs arrests, and was then himself taken into custody on July 10. Twenty-two others were arrested over the next three months and charged with distributing tracts and setting up an illegal organization.[9] In their December trial before the state security court at Médéa, the defendants responded to charges, but more important, they used the occasion to confront the government and assess the state of civil liberties in Algeria.[10] When the trial concluded, sentences ranging from six months to three years were handed down, and the defendants were dispersed to several different prisons. At the expiration of his own eleven-month sentence in June 1986, Ali Yahia was released from prison, but his liberty was short-lived. When political violence shook Constantine and Sétif later in the year, he and other associates in the unrecognized league were rearrested and sent to the desert south as a measure of "administrative detention," this time without formal charges or the opportunity to make a political statement.[11]

Ali Yahia's second arrest, in particular, generated international protest. According to Ali Yahia, the arrests were discussed within the European Community, and the president of the European parliament placed a call to

President Bendjedid. In efforts to extend the human rights activists the utmost support, the FIDH agreed to confer on Ali Yahia's organization the status of formal affiliation—and with it an international aura of legitimacy.

Meanwhile, Miloud Brahimi had engaged in talks with the Algerian government about the possibility of approving a human rights organization.[12] Some within the highest ranks were sympathetic; others saw in the proposal a disguised opposition party. By late 1986, as the Algerian government was coming under increased international pressure, a deal was struck. In exchange for formal recognition and full latitude concerning issues of human rights, the new organization would engage in no politics of opposition. In early April, Ali Yahia was released from prison, and on April 11, 1987, an Algerian League of Human Rights was formally accorded permission to exist. It was not, however, the league Ali Yahia had assembled in 1985. Instead, the new group's forty-six members were mostly personal associates of Brahimi's, drawn from a diverse array of professions. Represented were writers, filmmakers, journalists, religious leaders, academics, lawyers, and even sports professionals.[13]

Some efforts were made in 1985 to unite what remained three separate human rights groups. The gulf, however, proved unbridgeable. Ali Yahia's group was committed to opening the political system and was willing to be confrontational; it had the at least temporary advantage of international recognition. Brahimi had reached an informal agreement with Bendjedid himself that gave his group "full latitude in regards to human rights" in exchange for a commitment to abstain from oppositional politics.[14] Menouar's following, which had dissipated somewhat but remained roughly equal in size to each of the other two, defined themselves in opposition to the government and saw Brahimi's agreement as a betrayal of independence. The movement was fragmented, and from 1987 to 1989, the three groups operated independently. One was recognized internationally but remained illegal at home; a second enjoyed legal status in Algeria but was viewed as a usurper abroad; although initially supported by French leftists and with the largest membership, the third held no advantage on either of the fronts that mattered.

Under Miloud Brahimi's leadership, the formally recognized Algerian League of Human Rights gained respect and influence, at least among the Algerian political elite. Brahimi's discussions with high-level government officials continued, and through pressure brought to bear by the league, passports were returned to the formerly imprisoned Berbers, freedom of mobility was assured, and jobs were restored. During its first year in operation, the LADH issued reports on prison conditions, psychiatric hospitals in Algeria, and the status of children.[15] Of even greater significance in terms of both the immediate political climate and the more enduring patterns of political culture, to commemorate its first anniversary, the LADH hosted a national conference on censorship and self-censorship. For the first time in decades, ordinary people dared to speak out. Although the conference had been boycotted by the official press, the room was packed, and the seal of silence was finally and completely broken. Over the following months, an association of Algerian journalists was formed, and the press began to take more risks in political reporting.[16]

Not everyone privately critical of governmental repression cheered the LADH's 1988 program on censorship. The International Federation of Human Rights had reproached the authorized league about its connections with the regime. Within Algeria, many were suspicious both of the government's agenda in tolerating the league and of Brahimi's own designs. For Brahimi, the success of the conference on censorship was bittersweet. His own views of his actions differed dramatically from those of his critics, who alternatively saw the conference as self-promotion or the result of a private—and therefore compromising—deal with the authorities. Two decades of repression and self-censorship had effectively sealed most lips, and in the political context of early 1988, a conference opening the door to public criticism appeared either dangerous (presuming arrests to follow) or suspicious (assuming the conference were permitted).

Brahimi rejected both of these positions, pushing the boundaries of political behavior in pre–October 1988 Algeria. As an accepted member of the political elite, and personally confident in the presence of high-ranking officials, he was able to act, and often did act, with what for others would have been viewed as impunity. With social class and political connections providing a significant measure of insurance, Brahimi developed an interpretation of his agreement with the authorities that left the burden of proof to the law rather than to political sensibility. When it suited his purposes, he assumed that initiatives, however innovative, were legitimate if they could plausibly be conducted within the framework of Algerian law. To him it was ironic that while government officials had privately taken him to task about the conference, which in their eyes at least flirted with the taboo of politics, many Algerians sympathetic to notions of human rights also had reservations about it.

By October 1988, the subtleties of the *boulitique* ("politics") of the LADH were politically irrelevant. Out of the political disturbances that shook the Algerian polity to its core, the voice of the league emerged clearly. By October 11, the LADH was holding daily press conferences, and five days later, it issued a report on the use of torture by the security forces and called for the liberation of those arrested. Ali Yahia's group likewise declaimed the excesses. Jointly, their efforts helped embolden the press and expose the practice of torture, which was politically indefensible in the context of a mythology of equality. Brahimi's personal connections to the inner circle of government only increased the credibility of the charges and made abuses more difficult to deny. Reforms proposed by Bendjedid over next few months were in keeping with recommendations made by the LADH.

Governmental acknowledgement of issues that had been promoted by all Algerian human rights activists was not sufficient to eradicate enduring rivalries between what remained three separate groups. An active role in the October unrest vastly increased the visibility of human rights activists. The LADH's membership expanded rapidly: in 1989 it claimed 1,200 members and had regional offices in thirty-six of the country's forty-eight provincial districts. The group once led by Menouar was not vocal during the crisis, and in consequence it had shrunk to a dozen, who were integrated into the LADH in February 1989. In the meantime, Ali Yahia's group had renamed itself the Algerian League for the Defense of Human Rights (LADDH, as opposed to LADH), and in June it was finally authorized by the government. Rivalry between the two groups was thus formally institutionalized.

The voice of one or other of the Algerian human rights leagues was heard continuously through debates about the Gulf War, the Algerian state of siege declared in June 1991, and preparations for the December 1991 legislative elections. At times, however, it was difficult to assess how much support there was, or how cohesive the group that lay behind them was. Although Brahimi formally resigned from the presidency of the LADH in December 1989 and was replaced by Youcef Fethallah, he continued to cast a long shadow over both the organization and public discourse on human rights. Divisions within the LADDH also appear to have left Ali Yahia acting largely on the basis of his individual instincts and resources. Since early 1992, the voices of indigenous human rights groups have been nearly lost in the turmoil that has gripped the country, but the idea of human rights they introduced has not entirely disappeared from what political discourse yet remains heard in Algeria.

MOROCCO'S THREE HUMAN RIGHTS ORGANIZATIONS

The 1988 establishment of the OMDH in Morocco completed the panoply of indigenous human rights groups in the Maghrib, but the OMDH was not Morocco's first human rights group, and its own story must begin with that of its two predecessors and eventual competitors.[17] In 1972, the conservative nationalist Istiqlal Party had formed a Moroccan League for the Defense of Human Rights (LMDDH). A second organization, the Moroccan Association of Human Rights (AMDH) was founded in 1979 by a small group of USFP and PPS activists, at a time when publicity about the imprisonment of a large group of dissidents known as the Frontistes was gaining attention at home and abroad,[18] and roughly coincidental with Moroccan ratification of the major international human rights covenants in 1979. Both groups took it as their charge to promote respect for human rights through publicity, issuing what came to be infrequent statements concerning events in Morocco with some direct bearing on human rights and more frequent denunciations of injustices toward Palestinians, a safer issue. The league seems never to have been outspoken, even at such times of crisis as the 1981 and 1984 riots.

The AMDH was—and is again—the more active of the two. In 1982 AMDH activists inspired a meeting of regional bar associations to endorse a national plan for improving human rights conditions that featured strengthening safeguards in the penal code and enacting measures to comply with the UN's Standard Minimal Rules for the Treatment of Prisoners. That meeting also called for the release of all political prisoners.[19] The AMDH's early plaints, ironically, were loudest on the several occasions when its own members faced arrest and trial.[20] The general refusal of most newspapers to carry its communiques stifled AMDH efforts, and after 1983 its voice grew progressively fainter. Its existence was never formally acknowledged by the Moroccan authorities, and in May 1983 it was barred from holding a general assembly. The radical wing of the USFP, to which most AMDH members belonged, was simultaneously under attack, and within a week several of its most active members were under arrest. Their imprisonment, and the concurrent ascendance of the USFP mainstream, sent the AMDH into reclusion for several years.

While the two human rights associations lay dormant in 1987, a small group of activists within the USFP mainstream, led by the attorney Abdelaziz Bennani, began informally to discuss the possibility of creating a more active human rights organization in Morocco. Although Moroccan prisons were known to house several hundred political prisoners, and political repression was understood to be widespread, virtually none of the country's organized political and civic groups were in a position to act.

Over the course of 1987, informal discussions in homes and cafes expanded through personal connections to include men and women from small opposition groups such as the PPS, the OADP, and the RNI, as well as USFP activists and certain academics and jurists without political affiliation. Two conditions were imposed upon participants: first, that they profess a belief in international human rights principles, and second, that they declare themselves willing to work to promote those rights in a strictly nonpartisan context.[21] Initially, there were efforts to consolidate a sort of "human rights front" with the AMDH and the LMDDH, but they foundered on the issue of partisan politics.[22] Eventually, a preparatory committee of nearly forty people formed instead to draft what would become the 1988 OMDH charter.

Beyond concern for its nonpartisan character, the preparatory committee elaborated a number of issues. A background paper circulated to interested persons set out a brief organizational background and justified the formation of a human rights interest group by pointing to the inadequacy of legal protection for individuals, both in existing law and in its application. The document set out the new group's objectives, described its intended mode of action, and emphasized both its nonpartisan composition and its political autonomy. The OMDH aimed to raise individual and collective human rights consciousness, would work to strengthen human rights law and the judiciary, and would defend victims of violations. Working within existing law, members envisioned collecting legal texts, organizing colloquia, and providing relief to victims as the principal means of making progress toward their goals.[23]

The embryonic OMDH faced its first tactical—and substantive—challenge early on in a debate over the role the new human rights organization should ascribe to Islam. To many members of the preparatory committee, leaving Islam out seemed an open invitation to those who might attack the organization as inherently anti-Moroccan. For others, lip service to Islam seemed not only unnecessary deference to conservative social and political forces, but also betrayed the positive universality of the principles and standards upon which the new organization would be based and behind which it would take refuge. A compromise was ultimately reached, whereby Islam was to be recognized in the preamble to the OMDH Charter, while the main body would be built on positive law and reflect the principles enshrined in international human rights instruments to which Morocco was party.[24]

With the intricacies of the charter worked out, the preparatory committee laid plans to constitute the OMDH formally in an open assembly. A flurry of meetings began in April 1988 to broaden the organization's base. It was important to the committee that in addition to their commitment to human rights, the organization's founding members should represent varying concerns and be drawn from different professions.[25] Prominent individuals without political ties were actively recruited at this time. Among them was Madhi el Mandjra, an academic whose commitment to the cause of independence had propelled him into a career of political prominence, but who nevertheless remained nonpartisan. Preparatory committee members were agreed that they should in practice honor the ideals for which they stood, and accordingly they envisioned a formal, public constitutive congress that would allow them to make their entrance on the political scene "by the front door." By careful planning, those attending would include businessmen and bureaucrats, engineers and university professors, doctors and lawyers, and individuals devoted to the arts, letters, and culture. They would also, by design, include a noticeable female contingent.[26] With preparations complete, a list of the founding members was made public, and a gathering to launch the OMDH was scheduled for 28 May 1988 in the Rabat suburb of Agdal.

While freedom of association is guaranteed by Moroccan law, freedom of assembly is more limited, and so it happened that on the morning of May 28, members of the executive committee within the preparatory commission were called before officials to explain their intent. Officially, permission to hold an assembly was denied on the grounds that some of the founding members had been previously convicted of participating in illegal extremist political groups.[27] Less formally, Interior Ministry officials warned OMDH leaders that they were involved in "delicate questions" and sought information as to the group's origin and backing.

This setback posed a second tactical problem for the new organization. Mindful of reprisals directed at the AMDH in 1983 and aware that the group's future might well depend on the strategy devised at this juncture, members debated the stance they should adopt vis-à-vis participants with a political past. Some, for pragmatic reasons, wanted to part company. An opposing group argued the importance of standing on principle: what the government was calling political "crimes" were in fact the exercise of rights; it was for the promotion of such rights that the OMDH was forming, and what integrity would be left for the group if they compromised here? The latter argument prevailed; the organization would stand by the members under attack, who by international standards had done no wrong.

Plans were again laid for a constitutive assembly, and were thwarted in late June and again in September. The government abandoned its charge against certain members and retreated to a claim that the "moment was not opportune." The preparatory commission fired back that the government was interfering with constitutionally guaranteed rights of association and assembly.[28]

The OMDH faced yet another tactical challenge: as a survival strategy, should it back down from its earlier decision to hold a public first meeting to constitute itself formally? Government officials, who had been calling in key OMDH figures one by one to chide them for their apparent insensitivity to larger political realities, seemed willing to allow the group to operate as long as it didn't insist on this public meeting. Again, members debated the costs of a compromise. On one hand, giving up the public aspect would assure the group's immediate survival; on the other hand, if the group so easily gave up its own rights, how could it defend those of others? A small committee was appointed to make arrangements for a meeting to be held no later than mid December.

The Agdal meeting was finally held, and the OMDH was officially "born," with a national council and a 19-member executive bureau. The executive committee, made up in large part of political independents, was headed up by Omar Azziman, a law professor unaffiliated with any party. The title of founding president was assigned to Madhi el Mandjra, whose unflagging commitment to the OMDH idea had helped bring it to birth, and whose political prominence in Morocco was intended to shield the fledgling organization from future political assaults.

OMDH members worked feverishly in early 1989, inspired by their cause. They launched appeals to amnesty political prisoners and submitted several requests to visit prisons. They called for investigations about apparent deaths in detention, asked questions about the closing of a newspaper, and expressed concerns about the working conditions of striking coal miners. For operational efficiency, the OMDH rented premises and hired a secretary, and members set to work on an ambitious project to create a comprehensive catalog of Moroccan political prisoners that could be used in legal and medical intervention.[29] Just five months after its inception, the OMDH saw some of its work come to fruition in the release of some thirty-five political prisoners, most of whom had been held at Kenitra Central Prison since 1977 for crimes of opinion. Some Frontistes had been released before their sentences had expired a few years earlier, but this was the only sizable amnesty the king had ever offered this group of dissidents. Although certain celebrated prisoners, among them Abraham Serfaty, remained in prison, the OMDH had cause to celebrate.

The OMDH's candor and forthrightness earned it publicity, respect, and competition. The OMDH caught both the eye of the press and the attention of the two prior, albeit nearly moribund, human rights groups. During the early months of 1989, both of these groups sprang into action. The AMDH decision to hold its congress now met no resistance from the authorities, and it elected new leadership. In March, it issued a press release calling for a general amnesty to liberate political detainees and to allow repatriation of political exiles.[30] The AMDH's new leaders pledged to work closely with the LMDH, and on April 15 the two groups issued a joint communique. In 1990, all three groups combined to craft a single Moroccan charter of human rights.

Ironically, their unprecedented success in calling attention to the taboo topics of torture, disappearance, and imprisonment caused the OMDH to experience difficulties in 1990 and 1991. Success made rivalry with the parties predictable. During the USFP congress in late March, applause for OMDH observers recognized from the podium lasted some 10–12 minutes, and competition thereafter was inevitable. According to one participant, this was a moment of truth for Morocco's political parties: human rights was an issue around which Moroccans could be mobilized; by linking social and economic grievances to politics, the concept of human rights acquired enormous potential as a political weapon.

The OMDH's flush of success was short-lived: in less than a year, most of the organization's independent mainstays had left and OMDH leadership was in complete disarray. A feud between Madhi el Mandjra and the FIDH's secretary-general, Daniel Jacoby, resulted in el Mandjra's resignation from the OMDH: OMDH members recognized the measure of insurance provided it through affiliation with the international association, but the connection was not acceptable to el Mandjra.[31] Besides depriving the OMDH of el Mandjra's support, the FIDH affair had the unfortunate effect of pointing up serious divisions within the OMDH. By mid October, virtually all the politically independent members of the OMDH's executive bureau had resigned, and the governing national committee was forced to reconstitute its leadership.

A meeting was held in October 1989 to create a new bureau, and now the bulk of the seats went to representatives of four political parties. The loss of some of its most energetic and enthusiastic members stymied the OMDH, and several months passed before a new president could be named. It initially appeared that the OMDH would either dissolve or find itself in the service of political parties, but by 1991 it had largely rebounded. The baton of leadership was passed several times, and although there was no return to the 1989 fever pitch of activity, both the OMDH and the AMDH have in the interim established credibility in their denunciation of abuses and their call for correctives.

CONCLUSION

Women's rights groups and associations of lawyers and jurists added their efforts to the six Maghribi groups devoted to improving human rights conditions in their own countries, and although individual groups would continue to experience crises during the several more years covered by this book, by 1991 an indigenous human rights movement was firmly anchored in the Maghrib. The work of that indigenous human rights movement was reinforced by local groups with wider human rights concerns. In 1983, Arab professionals from across the Middle East had gathered in Hammamet, Tunisia, to establish an Arab Organization of Human Rights (AOHR). The declaration they produced argued that human rights abuse underlay many problems shared across the Arab world, and that the promotion and protection of individual liberties was the solution.[32] AOHR branches were established in Tunisia and Algeria, and Tunis was chosen as home for a new Arab-African Institute for Human Rights.

On a parallel track, Amnesty International groups were established in Tunisia and Algeria. Although they did not specifically condemn local human rights abuses, they shared an attachment to international principles, they emphasisized human rights education locally, and they denounced similar abuses in other parts of the world.[33] From a variety of angles, thus, North Africans working within the context of their own culture linked local concerns for civil and political liberties to the norms enshrined in the UDHR in 1948.

8 Challenging the Political Order

The emergence of not one, but two important social movements in the Maghrib at the end of the twentieth century is not a historical accident. Ideas for political action frequently germinate but more rarely take root and spread. Ideas that do find expression in social movements appear and develop when established structures and familiar patterns of social interaction that have provided meaning and order in some way now fail to satisfy widespread and salient needs. It is not personal misfortune multiplied, but rather shared discomfort at prevalent social change that gives rise to social movements. Conditions for the appearance of new ideologies, Robert Wuthnow has argued, are optimized when the existing moral order is disrupted and when disruptions are experienced collectively as alterations in the patterns of moral obligations that bind society.[1] In North Africa in the 1970s, such a time was ripening.

North African societies have in recent decades increasingly had to face the reality that political independence provides no palliative for the social upheaval associated with the waning of patriarchal order. Social disruptions have been most dramatic in Tunisia and Algeria, where the particular nature of the colonial experience produced a cultural divide between elites and masses, but the moral order has been challenged throughout the region. The social distance of elites often exacerbated disruptions, but the slow progress of economic transformation has more basically and pervasively undermined the established order of society as it spread. Formal education, the decline of agriculture, and the growing importance of urbanism have all contributed to expectations that Maghribi adolescents will not replicate the lives of their parents. By a multitude of technological changes, some mundane and others dramatic, the social universe of the Maghrib has undeniably been altered. It has not turned out to be the happy-ever-after dénouement promised by theories of modernization, but it is change.

A patriarchal system that for all of its tyranny had governed family relations and economic activities, created marriages, channeled the sacred, and mediated political relations has slowly been rendered impotent, its structures in shambles. Patriarchy provided moral order, and its decline necessarily poses uncomfortable questions about the nature of meaning in Maghribi society. As I argued in Chapter 3, the logic of patriarchal hierarchy required individuals to sacrifice personal interest to the greater welfare of the social unit, but thereby assured one's place in the social hierarchy. Whatever physical vicissitudes might arise, emotional security was guaranteed. As patriarchal authority eroded in the family unit, in the polity, and across society at large, moral obligations relaxed and individual liberties expanded. Insecurities and anxiety, however, increased as well.

Disruptions in moral order affect particular individuals and various groups within society differently, and sometimes in opposite fashion. In consequence, times of upheaval commonly yield a variety of ideological responses, some inevitably at odds with others.[2] Contemporary social movements in the Maghrib may be seen in that light. In many critical regards, the Islamist movement and the human rights movement are quite opposite, but both social movements are reactions to a patriarchal order under assault and to governmental difficulties in navigating the troubled waters of change. Their diagnoses and prescriptions constitute different responses to the same set of concerns.

The Islamist movement addresses the moment with designs to restore the power and respect of patriarchy. Particularly in Tunisia and Algeria, the institutions put in place at independence deliberately diminished the role of religion and the religious elite who were its cultural custodians. New political elites viewed Islam as an impediment to the work of government, or at least to the effective rule of governors. The emergence of a politicized Islamic movement from the mid 1970s on suggests that not all prospered—politically, economically, or emotionally—under the banners of modernity and socialism. In the Islamist movement many found a way to give voice to displeasure about the social management of power relations. "Islam" is the banner participants raise, but their principal distinction from other political groups and even from governments in power is not so much based on their practice of Islam's sacred rituals or on their endorsement of particular social and political goals as upon the nature of social relations and the structure of the social order they advocate. Several

Islamist leaders have acknowledged a profound social alienation, and Ahmida Enneifer attributes the early growth of an Islamist movement in Tunisia to pervasive social disorientation:

> The uneasiness was not just political, but much larger than that. We did not know any longer where we were going. Those who joined the ranks of the Islamists were those who realized that they did not know what to hang on to, that they were neither on the right nor the left, that they were rootless. All those who came from the countryside into the cities, and for whom there was no plan to anchor them.[3]

"Islam" provides a political frame that resonates well and legitimates feelings of discontent and discomfort, but the highly structured social and political relations within the Islamist movement also provide an emotional anchor in turbulent times. Islamists propose restoration of a fallen moral order.

The North African human rights movement also addresses issues of moral order but offers a different diagnosis and prescription. Whereas Islamists decry governmental inability to guide society and fulfill socioeconomic needs, human rights groups have focused on abuses of government power and the extension of civil liberties. Both movements are necessarily political to the extent that they locate the central problem in the conduct of government,[4] but human rights activists worry about too much governmental power rather than too little control. For human rights activists, the central problem resides in arbitrary powers exercised within the political system. Proposed solutions that protect and extend individual liberties necessarily entail a less hierarchical and less heteronomous society.

The objectives pursued by national human rights groups vary according to the prevalent patterns of state-society relations, and this is the place where we must draw on the analyses of national political dynamics explored in Part II. Although they shared a common commitment to promoting and defending human rights, groups across the region adjusted their work to address their own national contexts. In Tunisia, where the framework of law was theoretically in place, but was disregarded when convenient by Bourguiba and the political apparatus at his disposal, the Tunisian League of Human Rights (LTDH) has pursued two principal objectives. First, it worked to lend substance to the form of law. Playing boldly with the disparity between law and practice, the LTDH observed political trials, and in some instances its members offered themselves as defense attorneys. Academic seminars on political rights were also effective vehicles for encouraging private discussions and debates. Because Tunisian law nominally protected political rights—and, perhaps more important, established the intent to punish abuse of authority—such discussions, if carefully framed, could appear politically innocuous. Inasmuch as they promoted human rights, they were not.

A second objective, yet more tailored to the Tunisian context, was to create an independent voice that would not be drowned out by Bourguiba and the PSD. Over the past fifteen years, the LTDH has consistently promoted the idea of political pluralism. Statements on civil unrest in 1978 and 1984 implicitly contested the joint monopoly of the state and the PSD on political commentary and set precedents for the league as well as for others. Ben Ali's rapid endorsement of a human rights platform momentarily obscured the league's voice and created a crisis of identity within it, but even within that context the LTDH developed positions on provisions of the new electoral code. The league's message was muted with the loss of several key members enticed to command ministerial posts, but in time it reaffirmed its mission and strengthened its contrapunctual voice. During the Gulf War, admidst great controversy, it steered debate away from feverish nationalism toward international legal principles, and in 1991, when repression again gripped the country, it directed its criticism even at those who once had been of kindred purpose.

In Algeria, the agenda of human rights groups has been more basic. Political form with regards both to law and to government is more rudimentary, and the two competing human rights groups openly differed with regard to the objectives they pursued. The goal of the Algerian League for the Defense of Human Rights (LADDH) goal was ambitious: the Algerian political system needed a near-complete overhaul to establish the rule of law. The LADDH—primarily reflecting Ali Yahia's own voice—has with temerity held up a mirror to the Algerian government, exposing practices and situations to inform, and perhaps surprise, many Algerians and more outsiders. Its clear objective has been to shed light on behavior by the Algerian government that is deemed abusive by the international standards to which Algeria has adhered, and thereby to force a change in the practices of governance. While the LADDH has sought implementation, and even enforcement, of human rights standards, the Algerian League of Human Rights (LADH) has limited its efforts to the more modest goal of *promoting* human rights.[5] Many of its members have had access to the inner circles of power, and few have wished to provoke more instability than seems already in the offing. The LADH has not only spoken with a more moderate voice; it has pursued a more limited objective of opening political discourse and expanding the pool of political participants. That its 1988 conference on censorship was seen by participants as daring, and by the government as threatening, reflects the extent to which the Algerian system has been closed and the importance in that context of a perceived need simply to establish the legitimacy of human rights claims.

For Moroccan human rights activists, the principal objective has been to alter the monarchy's position vis-à-vis the law. The existence of a constitution notwithstanding, the king has never been bound by law, and in consequence neither law nor legal procedure carries full weight. The monarchy has dominated the political scene and the façade of law that barely masks its preponderant influence can easily be pushed aside. There are important similarities between Morocco and Tunisia in this regard, although in Morocco formal legal procedures have at times been altogether ignored. Moroccan human rights activists have concentrated on elevating the place of law in society and in governance structures and have made a key objective the straightforward, but politically hazardous, commitment to making visible the widespread but surreptitious practices thatclearly violate domestic and international law. Simply cataloguing and publicizing the cases of political prisoners has been a major thrust of the work of the Moroccan Organization of Human Rights (OMDH), and since 1990 the Moroccan Association of Human Rights (AMDH) has tested political taboos by openly questioning police practices. The purpose in these efforts has been to eliminate the notion that abuses are isolated and to illustrate the existing limitations of law and legal practice.[6]

Although specific objectives and the tactics used to pursue them vary according to individual groups and particular national contexts, across the Maghrib, human rights activists collectively challenge the underpinnings of political structures and processes. They have successfully created an issue, and as William Gamson notes, the sheer existence of a symbolic contest is a major achievement for the challenger.[7] A social movement's effectiveness at making its concerns heard, let alone having them addressed, is far from assured, but any measure of success depends foremost on its ability to mobilize social resources and exert pressure. Recognition of the importance of organizing activity for resource mobilization directs attention to questions of collective identity and the internal dynamics of particular groups. The political impact of human rights groups depends, of course, as much on external factors as on their own internal dynamics, but a significant part of what human rights groups might accomplish is a function of the extent to which their concerns resonate in society, how they assess structures of power and interact with them, and how they function as a group.

HUMAN RIGHTS AS A SOCIAL MOVEMENT

In Chapter 1, I argued that the success of the independent human rights groups has been partially dependent upon the moral force they have mustered and the strategies they have adopted. A survey of the interactions these groups have had with governments and the various tactics they have adopted makes it clear that their strategic choices (and ultimately their political significance) depend upon the microdynamics within the groups. Several questions in particular require attention. To whom have human rights groups appealed, and why have individuals—sometimes at considerable personal risk—decided to assert themselves on behalf of a class to which they do not belong? How have groups pursued their goals, and what concerns have governed their choices? To what extent are they bounded by the dynamics of North African political culture and their own national contexts? The body of theory about social movements developed over the past two decades supplies a framework within which to organize this inquiry. Specifically, our attention is directed to interrelated questions of recruitment and resource mobilization, the place of political discourse, and the actual organization of the human rights groups.

Recruitment and Resource Mobilization

Scholars once commonly attributed the rise of social protest movements to the predisposition of personality or socioeconomic grievances, but that thinking has generally been superseded by an understanding that social movements depend upon processes of social construction and upon shared social experience, which may or may not involve grievances.[8] Early models were not able to account for social protest that did not vary commensurately with the level of grievance, nor did they satisfactorily address questions about the social construction of meaning. Collective action was seen as the political response of the alienated and marginalized, rather than of the elites. Unlike the leaders of the Islamist movement, the principals in the early human rights movement in North Africa came from the privileged classes. Virtually all of the movement's leaders—across the three countries—were university educated, and either through professional status or family connections, or both, they felt that they should, and could, command respect. With regard to economic class and social status, they were indistinguishable from those whose claim to absolute power they challenged.

It is political passion that has set them apart, and a closer look at that passion points up the interrelations of ideas, grievance, and collective identity increasingly recognized as critical to the development of social movements.[9] In Tunisia the passion grew out of frustration with reform efforts within the PSD. Initial concerns were not so much with protecting human rights per se as with opening up the political system and redressing the political, and personal, wrongs that followed the PSD's 1971 Monastir congress. The passion that fueled the Algerian movements was somewhat different. Ali Yahia's group coalesced within the context of the Berber cultural movement, and while his own motivations in advancing a human rights agenda were born out of frustrations with a closed political system he had experienced firsthand, it was the sense of anger and injustice spread widely within the Kabyle population that created a popular basis for the first Algerian human rights group. For Brahimi and others who helped create the LADH, the passions were less connected to a political program or to particular grievances. In a political system that otherwise appeared entirely stalemated, the LADH offered a more or less sanctioned means of effective political action. Concerns it expressed about arrest procedures, detention and torture moved the LADH to center stage when riots shook Algiers in October 1988. The situation was quite different in Morocco, where the form of political and economic relations obscured the role of the state. In principle, access to politics and private enterprise was not restricted, and it was possible in Morocco in the 1970s to pursue power and profits, without ever confronting the seamy side of politics. Those circumstances undoubtedly delayed the formation of the OMDH, just as they diminished the effectiveness of the existing groups. By the time the OMDH was shaped, the discourse of human rights had gained respect internationally and across the Maghrib, and in consequence, of all the Maghribi groups, the OMDH at its creation projected the clearest purpose of promoting and defending human rights. The nexus of individuals who shaped the OMDH shared knowledge of human rights abuses in Morocco, knowledge that in some measure they had gained through professional experiences as lawyers, journalists, and university professors. They were decent people for whom the veil of innocence had been torn off. Their passion was born of outrage at human indecency. Time and the different cultural contexts shaded the various groups differently, but what all held in common was a fervent commitment: joining a human rights group in the Maghrib was for most not a casual affair.

The passion that inspired human rights activists was for the most part tempered with caution and political savvy. Elite backgrounds meant that activists understood the need to avoid direct threats to those in power. Just a few years before PSD dissidents began to shape the LTDH, they had witnessed the ouster—and treason trial—of the former planning minister Ahmed Ben Salah, and they well understood the risks. Groups in Morocco and Algeria likewise took stock of the local political context. Recruitment was almost always on a personal basis, and until the national law of association was changed in 1992, an application for membership in the Tunisian league required formal recommendation by an active member. Several scholars have noted the importance of social networks and personal connections in the anchoring of social movements. Mobilization is enhanced when groups share strong, distinctive identities and dense interpersonal networks, and preexisting friendships seem particularly important when the risk is high.[10] In the North African groups, activists were not necessarily known to one another at the outset, but great care was exercised to establish individual credentials through a chain of contacts and personal connections.

Most groups recognized the advantage of having a well-placed, politically unassailable member at or near the head of the group. Especially desirable was someone whose integrity could not be questioned—that is, someone who would make a credible public advocate for human rights but at the same time would not be viewed as threatening by the defenders of the state. The small group of individuals who spawned the LTDH considered these issues and deliberately recruited Saadeddine Zmerli to satisfy this purpose. As a physician practicing in colonial Algeria, Zmerli had belonged to the Algerian branch of the French League of Human Rights and was respected as an educator and a practitioner. Unlike the LTDH's actual progenitors, however, he had never played a role in politics and was not politically ambitious. The OMDH in Morocco made similar calculations, but as many of the founding members there were relatively unknown and had previously abstained from political involvement, they sought a politically respectable but uncompromised player whose own reputation would move their cause forward while minimizing the appearance of contentious intent. Mahdi el-Mandjra for a time supplied that need. Brahimi's connections within the inner circle of the Algerian political elite likewise afforded certain protections.

Where groups allowed passions to override their pragmatic assessment of political realities, stiff penalties could be exacted. In 1987, in the midst of political turmoil, the LTDH's secretary-general, Khemais Chemmari, was arrested for criticizing the prime minister. Members of the Moroccan Association of Human Rights (AMDH) and the Moroccan league were called in for questioning following a joint communique issued in 1989. The pragmatic wisdom of self-restraint is amply illustrated by the experiences of the LADDH in Algeria and the AMDH in Morocco. Under Ali Yahia's leadership, the LADDH only minimally diversified its Berber membership base and as a matter of principle it maintained a careful distance from both the FLN and those in seats of governmental power. It dared to operate openly before receiving official approval, and in return, its members were sent to prison. Somewhat more liberal laws of association in Morocco gave the AMDH more breathing space, but the outspoken leftists among its members are sometimes harassed—even to the point of arrest and imprisonment—and for many years the organization was effectively marginalized. While most activists sought to avoid such outcomes, it was ultimately a commitment to speaking out against abuses that bound them together. Maintaining that commitment often necessitated a careful balance between effective action and political risks that were by no means negligible.

If passions tempered by political pragmatism provided energy for the movement, the financial resources to sustain it were of only slightly less importance. Producing press releases and publishing reports involves certain expenses, and equipping an office requires more substantial investment. In Morocco and Tunisia, members reached deeply into their pockets, and thanks to their own relative affluence found the wherewithal to fund their causes. In Tunisia, early activists met in the office of Hammouda Ben Slama, a private physician; they soon were able to rent modest office space but waited several years to benefit even from a typewriter. The OMDH's purse was more comfortably lined, and from the outset it occupied spacious quarters in a residential area near the law school in Rabat. In Algeria, where private sources of income are less abundant, government funds have paid for for the LADH's office. Its members, mostly professionals, donate their services and stock supplies. The LADDH, by contrast, has not been provided with an office and depends almost entirely on the limited resources of its president.

Ironically, the activities of human rights groups have been sustained in part by neopatrimonial structures that undergird personal rule. As functionaries or as self-employed professionals, many activists are fairly well paid but relatively underemployed. Energies devoted to human rights groups create meaning and offer a path to social engagement that in some circumstances patrimonial linkage may also supply, but that income alone cannot.

The Role of Political Discourse

Onlookers at times dismiss the rhetorical battles in which social activists and defenders of the status quo engage, but such exchanges are deeply significant. Political discourse lies at the heart of the work of social movements. David Snow and his associates note that social movements don't simply carry forward well-formulated ideas: they engage in a process of constructing ideas, producing and maintaining meaning for antagonists and bystanders as well as for their own constituents.[11] Political discourse shapes political action, and social movements both borrow from and try to change public discourse. As Sidney Tarrow puts it, "collective action is the stage on which new meanings are produced, as well as a text full of old meanings."[12]

In the Maghrib, human rights activists were inspired primarily by the immediate political situations they confronted, and the different histories of individual groups and their various rhetorical emphases are explained by the local context. The Tunisian league pressed for political pluralism and the enforcement of civil and political rights for the most part already set out in law. The two Algerian groups differed in their strategies, but both sought to *introduce* the notion of civil and political rights. In Morocco, the three human rights groups joined together in efforts to make law more prominent in society and politics. Although all groups argue the indivisibility of civil and political rights on the one hand and of social, economic, and cultural rights on the other, it is clear from both actions and rhetoric that civil and political rights have thus far occasioned the greatest concern.

The cyclical nature of social protest makes the place and the shape of its initial appearance in any given cycle of particular note.[13] Early ideational frames of collective action within a cycle condition subsequent ones, and although the Tunisian league was not the very first Maghribi human rights group, its role as the first fully mobilized group has had implications for rights organizations across the Maghrib and in other parts of the Middle East as well.

That "human rights" emerged as a master frame of social protest in the Maghrib owes something to the fact that the protest cycle itself commenced in Tunisia. It is a paradox of political dynamics that relatively open governments are most likely to experience political protest.[14] The fact that Tunisian political rhetoric tacitly acknowledged and legitimized the idea of public liberties gave early activists there a political foothold from which to ratchet upward their claims to more extensive civil and political liberties. More than two decades of official discourse about human dignity had provided compelling rhetorical devices to political opponents who first gathered as the ad hoc council on public liberties. Habib Bourguiba and his political entourage within the PSD were able to expel them from formally designated political space, but they could not entirely silence them without incurring costs of their own.

Some critics now pose questions about the compatibility of Western-based notion of rights and the Arabo-Muslim cultural heritage, but those issues were not raised at the inception of the LTDH and may appear more a tactical ploy than evidence of a fundamental philosophical difference. Almost a decade before, the Tunisian government had ratified the International Covenant on Civil and Political Rights: a venerable tradition of political reformism solidly anchored the notion of individual-based rights within the bounds of Tunisian political culture.[15]

An individualist view of rights need not locate itself within the Western tradition or establish itself as anathema in the East. To assure coherence, Wuthnow argues, a moral ideology based on the individual minimally entails both rights and responsibilities: individuals are seen as capable of possessing rights; individuals are free to act and constitute the locus of choice; and individuals are conceptualized as having moral obligations. Moral accountability is meaningless without freedom, since any notion of moral obligation requires that an individual be free to reject the obligation.[16] Such a notion of freedom and individual rights and responsibility may be contested by many in Tunisian society inasmuch as it connotes the ability to make doctrinal interpretations that adapt universalistic ideas to particular situations,[17] but it is essentially compatible with the reform tradition that can be traced in Tunisian political history from Khayr al-Din Pasha forward.[18]

"Human rights" was a term gaining international currency in the late 1970s, and Tunisian activists seized upon the notion as a schema that could effectively organize and represent their own concerns. Such schemas, or "collective action frames" as they are identified within the literature on social movements, aid in efforts to locate, perceive, identify, label, and generally interpret events as they occur.[19] Frames once developed take on a power of their own. When drafting its charter in 1985, the Tunisian League accordingly found itself led through the debate by its own prior conceptualization of the issues as pertaining to *human* rights (as opposed to Tunisian, Arabo-Muslim, or male rights). In the process, it broadened and expanded the concerns within its purview and explicitly endorsed a universalist concept of human rights.

The terms of popular debate were likewise transformed. Discussions about the role of women in society that had once fallen under the rubric "status of women," for example, were subtly reframed as a rights issue. Women's groups formed in the late 1980s across the region use "rights" and "democracy" rather than "feminism" or "equality" to advance their claims. Similarly, political uprisings and governmental reprisals conventionally analyzed in terms of class struggle or social order were now seen through the prism of human rights. "Human rights" by the late 1980s had enough currency in the streets of Tunis to sustain conversational debate about the relative precedence of civil and political, as opposed to social and economic, rights. Moroccans and Algerians heard the term somewhat less frequently, but there, too, it entered public discourse. In Algeria the Gulf War was discussed in terms of human rights, and a 1993 sex scandal in Morocco centering on Casablanca's police superintendent was framed as abuse of power, violation of the public trust, and accountability—all terms within the Moroccan human rights lexicon.[20]

That Tunis was the birthplace of the contemporary Maghribi human rights movement was important for another reason. As already noted, periods of moral disorder frequently give rise to competitive ideologies, and human rights was not the only broad social movement to emerge in the Maghrib in the late twentieth century. The human rights and Islamist movements had parallel histories in Tunisia in the early 1970s, formulating alternative visions. The human rights movement arguably has a major role to play in the evolution of Maghribi politics and has successfully imposed its own frame on public discourse, but it is important not to lose perspective. Of the two contending movements, it is fundamentalist ideology and not human rights that resonates most deeply with the popular culture of the Maghrib. As it turned out, however, "human rights" conveyed a message of protest clearly and effectively enough that Islamist groups chose to adapt the language used by human rights groups, rather than vice versa.

Elements embedded in Tunisian political culture aided this evolution. Of the three Maghribi countries, Tunisia offered the human rights movement its greatest chance to take root and establish itself as an alternative to an Islamist movement. Neither Morocco nor Algeria had as strongly rooted a tradition of reform on which to draw, and in both countries governments openly opposed the domestic promotion of human rights, albeit in different ways and with different rationales. In Tunisia by contrast, Bourguiba had once used an as-yet-inchoate religious movement to combat more threatening challenges from the left, and in time, the government saw human rights as a tool to fight the Islamists. The LTDH perhaps unwittingly abetted the government in this regard with its failure to make bold appeals for the release of Islamists imprisoned in 1981 (although it did closely monitor their prison conditions), and, as explored in Chapter 8, a combination of elite status and a strict commitment to work within the framework of the law generally diminished perceptions of threat from the LTDH. International human rights groups, though, did take up the Islamist cases, and it was probably through that means that human rights discourse was introduced to the group then known as the MTI.[21] During the 1987 clampdown that targeted Islamists and their sympathizers, the league did strongly register its concerns. By that time, however, several Islamists had joined the LTDH and both movements were firmly implanted.

It was not simply tolerance for the philosophical notion of human rights that allowed human rights to come to the fore of political discourse. Islamism was also actively repressed. As a cornerstone of Middle Eastern culture, Islam possesses enormous legitimizing power. A movement of social protest tapping its power could threaten any government in the Arab world. Maghribi statesmen implicitly recognized that potential, and regimes in Tunisia and Algeria had sought to tame Islam soon after independence; in Morocco, its power was harnessed to the monarchy. In none of the three countries was the government in place willing to see Islam's potentially explosive power yoked to an opposition group, and in consequence organized Islamism has been met with harsh repression and its rhetoric has been vigorously contested.

There were thus multiple factors influencing the Tunisian human rights movement's delivery of its message, but while the government's intent to use it selectively and exploit it for its own ends must not be discounted, the LTDH's own success in altering political discourse in Tunisia was not negligible. Public discourse is not monopolized by any single actor, no matter how powerful, nor can its location be confined to a designated political space. As Carol McClurg Mueller notes, public discourse involves an interplay among media discourse, issue arenas, interpersonal interactions, and public opinion. In framing issues, defining grievances, and staging collective actions, social movements alter public discourse.[22] The LTDH managed to insert human rights into political discourse in Tunisia, and with its voice amplified internationally, it spread to other Maghribi societies and polities. In the early 1980s, it would have been difficult to predict that within a decade, the leaders of Algeria and Morocco would take up the theme.

Organization and Tactics

In addition to recruitment issues and political discourse, a social movement's effective micromobilization depends upon the strategies and tactics it adopts. As with political discourse, successful tactics must resonate within the political culture and call on constituents to act, perhaps creatively, with familiar means. Because contextual factors loom very large, there can be no single blueprint for effective action.

North African human rights groups initially faced two questions of broad tactical significance: how to structure their organizations and how to target their efforts. After extensive deliberations, each group developed different strategies, but as with questions of political discourse, the patterns established by the Tunisian league informed and influenced decisions in Morocco and Algeria.

The issue of organizing structures turned on two poles: who (and not simply *how*) to recruit, and what relationship to pursue with political parties. The first of these issues occupied groups most keenly in their formative period. Members talked about how large their group might become and whether or not they sought a mass-based organization. Drawing on experiences with the PSD, in Tunisia the choice was for an organization small enough to be monitored from, but not entirely dominated by, the center. In 1982 the league consciously limited the number of groups it would sponsor in Tunis.[23] In Morocco, the OMDH drew members primarily from professional circles in major cities; the resurgent AMDH attracted members of the OADP as well as more radical elements from within the USFP and set up branches throughout the country.

Membership policies reflect how the risk of participation was assessed. Both the LTDH and the OMDH understood that they were pushing the boundaries of politically acceptable action and recognized the importance of internal cohesiveness and trust. Their membership was deliberately drawn from professional classes who maintained important stakes in society. Not wishing to court trouble, they moved carefully. Algerian groups, too, were initially cautious, but Ali Yahia and associates within the Sons of the Martyrs group had already been chafing for several years and were not inclined to patience. And as noted earlier, for direct expression, they paid a price. As the LADDH developed, Ali Yahia came to exercise considerable personal discretion, and although by 1991 several thousand LADDH membership cards had been distributed, "membership" in the organization did not seriously engage many others besides him. Under Brahimi's wing, the LADH had much less to fear, and its several branches operated freely.

Relation to parties was the second major organizational issue faced by groups, and the more delicate one. The Tunisian league had originally feared that it might be swallowed by the PSD, but a more substantial threat actually came from the social democrats out of whose midst it had been formed. A fiction of separation was originally maintained by electing Zmerli, an independent, as president and by Mestiri's decision to maintain distance from the league. In 1982, the LTDH went so far as to close one Sahelian branch it thought would be overtaken by the PSD and refused to open another it judged dominated by leftists. Problems developed in 1985, however, when more than a third of the delegates to the league's congress and half of the candidates for the league's executive committee had strong connections to the MDS. The problem caused the league to reaffirm its commitment to nonpartisan action, and the immediate difficulties were finessed by expanding the executive committee (which in 1982 had been reduced to fifteen members). For the moment, at least, the league managed to stay its nonpartisan course.

As the Moroccan Organization of Human Rights was forming, it took heed of the Tunisian league's experience, as well as that of the two existing Moroccan groups. Both of those groups were affiliated with political parties, and as a result both were stymied either by political policies or political wrangling. The OMDH recognized these problems and discussed them with its counterparts in Tunis, but the issue in Morocco was not an easy one to transcend. Even from the beginning, the OMDH locked itself into party structures by permitting parties to send representatives, and following the fall 1989 resignation of most independents within the organization, the OMDH relied more heavily on party structures. Gradually it became associated with the USFP mainstream, and in January 1992 it elected Abdelaziz Bennani, a prominent USFP member, as its president. Ironically, the OMDH's growing links to the USFP have allowed the AMDH—formally affiliated with that party—to develop greater independence.

Algerian human rights activists considered the Tunisian experience as well, but without serious engagement. Although the Front of Socialist Forces (FFS) had resumed its activities in the late 1970s, and the Avant-Garde Socialist Party (PAGS) offered a venue for limited opposition within a partisan framework, in 1987 the FLN was legally and effectively the lone political party in Algeria. The question of party affiliation was thus a simple one, and for Ali Yahia, a known critic of the FLN, the matter was clear. Brahimi's group, on the other hand, might have accepted formal FLN linkage, but it was particularly covetous of affiliation with the International Federation of Human Rights Leagues (FIDH), whose guidelines in the interest of independence prohibited connection to any single party. In 1985, the FIDH had recognized the rival league, and that was the LADH's primary concern.

Allowing political parties to play a substantial role potentially involved both assets and liabilities, which each group had to weigh. Affiliation with parties risked the engulfing of the human rights groups, but allowed the possibility of harnessing organized energies and gaining access to party congresses, party presses, labor organizations, and so on. Furthermore, only preexisting organizations or cliques promised to counterbalance the strong personalities who emerged as leaders in some of the groups. Party connections by themselves were not necessarily either harmful or helpful to groups, but they posed the difficult question of trade-offs between principle and expediency, which in turn raised the specter of compromise. Groups recognized that they could be effective only to the extent that they maintained the requisite political independence, and the advantages of affiliation with parties had to be balanced against the potential costs of becoming embroiled in partisan struggles. To the extent that groups were committed to metapolitical goals rather than relational politics, the question was critical. If human rights groups sought to alter the political game, their task was in some degree to remove themselves from it. Overlapping roles and conflicting loyalties necessarily confused the concerns.

In this sense, a recent change in Tunisian law that appeared intended to weaken the league may in time strengthen it. A 1992 modification in the law of association (explored more fully in Chapter 9) prohibits overlap between party leadership and group leadership, and although the stipulation resulted in the league's temporary dissolution in 1992, its ultimate impact may well be to strengthen its metapolitical role. As with many questions of political strategy, no single path is clearly optimal. What does seem clear is that the stronger groups have wrestled with these issues, and it is the failure to address them rather than a particular resolution that most threatens a group.

STRATEGIC CHOICES

In addition to questions about organizing to maximize both integrity and strength within their inner circles, the human rights groups had to consider how to target their efforts. Specifically, they needed a strategy to guide interactions with the two components of society they sought to influence: government and public opinion. The different concerns of those two audiences created another set of tensions for them. Governments held real power, and disregard for the way human rights concerns were framed and presented was likely to exact costs. Modes of action that assuaged government sensibilities, however, tended to cultivate public criticism. A public disaffected with personal politics looked to human rights groups for saintly adherence to principle, taking seriously the moral dimension of human rights work and reacting caustically when the heroes proved more mortal than moral. Evidence of political calculation invited public criticism, but so did principled adherence to unpopular ideals. Moreover, even popular moral stances rarely rallied mass support. Most groups conceived of themselves as reformers rather than revolutionaries, and they faced a common dilemma: how to compromise without being compromised.

Four issue areas, with various relevance for particular groups, point up the political difficulties of crafting strategies that fully respect the principles to which groups subscribe. The rise of Islamism, the Western Sahara conflict, the Gulf War, and Palestinian rights have all tested the commitment and clear view of human rights groups in the Maghrib. Assessment of their performance is generally colored by the political preference of the observer. The object here is to discern the extent to which, across these issues, groups have indeed delivered a metapolitical challenge.

The Tunisian league was first to confront the issue of Islamism. Early on, the league had developed a tactical strategy of working with, not against, government. "Mass action," Zmerli cautioned in 1985, "could cause us to skid."[24] Press releases conveyed the LTDH's position to the public, but it preferred to use dignified, respectful letters or personal interviews to register its concerns with government officials. Through the tactics it adopted, the league presented itself as a loyal opposition, and from as early as 1981, the Islamist movement exposed the unstable nature of that oxymoron. The league dodged the difficult question at first. Although the 1981 trial of the officially unrecognized Islamic Tendency Movement (MTI) leaders prompted its first judicial intervention, its concerns were framed in the broader context of the issues of adequate prison conditions and rights of association. The 1984 amnesty extended to MTI leaders resolved a private quandary, but it resurfaced in 1987 and forced the league to clarify its position. The issue was not straightforward, in that many saw the Islamist movement as fundamentally intolerant and antiliberal. The participation of MTI members and other Islamist activists in the league threw the matter into relief. With clear purpose, through 1987, the league spoke out firmly against abuses and in advocacy of the MTI's right to exist within the law, winning the respect and gratitude of some and the ire of others. After Ben Ali acceded to power, the issue was again confused, this time by Mohammed Charfi in a voice the league well recognized. Charfi was elected president of the LTDH in March 1989; a month later, Ben Ali asked him to head the Ministry of Education. At the time, many speculated that his history within the LTDH would help ease tensions with Islamists at the University of Tunis. As minister of education, however, Charfi adopted a forceful anti-Islamist position that renewed debate and stirred controversy within human rights circles. Disappointment over the legislative elections in 1989 effectively ended Ben Ali's political honeymoon, but the facts that the league had new leadership and that the ministers they addressed included many old friends complicated matters. Another wave of repression again clarified the issues and renewed resolve to stand on principle in 1990, but in the meantime a central political truth had emerged. So long as the force of Islam could be mustered for purposes of protest politics, it would continue to force Maghribi human rights groups to clarify their own priorities.

The circumstances of context shaded this truth in Algeria and Morocco but did not fundamentally alter it. Ali Yahia clung steadfastly to principle and courageously provided legal defense to the Islamic Salvation Front (FIS) leaders Abbas Madani and Ali Belhadj, but politically he was marginalized. The LADDH denounced the January 1992 coup de main, but the conservative LADH was more equivocal. The OMDH in Morocco has confronted similar issues with regard to Islamism and was relatively slow to make public statements about cases that had, for example, been taken up internationally by Amnesty International. In Morocco, however, the issue is less prominent, in that the Moroccan Islamist movement remains largely inchoate and has not been targeted for repression nearly to the extent suffered by the political left. In 1990, the OMDH issued two press releases on behalf of al 'Adl wa'l Ihsan, apparently without political penalty.[25]

The OMDH (along with the AMDH and the Moroccan league) has faced a greater challenge of principle over the right of Western Saharans to self-determination. International human rights groups have generally remained neutral with regards to the Western Sahara, but the OMDH has instead steadfastly maintained the position that the Sahara is Moroccan. As a nominally independent group, the OMDH's position cannot be explained directly as an extension of a political party's own platform, and its advocacy of the official Moroccan position has set it at odds with its international affiliate, the FIDH.[26] Selective application of international principles on which the OMDH's work depends points up the great difficulties in transcending partisan, cultural, or national interests, but in this particular case, the near unanimity on the issue at home combined with only mild interest abroad has spared the OMDH political costs and embarrassments. Furthermore, it has won it favor in Moroccan political circles and has removed one potential cause for governmental attacks. At the same time, the political calculus has ramifications for its own actions and raises awkward questions about the group's full commitment to the international principles it has endorsed. Whereas the OMDH broke new political ground by cataloging and publicizing instances of political detention, it remained silent on the question of disappearances in southern Morocco and the Western Sahara. The strategy has undoubtedly spared the OMDH recriminations, but it also entails loss of an opportunity to challenge the most basic rules of Morocco's political game.

Human rights groups must monitor the mood not only of government but also of society at large. Even in societies with well-established, institutionalized civil rights traditions, an unpopular political stance or legal interpretation can be costly in terms of support. Where the objective of a human rights group is not simply to enforce legally guaranteed rights but to implant and develop respect for those rights, there are inevitably debates about how daring or how conservative to be, and whether to lead society or to be bound by its constraints. North African groups have at times been caught between wanting to respond to and spearhead popular human rights causes and not wanting to pander to public sentiments that threatened to undermine principles or distract them from more immediate concerns. Both the issue of Palestine rights and the Gulf War have tested their ability and resolve.

The Gulf War caused a crisis of sorts in the international human rights community. Many elements were at work: questions of international law; a double standard in international political practice, especially as concerned the Middle East; patterns of abuse by the Iraqi government in Iraq; and the difficulty of discerning truth and lies. For popular sentiment in the Maghrib, however, the issue was generally much simpler. The wealth and affluence enjoyed by the Saudis and Gulf emirates has long rankled in North African society, and from August 1990 on, Saddam Hussein was a hero.

Many human rights activists across the region felt themselves torn in different directions. As a body, Algerian activists were least troubled by conflict over principle. The LADH had a component identified as Arab nationalists, and although they stopped short of supporting Iraqi claims, both groups found unity and popular support in condemning the privations imposed upon the Iraqi people. The Moroccan OMDH was if anything more outspoken than its Algerian counterparts in condemning the West, but its position entailed more risk, and more debate, inasmuch as it differed from the Moroccan government's stance. The Tunisian league's position was the most complex, and most contested. At the outset of the conflict, LTDH leaders joined political parties in a march to express solidarity with Iraq and support the Tunisian government's decision not to follow Egypt into an alliance with the United States. But within the league, there was a complicated, multifaceted debate about the place of principle and international law. A Ba'thist contingent within the league openly supported Iraq, but others reasoned that international principles had to be upheld and that sentiments of political affinity should not be allowed to color the issue. Whatever the league's own position, it followed, it should be the same when Iraq invaded Kuwait as it would be had Kuwait invaded Iraq. There was not full unanimity on this position, and an article authored by the LTDH's president, Moncef Marzouki, expressing his own views sparked a long series of debates in the pages of the weekly *Réalités* and across a series of LTDH communiques. Marzouki castigated his countrymen for letting their passions and pain obscure other realities about the Gulf War and advocated support for the Iraqi people rather than Iraq's leader. His position was publicly attacked even by league members, and the LTDH as a whole lost popular support. Public disapproval amplified internal dissent over the war and the league's position, and for nearly six months it could focus on no other issues.[27] Meanwhile, a serious campaign of repression targeting Islamist dissidents was under way, and on that issue the league was nearly silent.[28] Although Moroccan and Algerian groups were not so internally divided, they, too, focused on little else during this period.

If issues of popular interest and import could sidetrack a group, they could also be used by groups to curry popular favor. The Gulf War was used this way in Algeria, in particular, and groups generally find it difficult to resist such opportunities if they do not involve obvious political costs. Among human rights groups in the Maghrib, the question of human conditions in territories occupied by Israel has most commonly served such purposes. Thus six months after the close of the Gulf War, as the Tunisian league was trying to refocus its energies, it seized upon a proposal from the LADH to host a conference on the rights of Palestinians in conjunction with the Arab-Israeli Peace Talks opening in Madrid. *Réalités* called the conference a "coup,"[29] and indeed it served to buoy the LTDH's beleaguered public relations. Contingents from all the Maghribi human rights groups attended, and delegates packed the conference hall in Carthage for an address by Yasser Arafat. In the Maghribi context, the conference was an easy success, but it required much planning, and the benefits were not necessarily long-lived.

A social movement's strength is in part derived from its ability to link its own cause to familiar, significant issues and experiences. Like community rituals or an external threat, local issues that inspire passion, but over which there is little division, can serve as rallying devices to consolidate energies and mobilize support. They can and do serve a positive function for groups, especially when rifts need to be bridged. Net positive effects are not, however, guaranteed. Whether a group is swept into a situation or deliberately chooses to engage its energies in issues that, however compelling, lie beyond its normal scope of activity and domain of influence, the result in either case may be to thwart, rather than to generate, new energies. Albert Hirshman has coined the term "social energy" to describe situations where joint efforts to achieve collective goals provide an inspiration of their own, so that as work proceeds, more energy becomes available than appeared at the start.[30] The possibilities of expanded energies are not boundless, however, and inevitably a group has difficulties in sustaining intense efforts. Actions in favor of popular causes may help unite groups and build support, but they may also distract groups from more difficult tasks.

As anecdotal evidence suggests, North African human rights groups have not always been guided by clear principle when confronting politically sensitive issues, nor have they been able to resist being drawn into issues that, while politically compelling, lay beyond their range of effective action. Internal politics has at times become mired in such issues. It is mistaken, however, to judge the movement's strength on such grounds. The measure of a group's commitment lies, not in its ability to avoid political snares or withstand distracting pressures, but rather in its resolve and ability to return to its principal objectives with clear purpose.

CONCLUSION

The human rights movements that began to emerge in the late 1970s were part of a broader protest cycle that concerned the nature of authority in the Maghrib. Their objectives were not always incompatible, but human rights activists and Islamists approached the crisis of authority from different angles, borrowing from different traditions within their immediate societies and beyond. The human rights movement in the Maghrib, no less than Islamism, is embedded in the culture of North Africa.

In part because it is an indigenous force, the human rights movement has offered a significant challenge to Maghribi states in the late twentieth century. They have contested the state's monopoly of political institutions through the medium of political discourse, and their emphasis on the preeminence of law directly challenges the framework of governance. The efficacy of Maghribi human rights groups in pursuit of these ends owes much to the fact that, for the most part, members are drawn from elite classes. Rarely since independence have social or political groups in the Maghrib enjoyed the cohesion, purpose, or resources to make their own voices carry. Human rights groups pose a challenge from within. The skills, energy, and financial and technological resources they have deployed do not depend upon the state, and thus far the absence of mass support has been compensated for by internal cohesion. They may operate independently, but at the same time, the interests they share with ruling elites mitigate the threatening aspects of their work. In politics the medium is often as important as the message, and the shared language allows human rights activists to press the claim that law is more important than leader.

9   Human Rights and Political Discourse

By 1978, each of the three Maghribi states had acceded to the two principal human rights covenants,[1] and within UN human rights bodies, individuals from the region assumed leadership positions. In 1981, the Moroccan delegate to the UN Commission on Human Rights served as rapporteur, and during his tenure on the Human Rights Committee, the Tunisian member actively pursued questioning of alleged violations by other African states.[2] In the international context, Maghribi statesmen paid homage to human rights, but at home it was another matter. No Maghribi state looked favorably upon the creation of a domestic watchdog group. At the same time, it was difficult to prohibit their formation. The fact that the nascent human rights movement's founders and activists were themselves members of the political elite and conformed even to the letter of the law made it difficult for those in power to portray them as a threat to the state. States and the men who ran them thus found it awkward to repress the groups by the familiar means of arrest and imprisonment, and instead initially employed delaying tactics to impede their development and obstruct efforts.

This approach shifted toward the end of the 1980s, as all across the Maghrib, governments moved from hostility to accommodation. Just as Tunisia was home to the first active Maghribi human rights group, its government was the first in the region to embrace the concept of human rights. From there it spread. As a political force human rights was so contagious that in Libya Colonel Muammar Qaddafi climbed aboard a bulldozer and posed for photographs as he prepared to demolish a prison. Algeria and Morocco moved more cautiously, but these governments, too, saw it in their interests to incorporate the language of human rights into official discourse.

Discourse is important to social movements, but it is no less so to the state. To a significant degree, the human rights struggle in North Africa has been a contest over political discourse. Statesmen who had been reluctant to permit groups even to operate began to promote human rights, inserting the notion of rights into their own rhetoric about domestic politics and responding through legal measures and specially created government bureaus to charges that international standards had been abrogated. This chapter seeks to explain the domestic dynamics that pushed governments to make that tactical shift, and it raises questions about consequences for the patrimonial state.

First, however, it must be recognized that the progressive legitimization of human rights concerns in official political discourse was only in part a voluntary concession, and in general the commitment remained shallow. In some cases, heads of state and governing elites saw human rights as a political device for advancing their own programs and enhancing their legitimacy; in others, they defensively tried to wrest political advantage from groups contesting the absolute quality of their power.

Even a shallow commitment, though, is not without significance. The dramatic change in states' tactics did not necessarily represent a fundamental change in political values, but it did signal an altered assessment of political dynamics. Moreover, the new tactics themselves affected the parameters of the political play, and beyond that, the legitimacy of a patrimonial framework of governance. Theda Skocpol has argued persuasively that the state influences political dynamics and political outcomes, not simply by the policies it pursues, but also by the parameters it helps establish for political maneuver.[3] By sanctioning a change in the language of politics, North African states legitimized new actions and raised new expectations. The respect for civil and political rights demanded by human rights groups across the Maghrib was at odds with the unlimited, arbitrary coercive powers of the state, and the credibility of states that now claimed their own interest in promoting human rights depended in part on a willingness to surrender some of those powers.[4]

The accounts of governmental response to the human rights movement to which this chapter now turns document a gradual transition on the part of Maghribi governments from bare tolerance to rhetorical embrace of the human rights cause at home. In the process, governments sanctioned the opening of space to reconsider patrimonial models of government, and even in the short run, state-society relations have been affected. Tunisia receives primary attention here because the richly documented interchange between the government and the LTDH lends itself well to an analysis of the impact of officially adopted human rights rhetoric. The Algerian government, like the Moroccan monarchy, adopted human rights discourse somewhat later, but the Tunisian and Algerian stories nevertheless have some features in common. In both of these countries, the emergence of human rights rhetoric followed an important shift in the regime itself, and pressures for change multiplied as that newly adopted rhetoric began to take effect. Through 1993, at least, the Moroccan monarchy has responded less to domestic forces than to international ones, but Hassan II has acknowledged an obligation to "defend the rights of Moroccan citizens vis-à-vis the administration and the state."[5] Governments have not been able to employ the concept of human rights without changing course themselves.

TUNISIA

When Zine el Abidine Ben Ali ushered human rights into the presidential palace at Carthage in November 1987, the irony was not lost on activists at home and abroad. For most of his career inside the state security apparatus, Ben Ali's professional responsibilities had placed him in opposition to those who promoted human rights, and his full embrace of human rights concerns upon assuming the presidency must be attributed to the power of the human rights idea combined with political concerns of the moment rather than to a long-standing personal commitment. Ben Ali rose to power by means that were legally open to question and without any clear social base of support. To make the matter more precarious, the Islamists at the time were demonstrably consolidating their own following. Ben Ali needed the firm backing of political elites, and human rights was a political concept that promised to rally support. The credibility of the LTDH during the political crisis that preceded Ben Ali's "constitutional coup" had made of human rights a potent new ideology and a new source of political legitimacy, which the new president sought to tap. Political necessity thus led the Tunisian government to endorse and promote the idea of human rights.

Ben Ali's first measures as president were taken in the name of human rights. Political amnesties and the legal reform of practices that facilitated abuses were given priority even over questions of elections and legal restrictions that hampered operations of the press and political parties. One of Ben Ali's first legislative initiatives was a bill to impose limits on *garde-à-vue,* the practice of incommunicado pretrial detention, which was widely linked to torture and ill-treatment. Measures to abolish the post of general prosecutor and the state security court quickly followed. It was in riding the wave of popular support for such reforms and seeking to harness to his own government the widespread respect and support enjoyed by the Tunisian League of Human Rights that Ben Ali also appointed two founding members of the league to his cabinet in July 1988. Saadeddine Zmerli was named minister of public health and Hammouda Ben Slama was asked to head the Ministry of Youth and Sports. Neither appointment involved substantial power, but they gained Ben Ali favor and much positive press. In official rhetoric, human rights would gradually come to be presented as a notable achievement, an acquisition, of Tunisian political culture, and its promotion during the first eighteen months of Ben Ali's rule clearly increased the power and legitimacy of the state and the new leader at its helm.[6]

Human rights rhetoric and efforts to capitalize on its appeal outlasted the honeymoon. The disappointment and cynicism that issued from the 1989 election, discussed in Chapter 4, returned Ben Ali's government to a defensive position vis-à-vis society and the desire for political pluralism. In the national assembly as elsewhere in the political system, it was patrimonial politics as usual. The Constitutional Democratic Rally (RCD) retained its monopoly, the personality of the president eclipsed all others, and a government that had espoused human rights became increasingly entangled in the contradictions between its words and its deeds.

Liberalizing measures enacted after the election evoked little interest. In June 1989, the Chamber of Deputies approved Ben Ali's proposal to restore civil liberties to more than five thousand ex-political prisoners, but for many this fruit was bitter. Just three weeks before, the government had refused to extend legal recognition to al-Nahda precisely because its leaders were not free to exercise their civil liberties. Islamists abandoned hopes of negotiating an opening for themselves with the new government and resumed their oppositional stance, staging informal rallies and distributing tracts. The government in turn responded by arresting Islamic activists and students (many of them with Islamist sympathies), and an atmosphere of wariness came to replace the political euphoria that had prevailed for the first year of Ben Ali's presidency. Press freedoms were gradually curtailed, and independent publications faced political censorship that was thinly veiled as technical problems. Others failed when financial backers under political pressure withdrew support.[7] Rumors of new internal security units began to circulate,[8] and in addition to Islamists, critics on the left were selectively harassed. In April 1990, the Tunisian league issued its first statement outlining concerns about abridgments of human rights by the new government. Although it had not hesitated to comment on specific cases, up to this point in the Ben Ali administration, the league had adopted a congratulatory attitude toward the government. The April memorandum made charges of widespread, systematic torture that could less easily be attributed to individual excesses. It thus constituted a serious rupture.[9]

The outbreak of tensions in the Gulf provided a diversion of sorts. It simultaneously redirected attention away from domestic politics and increased intensity in the contest between the Islamists and Ben Ali's regime. The Tunisian government had several issues about which to be concerned. As an Arab ally of the West, it received substantial amounts of military and nonmilitary aid. On the other hand, close association with the West was in many circles a political liability, and Ben Ali's appeals to Washington on behalf of the Palestinian cause had not received serious attention.[10] Within the greater Arab context, Tunisia was still recovering from a diplomatic blow to its national pride occasioned by the return of the Arab League to Egypt. Only months before the opening of a new headquarters building in Tunis, Cairo had reclaimed its statutory right to the organization's seat. In the end, Tunisia adopted a position of engaged neutrality with regards to the Gulf conflict. Like several other Arab states, Tunisia argued that Egypt had acted precipitously in endorsing the Western initiative in the Gulf. It abstained from the Arab League's early vote on the mission and steadfastly declined to participate in the allied forces, but it also withheld support from Saddam Hussein and throughout the conflict tried earnestly to walk the tightrope of neutrality.

It was not simply regional and global political concerns that influenced the government's position. Public opinion figured in the calculations, and in particular the apparent implications for the Islamist movement. On August 14, 1990, only days after Iraqi troops moved across the Kuwaiti border and the decision was made to move U.S. troops into Saudi Arabia, an estimated ten thousand people, led by representatives of a coalition of political parties and civic groups, marched through the streets of Tunis to express solidarity with Iraq and support for the Tunisian government's refusal to follow Egypt's lead.[11] The Gulf conflict heightened populist Arab nationalism: little sympathy was felt for the Kuwaitis, whose ostentation rankled sorely and was held up in contrast to the plight of Palestinian refugees, and dependence upon Western troops to defend the territory that housed Islam's sacred shrines was experienced by many as humiliation. Support for the coalition would have required blatant disregard of these popular sentiments and would surely have exacted a hefty political price.

At the same time, government officials gambled on the impact the Gulf conflict would have upon the Islamist movement. It was widely believed that Saudi money financed the Islamist movement in Algeria and Tunisia, and government officials hoped that the new fervor of anti-Saudi sentiment would also serve to discredit the Islamist movement.[12] Showing itself an ardent defender of Arabo-Muslim interests thus became a primary objective and upped the ante for the Islamists, who now found themselves battling the government against rhetorical weapons they alone had previously wielded. Demonstration followed upon demonstration, and violence erupted in early September when an Islamic activist was shot and killed by government troops while distributing leaflets outside a Tunis mosque. By October, the government had opened a full-scale operation to round up Islamist opponents of the regime.[13]

Ultimately, the government's policy of calculated neutrality in the Gulf conflict was no more successful at home than it was abroad. A rupture between popular sentiment and official policy was avoided, but Iraq lost the war, and U.S. aid to Tunisia was substantially reduced. Domestically, the Islamist movement suffered no evident loss of support either as a result of its alleged financial connections to the Saudis or as the consequence of targeted repression. The contest between Islamists and the government was at an impasse.

A review of policies under both Bourguiba and Ben Ali reveals little evidence that the Tunisian government ever intended to legitimize Islamist participation in national politics. From 1981 to 1990, successive governments alternatively repressed and courted the Islamists, but both policies were directed at the same goal of eradicating or disabling the movement, whether by coercion or by enticing its supporters to leave. By 1991, nearly all of the cards minimally consistent with public endorsement of human rights principles had been played, and the LTDH as self-appointed referee called foul when due process was violated. So long as Hizb al-Nahda adhered rigorously to the principles of nonviolence publicly endorsed in 1981, Ben Ali's government found it difficult to curb Islamist activities and at the same time stay within the bounds of its human rights commitments. There were nonetheless infractions around the edges. Moncef Ben Salem and a handful of others were sent to prison for a few years for political offenses that included defaming political leaders and spreading false news; activists and their associates were called to police stations for questioning, where some were abused; and hundreds of individuals were processed through the courts. Individuals suffered, but even so the Islamist movement survived.

The stakes were raised for all concerned in February 1991, when a handful of activists at least loosely associated with al-Nahda attacked an RCD office in the Bab Souika quarter of Tunis and set a fire that claimed the life of a night watchman. That event provided the basis for a change in official policy. Al-Nahda neither condemned nor condoned the attack, but cofounder Abdelfatah Mourou expressed regret at the slide into violence and resigned. Rachid Ghannouchi, by contrast, responded to journalists' inquiries by advocating continued confrontation as the only effective response to the government's own intransigence.[14] With the use of violence, whether perpetrated by al-Nahda or not, officials could more credibly claim a threat to state security and publicly justify use of the state's own muscle: the assailants were apprehended, prosecuted, and executed.[15] Even while the shock of the Bab Souika attack rippled through political circles, the government announced discovery of a plot with bigger designs. It charged that al-Nahda was actively seeking to overthrow the government and had drawn up a five-step plan to that end. Real or fictitious,[16] this plot allowed the government to seize the offensive and launch reprisals. In May, officials appeared on television to present details, and the security apparatus left few stones unturned in its efforts to interrogate Islamist leaders. From spring 1991 into the fall, thousands of Islamists, their family members, and their acquaintances were arrested or detained for questioning, many during nighttime raids. Reports of torture became common, and at least two individuals died under suspicious circumstances while in police custody. Few families were unaffected, and fear again gripped the country.

The relevance of this story is not that Ben Ali's government found means of clamping down on the Islamists, but rather that it felt constrained to cloak its actions in the formality of law. Governing elites appeared more mindful of society and the sensibilities of public opinion than they had been for several decades. Grounds had been found to portray al-Nahda as a threat and an enemy within, but the rhetoric of human rights retained its power, and care was exercised not to stray far beyond newly established parameters. The constitution was not suspended and no state of siege was declared: appearances conveyed social control and respect for law.

In some regards this strategy was not fundamentally different from those adopted by Bourguiba at times of domestic crisis. Faced with the Youssefist challenge in 1956, for example, Bourguiba had sought to legitimize repression and persecution through a judicial process. The innovation in 1991 was that a civic group made up largely of members of the elite who knew their way through the halls of power was committed to revealing, albeit discreetly, the state of the emperor's undress. The LTDH itself was not without foibles, though, and at times its vigilance waned. In 1989 and 1990, as the contest between government and al-Nahda heated up, the league carefully adopted a balanced position, criticizing al-Nahda's public position on civil and political liberties and its connection to sporadic violence at the university, but criticizing the state's abuse of its power too.[17] By the time the government's dragnet operation was under way in spring 1991, the LTDH was so enmeshed in its internal debate about Arab nationalism, the Gulf War, and international law that it could see little else. By June, however, it had found its voice again and took the government to task for apparent excesses.

Events that unfolded from June 1991 to June 1992 present an opportunity to study the relationship between human rights rhetoric and political practices in a context relatively untrammeled by the elements of political convenience prevalent in the first year of Ben Ali's presidency. As already noted, by 1991 few traces of the celebrated honeymoon remained. Virtually all important civic groups had been enjoined to denounce the February attack on the Bab Souika office of the RCD,[18] but prominent professionals also expressed concerns about the government's own practices. A statement calling for political liberalization circulated during the second half of 1991 and was signed by some three hundred well-known individuals. There was little celebration in April when Ben Ali created a Higher Committee for Human Rights and Basic Liberties,[19] and there was no longer any pretense about the Islamists' possibly being admitted to the official game of politics. Security forces and new walls reinforced the presidential palace in Carthage, and expansion of the security apparatus already known by and presumably loyal to Ben Ali offered the regime an independent base of power it had not enjoyed in Ben Ali's first years of rule.[20] The Movement of Socialist Democrats (MDS), which had not yet recovered from its humiliating electoral defeat in 1989, was in new state of political crisis, and other parties remained weak. Politics, nevertheless, had become confrontational, and the LTDH was at its fore.

Although as a "humanitarian organization," the league was not formally admitted to the political arena, Ben Ali tacitly acknowledged its importance to his effective governance. Bourguiba had ostracized liberal critics of his regime, but Bourguiba had held firm control over the ruling party and had not until the last decade of his rule had to contend with potent opposition. Ben Ali had anchored himself at Carthage, but his popular support came primarily from a party he had not long served as patron. The league's words fell on listening ears at home and abroad, and even if its support was no longer essential to undergird the regime, it was capable of producing embarrassment by exposing inconsistencies.

When the league issued a highly critical communique on 14 June 1991, it was thus treated seriously. Four weeks earlier, on 18 May, the league had used its customary diplomacy to register concern about abrogated arrest and detention procedures and frustration with exchanges at the Interior Ministry. Now it spoke directly of deaths in detention and torture and announced plans to establish its own commission of inquiry. The league's summary press release omitted the details included in a nine-page memorandum sent privately to Ben Ali, but its language was stern:

> In the context of its humanitarian responsibilities, the League has always pressed for greater individual and collective liberties, and for furthering and deepening the democratic process. It has always and absolutely rejected, as it does now, the idea that maintenance of order should be to the detriment of values essential to the respect for human rights.
>
> It is with this background, and in reference to its basic principles, that the Executive Committee declares [that] the League has decided to establish a special committee to inquire into suspicious circumstances surrounding the death and burial of Abderraouf Laribi. . . . The League fears that this death, as well as others, may be linked to conditions of detention and interrogation. . . . It also expresses its most serious concern regarding the greater and greater number of complaints of possible extended torture. . . . The League profoundly regrets that its numerous and repeated appeals to the Government during this crisis have borne few fruits and hopes for improved collaboration, in the interest of Human Rights, the reputation of our country, and the State itself.[21]

Through private circles the communique circulated widely; it was reported more circumspectly in the Tunisian press. The Interior Ministry issued a reply memo discounting allegations of abuse, but less than a week later Amnesty International had released a statement making similar charges. Ben Ali convoked a meeting between human rights activists and Interior Minister Abdallah Kallel and Justice Minister Abderrahim Zouari,[22] where the LTDH's president, Moncef Marzouki, contended that the league had issued its statement only when efforts to work with the Interior Ministry had collapsed. He reiterated concerns for an investigation.

By the end of June, the league had agreed not to proceed on its own, and under the aegis of the Higher Committee, a National Commission of Inquiry headed by Rachid Driss, a retired diplomat, set to work investigating the league's charges. The six-member commission, which included a representative from the league, was to have full access to government personnel and records. According to the Tunisian newsweekly *Réalités*, the minister of interior was instructed to meet with league officials posthaste. To emphasize his own commitment to human rights to the domestic and international communities before whom he had been embarrassed, Ben Ali also created the special post of principal presidential adviser in charge of human rights.

Meanwhile, arrests, accounts of torture and ill-treatment, and new reports of death in detention continued to accumulate. The league issued statements of protest, but its communiques were generally ignored by the press. The Driss Commission, as it was popularly identified, conducted its investigation over the summer months, meeting with Abdallah Kallel, representatives of the LTDH, defense attorneys, and prosecutors, and visiting several prisons in or near Tunis. In late October, it submitted its report to Ben Ali, and a summary statement was distributed to the press. Tunisians who had hoped for full disclosure—including most prominently those members of the league who had argued for placing confidence in the Driss Commission—were both disappointed and distressed at the outcome. Rather than acknowledge and illustrate systematic abuse, the summary spoke in general terms of individuals who had been deprived of their rights as a result of individual zeal, lauded the open atmosphere in which the commission had been allowed to act, and made a series of policy recommendations.[23]

Over the next few months, league spokespersons repeatedly pressed for public release of the report and were joined in their appeal by Amnesty International and other international human rights organizations. So long as the report remained confidential, they argued, details of the commission's investigation of alleged deaths in detention and abuse of power were withheld from public scrutiny. No casual observer could discern where the truth lay in the volley of charges and countercharges between human rights groups and the government that ensued. An Amnesty International report issued in March 1992 providing extensive documentation on mishandled arrest and detention procedures, torture, and death in detention was firmly rebutted by the government in a statement that took refuge in the Driss Report and refuted specific claims attributed to AI. In a firm reply of its own, AI defended its evidence and chided the government for misrepresenting its claims.[24]

Ben Ali was caught in the contradictions of his regime. In presidential speeches, human rights figured prominently as part of the heritage of November 7, but he could not effectively use the rhetoric of human rights to bolster the legitimacy of his government and simultaneously appear to sanction egregious abuses. The human rights rhetoric had a power of its own and imposed limits on acceptable policy. In April, he instructed the Driss Commission to report on the implementation of its earlier recommendations, and results of this second investigation were made public. According to the published report, several official directives on appropriate police conduct had been issued and posted in police stations, and a training program on community relations had been inaugurated; 116 police officers had been judged to be implicated in 105 cases, and 55 officers had received sentences. Monetary reparations were to be made to the families of five individuals acknowledged to have died in detention.[25]

Trials of Islamists involved in the alleged plots were set for late July, and as that date neared, the government took further steps to better public relations, and in particular, international relations. July brought top officials from both Amnesty International and the International Federation of Human Rights to the presidential palace in Carthage, and although the military tribunals before which the defendants were to be tried normally proceeded in camera,[26] assurances were issued that international observers would be admitted. The government went to great lengths to explain its legal procedures, preparing information packets in several languages and comparing its procedures to European ones.[27] The trials eventually took place in July 1992, and while in the eyes of international observers they failed in several regards to comply fully with international standards, the proceedings did point up the Tunisian government's concern for its image with respect to human rights. Moreover, the sentences were not as severe as many had feared.

In the meantime, relations between the Tunisian League of Human Rights and the government had deteriorated. Tensions had risen, then subsided after the Driss Commission was established. They mounted again in October 1991, when the league appealed for the commission's report to be made public.[28] In December, they sharpened further when the league issued a communique reiterating grave concerns about reported deaths in detention, abuse of preventive detention, and house-to-house searches. The government promptly dismissed the charges as false and reminded the league of its strictly humanitarian mission.[29] Late in January, Marzouki was questioned by police about league positions; the authorities later explained that their concerns arose from an interview he had given to a foreign radio station.[30]

These difficulties, however, paled beside the more serious changes in the law of association hastily proposed by the government, approved by the Constitutional Council, and presented to parliament for passage into law in early March. The law of association had already been liberalized shortly after Ben Ali assumed office, and in the interim no pressures had emerged for additional alterations. (By contrast, many complaints were popularly registered against the revised electoral and press codes.) Although seemingly innocuous, the proposed reform was framed in such a way as to deprive the LTDH of two pillars of its strength: carefully scrutinized membership and the participation of members active in political parties. The proposed legislation severely limited restrictions on membership and stipulated that leaders of political parties could not simultaneously hold positions of responsibility in general associations.

The government repeatedly denied that it was targeting the league and instead presented the reform as an advance in democratization, but the dynamics of the bill's preparation, debate, and interpretation all suggested otherwise. Five year's before, the Interior Ministry (during Ben Ali's tenure as minister) had already sent an ominous letter to the league raising concerns about a host of very minor legal irregularities and its troublesome membership policy.[31] When the 1992 legislation was introduced to the RCD-monopolized parliament, RCD members loyally stressed the need to separate politics and civic associations. In praising the debate about the new bill, Interior Minister Kallel made clear the government's intent to prevent associations from running their affairs as thinly disguised political parties.[32] Although 41 of the country's 5,000 associations were nominally affected by the change, in the popular view, only one organization truly fit the bill.

The league fought energetically to prevent passage of the law, but although the measure was discussed at length in the parliamentary chamber and in its hallways, in the end, the LTDH was unable to win even a single vote in the RCD-monopolized assembly. A subsequent ruling by the Interior Ministry on the league's classification as a "general association" made the defeat complete. It was given until June 14 to make its structures and its membership procedures conform to the new law. When Sihem Ben Sedrine, a member of the league's executive committee as well as of the political bureau of the Socialist Progressive Rally (RSP), refused to resolve the immediate crisis by relinquishing leadership in either body, the league was forced to dissolve itself. Subsequent efforts to convoke a special LTDH congress failed, and the activities of the most venerable human rights organization in the Arab world were suspended.

In March 1993, an administrative court's extraordinary decision to reverse the Interior Ministry's earlier decision on the league's classification allowed it to reconstitute itself. In anticipation of the World Conference on Human Rights in Vienna, it resumed operation with renewed commitment. Within Tunisian society, however, there was much discouragement among human rights sympathizers. Many were disheartened: for all the human rights fanfare, little had changed, and in some ways the situation was worse than it had been during Bourguiba's thirty-year rule. Little progress had been made toward either of the league's main objectives, preventing abuse and promoting political pluralism. According to *Le Monde*, some three thousand Islamists remained in Tunisian prisons, and reports of torture had not diminished. Members of the Tunisian Communist Workers' Party (Parti des Ouvriers communistes tunisiens, or POCT) had recently been harassed, and several of its leaders were arrested for belonging to an unauthorized organization. The MDS had suffered major internal divisions, and those who originally sought to turn it into a full-fledged opposition party were ousted or resigned. Other legal parties exercised little influence, and the UGTT remained weak. Despite the fact that changes in the electoral code were made to award a number of parliamentary seats to opposition parties, legislative elections in March 1994 generated little more enthusiasm than had the creation of a special council to resuscitate the National Pact of 1988. Tunisians in general showed slight interest in such political reforms.

Many of those who sought broad change looked at these developments with deep pessimism and concluded that the human rights movement had had little impact, but from another angle the response of the government to the league and the human rights idea remained significant. As explored in Chapter 3, Bourguiba met with little resistance when he created, used, and altered laws to serve his own ends. In a different era and with a different background, Ben Ali was less able to impose himself on the political system. He used an ambiguous constitutional passage to initiate his rule, and legal reforms provided popular legitimacy. As the story of the law of association makes clear, presidential control of parliament through 1993 at least remains complete and unchallenged. The reforms, however, have made obviously arbitrary exercise of power more difficult. Ben Ali must be more mindful of the law than was his predecessor, and the difference lies with society, operating through human rights activists and the support they have generated.

ALGERIA AND MOROCCO

The governments of Algeria and Morocco also incorporated human rights rhetoric into political discourse in the late 1980s, but to somewhat different ends. In Tunisia, Ben Ali's adoption of human rights language allowed him to establish his own reform platform and distance himself from unpopular policies. In Algeria and Morocco, the task for established rulers was to reorient political rhetoric—and to a more limited extent, actions and policies—without undermining their own control.

The Algerian government did not readily embrace the idea of human rights. Not only were Ali Yahia and several of his associates imprisoned from 1985 to 1987, but in the UN Economic and Social Council, Algeria used its influence to prevent the regional Arab Organization of Human Rights (AOHR) from receiving consultative status.[33] It was primarily the wave of international concern for the imprisoned human rights activists, channeled through the FIDH, that pushed the government to reverse field. To deflect criticism, the government opened dialogue with Miloud Brahimi and encouraged development of an independent group that would nonetheless be sympathetic to the official point of view. Human rights activists who joined Brahimi, as well as those who risked arrest with Ali Yahia, were committed to their work. Apart from the amnesty extended to Ali Yahia and the Berber activists, however, there is little to suggest that the government took them or their concerns seriously in 1987.

Popular reaction to the government's handling of the October 1988 riots turned the tide. The coalescence of several professional groups and the outcry of public protest against torture and ill-treatment was unprecedented in the history of independent Algeria. Ali Yahia was perhaps to be dismissed as a political malcontent, but the Algerian League of Human Rights (LADH) was drawn largely from the class of professional and technocratic elites, and a newly formed Committee against Torture also demanded attention.[34]

The LADH had been approved primarily to placate foreign critics, but its outspoken reports in 1988 helped mobilize a public outcry within Algeria. It was in response to discontent at home that Chadli Bendjedid embarked upon a reform program that culminated in a new constitution and contested elections. The 1989 constitution provided rights of association and assembly, guaranteed free expression, and affirmed judicial independence. Several measures intended to implement the constitution were directly related to the protection of human rights and responded to popular concerns arising from the October riots. First, the state security court at Médéa, which had been used intermittently to try individuals accused of political crimes, was abolished. Soon thereafter, restrictions on the press were lifted, and a new law of political association opened the door to scores of new civic groups and political parties.

Overnight, Algeria's tightly controlled and self-censored society was transformed, and for a brief time thereafter, associational life flourished. The fractious FLN continued to monopolize power structures, but the newly established opposition press carried lively debates about policy and government performance. Both human rights groups commented freely on, and almost certainly influenced, elaboration of an electoral code. The government did not go so far as to prosecute security personnel accused of abuses during the 1988 riots, but prisons were gradually emptied of political detainees, and according to Amnesty International, the practice of torture was for a time virtually eradicated.[35]

The Algerian government was anxious to avoid criticism at home and abroad. Bendjedid did not use human rights rhetoric as extensively as Ben Ali in Tunisia, but he nevertheless showed new sensitivity to appearances, and restrictive measures were now often accompanied by a nod to human rights. To counterbalance the effects of the state of siege declared in June 1991, for example, Bendjedid created a new human rights dossier and named Ali Haroun minister delegate for human rights. The appointment was largely symbolic, but it was important in that it acknowledged new forces at play in Algeria and across the region. Two months earlier, Ben Ali had named a presidential adviser on human rights, and just prior to that, King Hassan II had created a royal consultative council. Algeria had lagged behind in the Maghribi competition to demonstrate commitment to human rights, but Bendjedid took the lead for his country by elevating Haroun's appointment to ministerial level.[36]

When the political system collapsed in January 1992 and Mohammed Boudiaf returned from exile to head the newly governing High Council of State (HCE), human rights did not disappear from official discourse. The state of emergency that was declared in February 1992 suspended only parts of the constitution, and through its president, the HCE pledged restraint. Even as the security forces began to round up thousands of people and sequester them in Saharan camps, Boudiaf publicly announced that there would be no physical or mental abuse and made a personal commitment not to tolerate excesses. Furthermore, since in the interim Haroun had joined the HCE, Boudiaf used his presidential powers to replace the ineffectual Human Rights Ministry with a new Observatoire des droits de l'homme. In keeping with the style of collegial rule to which Algeria had returned, the Observatoire was conceived of as a corporate body. Its twenty-six members were nominally independent; and they were charged both with promoting human rights and with acting on any allegations of human rights abuse.

Concern with human rights continued to be rhetorical, but some substance was lent the public pronouncements when, despite the declared emergency, the HCE opened Algeria's borders to international human rights investigators. Both the International Committee of the Red Cross and AI, as well as the LADH, were granted access to the detention camps. Like Ben Ali in Tunisia, the HCE was concerned to legitimize a takeover that had raised eyebrows abroad and protest at home.

The Algerian HCE was less heavily invested in human rights rhetoric than Ben Ali was, however, and the concerns of Algerian society were less troublesome. Algerian leaders were not in the habit of appealing to popular sentiment, and in elite circles fears about security and the threat of an Islamist takeover substantially reduced interest in liberal reform. Some members of the Algerian elite did want the government to protect individual liberties, including the free choice of elected representation, but for many political leaders the outcome of a political contest was clearly more important than the process. Indeed, the notion of human rights was itself used to explain and justify abandoning the project of political reform. Haroun was among those who portrayed the January intervention as an effort to save democracy and human rights:

> As human rights minister, I believe that when an exceptional situation in a nation's life occurs, at that point it is a question of defending the whole of this nation, because what threatened us after 15 January was an Islamic state. . . . I say that I defend human rights by doing what is necessary so that my country will not undergo the situation that is being experienced in certain countries in the Middle East and East Africa.[37]

By mid spring there would have been little cost within Algeria to abandoning human rights rhetoric altogether, and no obvious price was exacted for retaining only lip service. Many were happy and relieved to settle for rhetoric that echoed liberal values, even if there was less than full commitment to democratic ideals. In any case, by July, events had overtaken discussion and debate about Algerian politics. The assassination of Boudiaf intensified concerns about security. A full-scale but fragmented insurgency was under way, and neither the army nor the national police could fully control its own ranks, let alone restore order to society. Amnesty International sent observers to Algeria three times between August 1991 and December 1992 and reported in February 1993 that human rights violations were becoming institutionalized. Under the emergency legislation, many detainees were subjected to prolonged incommunicado detention, and via a special antiterrorism law enacted in October 1992, special courts were empowered to impose double sentences in an accelerated procedure that abridged due process. About 1,000 individuals remained in detention camps and torture had again become common.[38]

Within Algeria, either concerns about such practices or the voices that expressed them had been submerged. The Observatoire declined a proactive role in curbing abuses of power and focused instead on children's rights and the shortage of medical supplies. It condemned Islamist violence but remained silent on the new judicial procedures.[39] The LADDH continued to issue periodic statements, and one report on torture received substantial attention both in Algeria and France. More commonly, its communiques were ignored. The LADH was potentially more influential, but it exercised caution. Shortly after the emergency was declared, a league delegation visited an internment camp and issued a communique critical of arrest procedures and detention conditions.[40] Brahimi spoke out on press freedoms,[41] but then, borrowing the LADH cachet, he and Menouar as founding presidents ardently defended the emergency procedures: "All of the criticisms . . . against the interruption of the electoral process [can]not escape this truth: the republic had to be saved."[42] After that pronouncement, the LADH spoke only with a timorous voice.

The LADH was the first civic group in Algeria permitted to act free of government control, and the human rights idea it and other activists promoted helped dismantle a repressive system of governance that for many reasons was no longer tenable. Algeria's patrimonial system had enforced heteronomy to the point where Algerians commonly acknowledged their own self-censorship. The gap between state and society had become so large, and governmental responses to pressures for change came so late, that the state all but collapsed. Amidst the political chaos of 1993, however, an independent press did manage to survive despite efforts to curtail it, and in the spring there was still a sufficient number of civic organizations active in Algiers and other cities to organize thousands of people in a march to end the violence, whatever its source.[43]

The Moroccan monarchy was not as fragile as the Algerian state, but for most of the 1980s, King Hassan II was no more enthusiastic about human rights than were Algeria's political leaders. He commonly dismissed human rights concerns and regularly denied that Morocco held any political prisoners. By any account, his decision in 1990 to create a Consultative Council on Human Rights (CCDH) was an extraordinary event. The story behind the royal human rights council involves a host of international actors and so is left to the following chapter, but the actual politics of the CCDH directly involved domestic actors. That politics is a prism through which to view subtle shifts in the parameters of more general political activity.

As explored in Chapter 6, the Palace closely monitors Moroccan politics, and the king controls the political agenda. Initial openings in the domain of human rights—including permission for the Moroccan Organization of Human Rights (OMDH) to organize—did not signal change; they were designed to appease international critics without significantly altering political dynamics at home. As early as 1989, however, there was evidence that the OMDH might not fit well into the royal schema. The new human rights organization politely violated political taboos, and within six months it had become the darling of opposition parties. Only internal dissent seemed capable of dissipating its energies, and by April 1990 even those problems seemed soluble. The Moroccan Association of Human Rights (AMDH) and the Moroccan League of Human Rights (LMDH), had moreover, renewed their own efforts to promote and defend human rights.

Human rights had worked its way onto the national agenda, and the monarchy, somewhat tardily, sought control of it. On May 8, the king convened his new council, saying, "We have decided that this meeting should be dedicated not to the creation of a state of law, but to the completion of a state of law—a state that once and for all puts an end to hearsay about human rights. We would like to settle this issue."[44] The 36-member CCDH consisted of five government ministers; nineteen representatives from political parties, human rights groups, and civic organizations; and twelve academics and other prominent individuals.[45] It was nominally established as an independent body, but its expenses are paid directly by the Palace, and Hassan II made clear his intent that it should not transgress the political dictum of respect for God, king, and country.[46] The council initially set up three working groups, two of which corresponded to concerns about pretrial detention and prison conditions that had been raised in an Amnesty International report. The third group, including many of the council's most illustrious members, was responsible for relations with international organizations. Critics dismissed the CCDH as a propaganda tool, and the AMDH refused to participate.

The CCDH has, in fact, played to the Palace. Its statements regularly laud the civic virtues of both monarch and monarchy, and in 1992 its secretariat rejected lists of several hundred names submitted by the three domestic rights groups and publicly denied their claim that the government holds political prisoners. The CCDH serves the government, but in a limited way, it has also carefully criticized official policies and practices, proposing reforms or advising restraint. Such initiatives merit closer consideration, not because they dramatically advance the protection of human rights, but because they test the limits of politically acceptable behavior and the popular *perception* of such behavior.

The CCDH has never been bold, but it initially took its charge seriously. Its first memorandum to the king cautiously suggested a political amnesty, but it was ignored. The working group on pretrial detention, which included the OMDH representative, subsequently recommended legal reforms to establish clear limits on the allowable period of *garde-à-vue* and preventive detention, reforms that were enacted, albeit after a year's delay. Gradually, the CCDH was brought under control. It sought permission to investigate the 1990 riots in Fez, but that inquiry quietly died. In 1991, working parties issued solicitous memos to the king and offered suggestions for safeguards, which were subsequently implemented, but to little effect. Torture remained widespread, and there were at least five deaths in detention under suspicious circumstances in 1991.[47] In 1992 and 1993, the CCDH turned its attention to the less contentious issues of human rights conditions in Polisario-controlled camps at Tindouf (in the Algerian Sahara) and the representation of Morocco in international human rights organizations.[48]

The CCDH was created to deflect criticism, and its significance relative to human rights practice lies, not in its power to effect change, but rather in its inability to resist pressures for change. The gradual disengagement from provocative issues suggests successful resistance, but it comes with difficulty and with cost. In 1991, a small group of CCDH members issued a maverick protest about judicial process,[49] and in 1992, the CCDH leadership could not risk putting lists of political prisoners before the entire council for discussion. Furthermore, the OMDH has protested apparent manipulation by the government and at one point threatened to withdraw its representative. The work of domestic human rights groups, and their regularly reported communiques, has tested CCDH credibility, created a competitive atmosphere, and put pressure on even those members with the greatest interest in defending the status quo.

King Hassan II has also registered the pressures of human rights rhetoric. In establishing the CCDH, he acknowledged that he needed to share responsibility for the oversight of human rights.[50] Two years later, in the 1992 constitutional reform that many with access to the Palace saw as significant, the king himself drafted amendments that made reference to human rights and ceded tightly held powers of appointment to the prime minister. In 1993, then, following legislative elections, he created a Ministry of Human Rights; its credibility was enhanced by the ministerial appointment of Omar Azziman, widely respected as a law professor and for his early role in the OMDH. Both the constitutional reform and the creation of a new ministry are symbolic gestures, inasmuch as the king retained power to dismiss the prime minister and suspend parliament, and insofar as the new ministry's role lacks definition, but they nevertheless signal that concern about rights and accountability has been heard in the Palace.

CONCLUSION

In this chapter, to bring the interplay between human rights activists and national governments into focus, I have presented the emergence of human rights in official discourse as the governmental response to pressures mounted by domestic nongovernmental human rights groups. As has been acknowledged throughout the book, many other factors were also at work. Political and economic privations across the Maghrib added to the resonance of the rights idea, and governments also understood that rights rhetoric could be used against the Islamist opposition. Many readers will anticipate that pressures from abroad made their own substantial contribution, an element of the analysis to be addressed in the following chapter. In the final chapter of the book, I return to the broader context, but at this juncture we should focus on the significance of governmental response to pressures that emanated from several quarters but were most clearly articulated at home by human rights groups.

Concern about human rights constrains a government's arbitrary exercise of power, even if it does not necessarily reduce its ability to govern. It is understandable, therefore, that governments resist the pressures put upon them by human rights advocates. The Moroccan and Algerian authorities are hardly alone in their fear that human rights reform will undermine governmental control. Ben Ali's government in Tunisia excepted itself from the rule only during the short period when human rights reform served the very important political purpose of legitimating the new regime. Confronted with real opposition—on the political left as well as by Islamists—the government reinforced its security apparatus and engaged in abuses reminiscent of an earlier period.

Governments have been reluctant to change their ways, but rhetoric is a somewhat different matter. Even when it again corralled regime opponents and muffled the press,[51] for example, the Tunisian government did not abandon the discourse of human rights. However much they may resist actual reform, Maghribi governments have sanctioned the notion of rights, not simply in distant international instruments but in their own political discourse. Political rhetoric and political reality are not to be confused, but the power of political discourse should likewise not be discounted. To follow Skocpol's argument, in adopting the language of human rights, state leaders reset the parameters of what may be considered legitimate political concerns.

10 The International Dimension

The political drama of human rights in North Africa has only partially been staged behind the barriers of national sovereignty. States of the Maghrib are not impervious to international pressures, and although important domestic forces were marshaled in the cause of promoting and protecting human rights, international actors also wielded influence.

There is nothing original in the observation that external actors and events can influence a domestic situation. Indeed, foreign policy may be explicitly designed for that purpose.[1] The challenge for scholars has been to trace and analyze the interchange between domestic and international forces. Over three decades, several models have been developed to assist in analyzing the impact of outside forces. "World systems," "dependency," "dependence," "interdependence," "transnationalism," and "multicentrism" are all now familiar terms in the lexicon of international relations. The dependency and the world systems approaches were developed to analyze the impact of stronger, powerful "core" states on the weaker "periphery," and economic interests were of central concern to them. Alternatively, models of interdependence emphasize relations of mutual interest (albeit of potentially asymmetrical importance) that involve nonstate as well as state actors. Recently introduced multicultural models seek to recover masked history and establish non-Western actors as agents in historical accounts and in the analysis of contemporary events.

Studies of the Maghrib have frequently traced the impact of international economic forces on the region, but the impact of international political forces has been less well studied. In the contemporary period, these are no longer confined to states and their foreign policies, nor even to intergovernmental organizations. With the proliferation of communications technology, which includes both products and services—telephone, micro-

194

computers, facsimile, electronic mail, communications satellites, air travel, and international express mail delivery—the international press and global interest groups have also flourished. The same changes that have allowed such actors to gather strength have eroded states' control over international affairs, and while the state's demise is not imminent, the importance of nonstate actors likewise should not be discounted. The stage on which world actors now play has become crowded, and as James Rosenau has noted, the frequent interchanges sometimes produce unintended and unexpected results.[2]

In Chapter 2, I argued that international forces are one of three elements that have afforded North African human rights groups a measure of protection, helping assure their survival and enhancing their effectiveness. In this chapter, the interactions between external and domestic players are scrutinized more closely. Western states have played a prominent role, but they were neither alone in wielding influence nor the first to take action. Less recognized actors include exile groups, the international press, international organizations, and interested parties from within the region. It is the supportive role played by these actors that is the focus of attention here, although it will quickly be recognized that outside actors are not always helpful.

Even when they have been sympathetic to human rights groups, not all of the efforts of international actors have had a salutary effect, or at least not all of their effects have been unequivocally supportive. No international agency had as its principal goal to advance the work of the domestic human rights groups, and in some cases, contributions were made (and injuries inflicted) accidentally. Outside actors have independent agendas, which may involve their own self-interest or subtle philosophical differences, and these have not always meshed with the goals of the Maghribi human rights groups.

SOLIDARITY GROUPS

In the 1970s, expatriate and solidarity groups in Europe created a backdrop for the politics of human rights in North Africa.[3] Expatriates—mostly students—were well informed and often impassioned about politics in their home countries; consequently, they were among the first to call public attention to problems in the Maghrib. Their principal contribution to both the domestic and the international human rights movements was to make abuses more visible.

The shape of expatriate activities was commonly influenced by politics at home. Tunisians organized themselves in opposition to the PSD and issued calls for pluralism. Ahmed Ben Salah, exiled in Geneva, had a small but loyal following, and many Tunisian liberals who parted ways with Bourguiba in the 1960s established themselves in France. Bechir Ben Yahmed began publishing the weekly *Jeune Afrique* in Paris, and others, including the journalist Habib Boulares and the diplomat Mohammed Masmoudi, advocated pluralism and provided commentary on their country from abroad. Algerians also rejected single-party rule, but the FLN was itself positioned on the political left. From remaining space, dissidents carved out radical alternatives that did not easily accommodate the notion of individual rights. Moreover, fear dominated politics abroad as at home,[4] and Algerians were more circumspect in public discussions of their national politics.

Alone of the three sets of expatriates, Moroccan dissidents abroad formed solidarity groups rather than political parties. Morocco's was the only political system not monopolized by a single party, and in the view of many student activists, to join a party was to enter the political game they rejected. They joined French sympathizers to form the Committees for the Struggle against Repression in Morocco (CLCRM) and the Association of Families of the Disappeared in Morocco (AFDM) Their news bulletins, information sessions, and occasional demonstrations captured modest attention from the press.

In the 1980s, groups abroad were better able to serve, and to use, the domestic human rights movement. While the CLCRM and AFDM continued their activities, in 1985 another group of Moroccan students organized a new solidarity group and called it ASDHOM—the Association for the Defense of Human Rights in Morocco. Common language, however, did not necessarily make fast allies. When human rights groups became active in Morocco after 1988, ASDHOM cooperated with the Moroccan Association of Human Rights (AMDH) but was more critical of the elite-based and less confrontational Moroccan Organization of Human Rights (OMDH). Similar differences emerged between the Tunisian League of Human Rights and Tunisian Islamists who established themselves abroad, in the United States and England as well as in France. As targets of repression, Islamists provided information to all those concerned about human rights practices in Tunisia, but their appropriation of human rights language and circulation of the LTDH's own communiques made many activists nervous. The political caution of domestic human rights groups likewise brought scorn from more radical expatriates. Such tensions have not put insurmountable barriers between parties of common cause, but as local human rights groups established their own credibility, they have tended to rely less on expatriate support.

INTERNATIONAL HUMAN RIGHTS GROUPS

International human rights groups put direct pressure upon governments in the Maghrib, but they also lent considerable support to domestic human rights groups. The International Federation of Human Rights Leagues (FIDH) and Amnesty International (AI) combined to form the backbone of the international human rights movement visible in the Maghrib, but other international organizations had influence as well. The Arab Organization of Human Rights (AOHR), for example, maintained headquarters in Cairo but held its first conference in Tunisia and returned for an annual meeting in 1990. Local AI groups in both Tunisia and Algeria served to remind authorities that some North Africans had an interest in human rights irrespective of political context. Additionally, a number of smaller groups based in Western countries made Maghribi human rights issues a concern. Several medical groups and law associations were assured an audience in Europe, and in the United States both the Lawyers' Committee for Human Rights and Middle East Watch issued periodic reports.[5]

Scholars have recognized the role that international human rights groups have played in expressing opinions of "global society" or creating pressures for democratization, but less attention has been paid to the effect of such groups on domestic nongovernmental organizations.[6] In North Africa, their actions were critical. Divergent interests, reflected in different mandates, strategies, or power dynamics, did at times strain relations between the two sets of human rights groups, but in general they acknowledged a tacit partnership.

The work of international groups lent support in several important ways. In the first place, they increased the visibility of local human rights groups and clarified governmental responsibility for abuses. They raised the public outcry that caught the attention of both the international press and foreign governments. Sending missions, publicizing reports, and—particularly in the case of AI—mobilizing a vast membership who multiplied AI's own efforts by approaching individuals with influence, the media, and their own governments put the issue of human rights where it couldn't be ignored.

Secondly, to the extent that international human rights groups commanded credibility and respect in the global arena, they extended protection to the domestic groups. Some Maghribi human rights activists had never had much significant contact outside their countries; now international visitors from well-known organizations sought them out. The pragmatic benefits were quickly recognized. The international protest over Ali Yahia's arrest in 1986 and the FIDH's swift action to affiliate his group registered both with the Algerian government and with the other Maghribi human rights groups. As a measure of protection for the LTDH, Khemais Chemmari was made an FIDH vice president, and his arrest in the final months of Bourguiba's rule generated hundreds of letters and telegrams. When in a moment of irritation with the FIDH, OMDH members considered severing their affiliation, political wisdom prevailed: "They send lawyers, and someday we might need them."

In addition to the promotion and protection international groups provided indirectly, the FIDH in particular has offered direct assistance to North African groups. Until recently, it was FIDH policy not to assume responsibility for creating national affiliates, but at the invitation of OMDH founders, it did assist in that group's formation. More generally, the FIDH has served a clearinghouse function that allowed North African activists to profit from the experience of other groups. At times its engagement in local or regional relations has provoked anger within the groups, but at other times, it has made valuable resources available to the Maghribi groups. In 1990, for example, at its recommendation, Khemais Chemmari was awarded a prize by the French government to support a program of human rights training in Geneva.

Finally, the research work done by international human rights groups helped increase the effectiveness of domestic groups. Outside groups with well-established reputations were often in a better position both to obtain and to publicize sensitive information. AI's 1991 questions about deaths in detention, for example, reinforced and amplified the Tunisian league's own expression of concern. Domestic groups generally found it politically safer, and easier, to raise an issue domestically after it had been broached abroad, and vocal protest by international groups reduced the semblance of threat in the domestic groups' more discreet approach.

INTERNATIONAL PRESS AND PUBLIC OPINION

Like the chorus in a classical Greek play, the international press reflected, shaped, and amplified the drama of human rights in North Africa. Through the 1980s, the French press increasingly depended on the LTDH for reliable information about political developments in Tunisia, and as other groups emerged it followed them closely. Wire services disseminated communiques that the domestic press was apt to ignore, and prestigious papers like *Le Monde* reported them regularly. There was a natural sympathy between journalists and rights activists, and many stories focused on the groups themselves. Such attention created a protective shield around the groups, inasmuch as harassment was likely to bring adverse publicity to state authorities.

The international media has also had substantial impact in galvanizing public opinion and establishing a record in the world of international politics. Even slight publicity may place an otherwise obscure item on the political agenda: *Le Monde*'s 1989 story about a virtually forgotten five-year-old hunger strike in Morocco aroused interest and protest. Shortly after that story, the International Commission of Health Professionals and the Association internationale des juristes démocrates sent a joint fact-finding mission that issued a lengthy report.[7] A year later, Gilles Perrault's exposé of human rights issues in Morocco contributed mightily to a diplomatic crisis. Maghribi elites may denigrate the European media, but they listen to them, watch them, or read them for information, and find access to them even when particular publications are banned. Stories in prominent news publications and broadcasts on Radio France internationale helped shape opinion in the Maghrib as well as Europe.

Not all human rights coverage, clearly, is attributable to moral indignation or dogged investigation. If the press stimulates political opinion, it also responds to public demand. As reflected in the growth and spread of international human rights organizations, the world's attentive public was also showing greater awareness of and interest in human rights concerns. The press responded to market forces. Because interests rise and wane, however, the economics of media coverage points to one obvious liability for any group whose effectiveness depends exclusively upon publicity. The international press has generally been favorable to Maghribi rights groups, but in the best of times, its coverage is not constant. Even the interest of the French press fluctuates, and journalists from other European and U.S. papers cover the area erratically. More important, political interests shift, and in Europe both the politics of the Gulf War and rising fear of politicized Islam in Algeria and Tunisia tended to counterbalance concern for human rights. Governments also intervene to influence the dynamics. All Maghribi states have ministries of information and supply the media through state-run press agencies. The Tunisian government, for example, has gone to great lengths to produce and distribute its own view of both Islamism and human rights to the foreign media. Publications with critical views are often banned or particular issues seized, and individual journalists may be punished. In 1991, the Tunisian authorities expelled Reuters' chief North Africa correspondent for reporting on abuses,[8] and a year later the Algerians curtailed access to all foreign journalists. Alternatively, good behavior may be rewarded. Hassan II has preferred to woo the foreign media, inviting prominent journalists to his palace or to gala events. Human rights groups continue to benefit from the press, but they do not control it.

WESTERN STATES AND INTERGOVERNMENTAL ORGANIZATIONS

Western states have over time shown exceptional interest in North African human rights issues. In the power-driven world of interstatal relations, however, moral concerns embedded in foreign policy cannot be taken at face value. States rarely if ever sacrifice objectives conceived of as economic or security interests to moral purpose. That is not to argue, though, that morality has no place in foreign policy, a position long espoused by the realist school of international relations. Moral concerns may recede in the face of threat, real or perceived, but they regularly resurface in policy discussions. In practice, many policy makers do take them seriously. Moral concerns need not be "pure" to find their way into policy, and both France and the United States—the two countries with greatest influence in the Maghrib—have a long history of incorporating morality into their diplomacy. In both countries, the conceptual bridge between human rights and national interest was easily constructed.[9]

As noted in Chapter 2, the contemporary foreign policy emphasis on human rights concerns originated in the United States, and more precisely, with the U.S. Congress. Criticism was facilitated for the Congress, as it was for the European parliament, by its only distant responsibility to oversee foreign policy. The United States maintained friendly relations with Maghribi states but recognized no vital interests in the region. Algeria had broken off diplomatic relations with the United States in 1967 following the Arab-Israeli war, but these were restored in 1974; the 1986 attack on Libya quieted the foreign policy preoccupation with Muammar Qaddafi. Congress recognized the long history of positive relations and registered pressures from foreign lobbyists. By the late 1980s, though, congressional representatives were also listening to human rights concerns expressed by constituents and documented in the human rights reports they commissioned from the State Department. Foreign aid has rarely been a popular cause, and in the annual review of military and aid appropriations, Congress found it easy to scrutinize records more closely.

Even if irritating, human rights concerns expressed by friendly states were not easily ignored. At very least, the human rights practices of Maghribi states were detailed in the State Department reports—which were paying close attention to the domestic human rights groups. Stronger external linkages meant that Morocco and Tunisia were more affected than Algeria, and both countries have attempted to reduce the criticism. After 1990, one by one, the Moroccan government closed long-standing human rights dossiers featured in the reports, and in 1993 it invited an American firm to observe parliamentary elections. Tunisia has also polished its image: English-language publications distributed by its embassies regularly insist on the Tunisian government's commitment to human rights.[10]

Foreign governments with strong diplomatic ties exert the most influential and the most direct human rights pressure, but competing concerns may dilute the message. International organizations that act as agents for states are also prone to equivocating, but they have proven more effective in promoting and defending human rights than many analysts anticipated.[11] As the most sovereignty-bound agency, the UN Human Rights Commission is usually constrained by the political agenda its members promote, but other bodies extend greater autonomy to representatives. The UN Human Rights Subcommission on the Prevention of Discrimination and Protection of Minorities has received several reports on Morocco, and as parties to the ICCPR, all three Maghribi states are bound to submit periodic reports to the independent Human Rights Committee. Consisting of eighteen experts uninstructed by their governments, that body has showed exceptional independence since its creation in 1978.[12] Individuals as well as human rights organizations may submit reports to it, and both Tunisia and Morocco have been reviewed critically by it in recent years. Such bodies have only limited weight in the international political system, and of themselves they have little influence. They do, however, relay political messages of the sort that diplomats seek to avoid. Few states are impervious to the embarrassment that accompanies exposure.

TRANSREGIONAL EFFECTS

Western states and international organizations have affected the Maghribi politics of human rights, but forces ranging from public opinion to individual leaders have in several ways also created transregional effects. First, they may create a demonstration effect. Pressures generated from within the region may be less visible to outsiders, but for Maghribi leaders they may have greater impact than more distant forces. Secondly, in both diplomatic circles and before domestic audiences, they reduce the credibility of a government's claims that reforms cannot, or should not, be implemented. Finally, at another level, Maghribi human rights groups have themselves profited from mutual solidarity.

As suggested in Chapter 9, governments themselves originated some transregional pressures as by-products of domestic policies. In 1989, Maghribi states joined to form a regional economic union, and at the time much was made of North African political solidarity. In fact, relations within the region had long been rivalrous,[13] and little has been done in the interim to further the Grand Maghrib project. Governments within the region have regular, direct contact, but many transnational interactions are routed through France. Diplomatic overtures notwithstanding, transportation systems across the region remain underdeveloped, and intraregional tourism and trade have only marginally improved. The scarcity of factual information and firsthand knowledge of other countries in the region has not, however, hindered the construction of unflattering national images from country to country. Competition is amicable but real, and in the late 1980s, it extended to questions of human rights.

Reform launched first in Tunisia and then in Algeria had repercussions throughout the Maghrib. Even Colonel Qaddafi, who appeared least receptive to international principles, and in the recent past had launched a "liquidation campaign" to remove political foes, amnestied political prisoners and embraced the notion of human rights. Beyond whatever reforms they entertained at home, human rights provided statesmen with language with which to frame their common concerns about the Palestinian cause, and at the creation of the Arab Maghrib Union, they included a commitment to protecting rights in the official charter.

A door was thus opened for the press, who in the atmosphere of intraregional competition often indulged in critiques of a neighboring government not readily permitted with their own. The practice was gradually extended to coverage of human rights concerns. Interviews with human rights leaders and stories about human rights practices in neighboring countries promoted public awareness of the human rights movement and of human rights abuses prevalent in the region.

Most directly, a regional effect that involved both cooperation and competition operated directly among the human rights groups. For nearly a decade, the Tunisian league was alone in the region, and for external support, it turned to the FIDH and some of its national affiliates in Europe. Inter-Maghribi relations between human rights groups were inspired primarily by the LADH, anxious to establish its legitimacy. The Tunisian league had sent an observer to the trial of Ali Yahia's group in 1986, and in 1987, the latter's newly authorized rival, the LADH, sent its first official correspondence to the LTDH. The LADH subsequently promoted the idea of a regional meeting—which the FIDH dissuaded Tunisian activists from attending, seeing it as an effort to undermine the Algerian league it had first affiliated.[14] However equivocal the sentiments of regional solidarity, the 1988 meeting produced a joint document (the Declaration of Nouakchott) and allowed activists across the region to become acquainted with one another and compare experiences. Despite its boycott of the meeting, as the best-established group in the region the Tunisian league retained its influence and was readily integrated into the emergent network. Following Nouakchott, groups disseminated communiques among themselves, attended each other's national conferences, occasionally coordinated meetings and actions, and even mediated disputes. Beyond the pragmatic dividends of such exchanges, Maghribi activists in this way came to see themselves as part of a larger—indigenous—force, and their efforts were thereby reinforced.

THE MOROCCAN CASE

The full impact of international forces upon the North African politics of human rights cannot be conveyed in a simple introduction of the cast of players. Actions were frequently coincidental, and actors often collaborated unwittingly. Even an additive analysis that presumes a cumulative effect is misleading in that it underestimates the interactions among actors, which in many cases amplified (or confounded) the effect of any single actor and of the local groups. Although in all three countries the politics of human rights has involved complex interchange among myriad actors, the Moroccan case is an exemplar and bears examination.

The relative importance of international factors is conditioned by the culture of domestic politics and international involvement. In important ways, Morocco differed from its neighbors. By comparison within the region as a whole, Tunisia's political system has been tolerant of internal criticism, and with relatively little outside assistance, the Tunisian league became the focal point of human rights demands and pressures. Ben Ali's expressed interest in human rights, of course, enhanced that role at an important political transition. Until 1987, Algerian leaders had not had to put up with independent political voices, but relative isolation made Algeria less susceptible to Western pressures. Algeria maintained important relations with France, but it did not receive aid or purchase arms from the West; nor was it at that point beholden to international creditors. Moreover, foreign journalists found access difficult. By contrast, Morocco was closely tied to the West, and the Palace tightly controlled political initiative. It also had a serious human rights problem.

Morocco's record from 1970 to the early 1990s is sobering. It included patently unfair trials, involving hundreds of political prisoners; prolonged incommunicado detention connected to systematic torture and some instances of death in detention; hundreds, and perhaps thousands, of forced "disappearances" in southern Morocco and the Saharan territory; and for certain military prisoners, detention under life-threatening conditions extending beyond the expiry of a legally imposed sentence. The family of General Mohammed Oufkir was being held in unacknowledged detention in apparent retribution for Oufkir's 1972 treason, and the Boureqat brothers, courtiers of mixed French and North African parentage, had disappeared in 1973 without a trace. In some way or other, all of the cases involved political dissidents, and developments were monitored from a distance by expatriates and French sympathizers. Several political prisoners wrote and published memoirs, to little effect. Human rights abuses were brushed aside or explicitly denied by Morocco's king. To numerous journalists, Hassan II denied charges that Morocco held political prisoners, and in December 1989, before an international television audience, Hassan II declared, "If one percent of the human rights violations suggested by Amnesty International were true, I wouldn't get a wink of sleep."[15]

On the occasion of national or religious holidays—including the Prophet's birthday—the king had frequently pardoned numerous prisoners convicted of crimes or civil offenses, but political prisoners rarely benefited from such measures if their offense transgressed the bounded code of God, king, and country. The first hint that important changes were in the offing came in May 1989, when thirty-one Frontistes imprisoned since the 1970s were released from Kenitra's Central Prison. Two years later, other prison doors began to swing open, and by early 1992 more than four hundred of the world's longest-held political prisoners had been set free.

Temporarily leaving aside any questions about the significance of these developments for structural change, the immediate task is to explain what lay behind the measures of clemency and what had overcome resolute resistance. The circulation of information in Morocco and the creation of effective domestic pressure groups are essential elements in the story, but overall, the leverage of international influence was paramount.

The international stage was being set toward the end of the 1970s, when human rights covenants took force, and respect for the cause of human rights increased when Amnesty International received the Nobel Prize for Peace. In the United States, Congress pressed for implementation of laws it had passed linking aid to human rights performance, and its creation of a Bureau for Human Rights and Humanitarian Affairs within the U.S. State Department established human rights as a legitimate foreign policy concern. As a product of all these developments, the international press gradually began to feature stories about human rights and human rights activists.

Morocco did not escape international attention apropos of human rights in this period, although it came primarily from within the sector that may be labeled "global society": political solidarity groups, international interest groups with legal or human rights concerns, and, to a somewhat limited degree, the international press. Moroccan trials were attended by several European observers, and irregularities were noted. In France and other European countries, Moroccan exile groups sought attention from the press, and through it from the European public and European governments. The net impact, however, was slight.

Western governments for the most part did not allow such issues to disturb their good working relations with Rabat. In fact, France and the United States competed for influence there, and in so doing effectively shielded Morocco from international pressures about its human rights record. France, Morocco's primary partner in trade, aid, and investment, was generally reluctant to criticize. French papers ran accounts of the 1981 Casablanca riots as headline stories, but the French government's own worry was about the regime's stability. U.S. concerns in the early 1980s revolved around arms sales and transit rights for the U.S. Rapid Deployment Force. A congressional delegation led by Stephen Solarz traveled to Morocco in 1979 and recommended against military support for Morocco in its Saharan engagement, but the concerns were not openly linked to human rights.[16] A joint U.S.–Morocco military commission was set up in February 1982, and a transit rights agreement was concluded shortly after the king's visit to Washington in May. France in the meantime had installed François Mitterand and the Socialist Party in the Elysée Palace, and with official French sympathies expressed for the Socialist Union of Popular Forces (USFP) in Morocco, relations between Paris and Rabat deteriorated.[17] The

United States profited from that disharmony, and by 1983, Morocco was acclaimed as the United States's closest Arab ally.[18] During his first term in office, President Ronald Reagan sent his special envoy Vernon Walters to consult with Hassan II several times, and in Rabat, U.S. Ambassador Joseph Verner Reed affectionately referred to the monarch as "our king."[19]

In 1984, however, relations between the United States and Morocco veered onto difficult terrain, with important repercussions for the prominence of human rights issues in bilateral diplomacy. Hassan II's decision to conclude a treaty of union with Libya in August 1984 opened him to serious criticism in Washington. Where diplomatic breaches warranted, Congress was taking the human rights country reports more seriously, and Morocco's human rights performance was increasingly subjected to scrutiny. In 1986, concerned that military aid might be slashed in the very year in which the United States and Morocco were celebrating their bicentennial of bilateral relations, Hassan II abruptly canceled a trip to the United States and instead stunned the Arab world by inviting the Israeli prime minister, Shimon Peres, to Morocco for a meeting intended to advance the Arab-Israeli peace process. He also severed the Libyan accord, which in the meantime had accomplished the purpose of halting Libyan support for the Polisario Front.

About this time, the voices of human rights groups began to resonate in official circles. In 1986, in conjunction with an international campaign, Amnesty International released a short report on the use of torture in Morocco. In France, Mitterand was pressured to convey concerns to the monarch.[20] In London, AI supporters demonstrated against torture when King Hassan visited Prime Minister Margaret Thatcher.[21] Expatriate groups and human rights activists had publicized Morocco's record during Hassan's visit to the European parliament in December 1986, and two years later, the parliamentarians in Strasbourg passed a resolution calling on the European parliament's president to convey their concerns to the Moroccan government.[22]

The balance of political forces across the Maghrib was also shifting. By 1989, both Tunisia and Algeria had taken important steps to improve their human rights performance. In Morocco, however, political arrests and trials continued, and stories of torture and death in detention circulated among dissidents. From a comparative view within the region, its record was looking worse.

Efforts to create a politically independent human rights organization both augmented interest in the situation and gave outsiders a place to focus their own energies. The emergence of the OMDH at the end of 1988 substantially altered the dynamics of the Moroccan politics of human rights. Human rights stories on Morocco began appearing regularly in the French press. Just before the 1988 Franco-African summit in Casablanca, for example, *Le Monde diplomatique* ran a lengthy story on the king's intransigence on long-standing human rights issues.[23] French journalists closely followed the OMDH's birth pains and, with Mahdi el Mandjra's help, made it a cause célèbre.[24] A press conference at OMDH headquarters in June 1989 brought attention to three long-term hunger strikers who lay near death and also made clear *Le Monde's* admiration for the new rights organization: "In reacting publicly, the OMDH . . . showed its independence with regard to the government on a delicate dossier."[25]

Recognition of the OMDH had hardly solved the monarchy's growing public relations problem. On the contrary, in 1989, the OMDH had energetically set about adding its own voice to the din. The release of selected political prisoners in May 1989 was welcomed, but it redressed only a fraction of the concerns of human rights activists, and it also added momentum to the forces pressing for a general amnesty. Even in the United States, difficult questions were being asked at high levels. The language in State Department country reports was in subtle ways becoming more critical of Morocco. During the 1989 foreign aid deliberations, the U.S. Senate Appropriations Committee elaborated concerns about "severe human rights abuses" and asked the State Department to monitor the situation closely and convey its concerns to the Moroccan government.[26]

This was the backdrop for what seemed no more than a squib but proved in hindsight to be the first salvo in a diplomatic war over human rights. During a televised interview broadcast across Europe and parts of the Maghrib in December 1989, King Hassan denied allegations of abuses, as he had many times before, and openly invited Amnesty International to send a research mission to Morocco. AI raised the ante with a press release that welcomed the invitation but also documented a history of denied access.[27] The pressure was on, and this time the invitation was honored. AI's delegation arrived in February, met with a specially constituted "Committee for Dialogue with Amnesty International," and presented its as-yet-unpublished concerns about *garde-à-vue* detention to the king.[28] When AI delegates returned a few weeks later to prepare for a second meeting, they were called in for questioning and expelled to London. In the interim, AI had published its *Human Rights in Garde-à-Vue Detention in Morocco,* which King Hassan viewed as a clear breach of diplomatic protocol. In response, the Moroccan government placed lengthy advertisements in Europe's major papers, denouncing—but not refuting—the report.[29] The result was to heighten interest in the matter and raise questions about intent as well as practice.

At the time of the AI report's release, the OMDH was in organizational disarray, and its members did not comment on the report or promote its distribution. Their interest, however, had not waned. Only weeks before, representatives from all three human rights groups had met with the Moroccan Bar Association and the Association of Jurists to elaborate a Moroccan Charter of Human Rights. As a political idea, human rights was gathering force among the political classes, and the government's efforts to organize a countercharge by forwarding half a million protest messages to France generally backfired—at home as well as abroad.[30] Interest in human rights spread with the story of the expulsion of the AI delegates and with the AI report, which circulated widely despite (or, more likely, because of) its having been denounced. Political parties began to pick up the theme, and the Moroccan press became more outspoken. It was in this context that members of parliament filed the motion of censure discussed in Chapter 6 and political parties began to speak openly of human rights issues in their congresses and newspapers. It was also in this context that the king appointed his Consultative Council on Human Rights.

Abroad, two diplomatic fiascoes were gathering shape, and both concerned human rights. Before the end of the year, Morocco would face serious embarrassment in France and before the UN's Human Rights Committee. In both cases, King Hassan II's government underestimated the interest and the influence of global society.

Serious troubles with France commenced, ironically, in the context of an initiative intended to improve relations. In February 1990 a Franco-Moroccan committee that had been working together for about three years announced plans to stage a year-long series of events to promote Moroccan culture and strengthen ties between the two countries. "Temps du Maroc" ("Moroccan Times") involved executives from Club Med, Peugeot, and Saint Laurent among others, and was headed on the French side by the former foreign minister Michel Jobert. The French minister of culture, Jack Lang, was to oversee the production. "Temps du Maroc" may have been intended to renew amity between France and Morocco, but it also provided a perfect rallying point for human rights activists.

Throughout the spring and summer, rumors circulated about the king's intent to issue a general amnesty prior to the opening festivities, but appropriate occasions came and went without event. The creation of the CCDH did no more to appease critics than had official recognition of the OMDH. By late August, the French government's expectations of human rights reform had diminished, Mitterand was under increasing pressure to exert pressures of his own, and Lang had relayed a personal wish to see the Frontiste leader Abraham Serfaty and his comrades released by the time of the production's opening. Jobert warned Hassan II that he had an image problem.[31] The human rights issue was not going away, and King Hassan, under pretext of concerns about the emerging conflict in the Gulf, notified the French press that he was canceling the entire series of events. The press in turn openly speculated about the "real" reasons for the abruptness of a decision that left Hassan's French partners in an embarrassing lurch.[32]

Relations between France and Morocco quickly slid to their worst level in decades. Salt was poured on Morocco's wounds by the appointment of Georges Kiejman, an outspoken attorney to the Oufkir family, as assistant minister of justice and by Danielle Mitterand's decision to participate in an Algerian press conference on Saharan refugees as head of France Libertés. Moroccan irritation was only compounded when, in early November, Mme. Mitterand announced that she would visit the refugee camps in Tindouf, Algeria.

In the meantime, Gallimard published Gilles Perrault's scathing exposé of the Moroccan monarch, *Notre ami le roi*, and with interest in Morocco heightened first by the Amnesty International affair and then by the "Temps du Maroc" fiasco, it quickly sold 100,000 copies and went into a second printing. The book was banned in Morocco, but Moroccans abroad transmitted large sections of it by facsimile, and it circulated widely—if clandestinely—there, too. Morocco charged that France had unleashed a campaign of defamation, and sued for banning of the book—specifically, of a chapter dealing with the 1973 arrest and disappearance of the Boureqat brothers.[33] Morocco lost that court battle, but pursued another when government-sponsored radio and television programs featured interviews with Perrault. The government yielded this time, and in further efforts to repair the damaged relationship, Foreign Minister Roland Dumas persuaded Mme. Mitterand to set aside her travel plans.[34] Human rights remained a central focus of French foreign policy, however, and when riots broke out in Fez in December, the French government reminded Rabat of its concerns.[35]

At UN headquarters in New York, a second diplomatic stew was boiling over. By 1990, Morocco was four years late in submitting its report to the Human Rights Committee (HRC) and risked a reprimand for delinquency at a time when it was already under fire over human rights. Its 1981 report had generated only discreet criticisms, and rather than face the alternatives, the government drafted a perfunctory and self-congratulatory re-port[36] and deployed a fairly low-level delegation to present it at the com-mittee's November meeting.

Times, however, had changed. For one thing, the committee itself had more experience in reviewing reports. For another, the OMDH had pro-cured a copy of the report and in a publicly distributed memorandum con-tested the assessment of both law and practice in Morocco. Furthermore, human rights monitors as diverse as the New York University Interna-tional Human Rights Law Clinic and ASDHOM in Paris prepared detailed reports that identified numerous discrepancies.

Committee members responded to Morocco's initial presentation with tactful questions, but when delegates defended the monarch's discretionary powers in apparent contravention of ICCPR provisions, they met with direct challenges. The experts from Japan, Britain, France, Ecuador, and Egypt variously raised issues of disappearance, detention centers, deaths in detention, and measures to prevent torture. Several others inquired about the Oufkir family.[37] These topics were taboo in Morocco and had never been publicly broached in diplomatic fora, and now reports from the committee made them part of the public record. Further, the committee's inability to complete the Moroccan review in the originally allocated time necessitated a second session and gave critics of the regime and human rights activists a second wind. When the committee reconvened in Geneva in July 1991, French television cameras were waiting, and journalists re-minded their readers that Rabat owed explanations about the military prison at Tazmamart.[38]

Since the United States had not yet ratified the ICCPR, and so did not participate in the Human Rights Committee, it had no more direct interest in the HRC's deliberations than it had in the "Temps du Maroc" affair. By early 1991, however, Hassan II's government was under such steady fire in Europe and international bodies that even Morocco's support of the al-lied forces in the Gulf could not shield it from human rights criticism in the United States. In June 1991, during hearings on North Africa held jointly by the U.S. House foreign affairs subcommittees on Africa and hu-man rights, the Moroccan record was again subjected to scrutiny. It was another irony that the hearings were prompted, not by concerns about Morocco—which in fact had just been handsomely rewarded for its coop-eration in the Gulf War—but by the deteriorating situations in Mauritania and Tunisia. Amnesty International, however, was in the midst of an inter-national campaign on Morocco, and its Washington office brought the Mo-rocco dossier forward. Committee members heard and responded to oral testimony about the military prison of Tazmamart, allegedly written by a prison guard:

> Open the first cell; it is empty except for a stretcher to carry the dead and a big torch. The second cell is empty too. Open the third and your blood freezes at the sight of the human corpse lying on a cement shelf: a skeleton with a long thick beard hanging down over his chest, long dirty hair like primitive stone age man's; long nails looking like serpent's claws. . . . [39]

Among the inmates at Tazmamart was Lt. Mbarek Touil, the Moroccan husband of an American woman.

Interest in Washington amplified concerns newly expressed in Morocco. Tazmamart was a name and location unfamiliar to most Moroccans, and questions about the military personnel implicated in the 1971 and 1972 attempted coups were long forgotten in Morocco. Undoubtedly feeling pressure both from Amnesty International and from exile groups in Europe who had not laid the cases aside, the OMDH had just weeks before made public mention of Tazmamart. The silence was broken. The Palace continued to deny even the existence of a prison at Tazmamart, but Moroccan human rights groups, the Moroccan press, and Moroccan elites were suddenly abuzz.

Pressures within and without Morocco mounted, and the possibility of awkward questions being posed during the king's scheduled state visit to Washington in September increased steadily. Presumably to reduce the chances of embarrassment, the impossible was made to happen. Serfaty and forty others were released from prison.[40] Almost simultaneously, a highly placed Moroccan official leaked news to Reuters that Tazmamart had been emptied and razed. Stories ricocheted from France to the United States, and with the help of a public relations firm in Washington,[41] the news was quietly circulated. Washington insiders speculated that Hassan feared public demonstrations on behalf of Lieutenant Touil. In any event, an advertisement mentioning Tazmamart was placed in the *Washington Post* by Amnesty International and the news was publicly available to those beyond the loop of political bruit. Ironically, it was not until King Hassan II returned to Morocco from a visit little-remarked-upon in Washington that it began to circulate openly in Morocco.

By mid 1992, virtually all of the well-publicized long-standing human rights dossiers in Morocco had been closed. Early in 1991, the family of General Oufkir was finally released to freedom, and in June that year, some three hundred of the "disappeared" Saharans for whom Morocco had never acknowledged responsibility quietly reappeared. The thirty survivors of Tazmamart were gradually returned to society; thirty-one others had died. In December 1991 the Boureqat brothers also reappeared; it turned out that they, too, had been held at Tazmamart. According to human rights groups in and out of the country, Morocco continued to hold hundreds of political prisoners, but the most diplomatically troubling cases were closed. The king had established the CCDH, changes to the constitution paid lip service to human rights, and Moroccan diplomats hailed 1991 as the year of human rights. "Human rights" had been inserted into the rhetoric of a political system hitherto tightly constrained by the triad of God, king, and country.

There is little to suggest that in nodding to human rights, the Moroccan government was voluntarily altering its policies or recognizing the errors of its past ways. Not only did Hassan II repeatedly deny the existence of the jails he ultimately emptied and the political prisoners pardoned, but as late as 1990 Interior Minister Driss Basri shrugged off the concerns as a pack of lies, citing a Moroccan proverb: "The bereavement is intense, but the deceased is a mouse."[42] In 1992 Hassan II offered only a terse remark about the prison at Tazmamart: "That chapter is closed. It was; it is no more."[43]

Given the Moroccan political system and the elements of political culture outlined earlier in this book, it is doubtful whether domestic forces in Morocco could ever have broken through the many-tiered barriers to introduce human rights as a legitimate concern. Indeed, co-optation of the Moroccan League of Human Rights (LMDH) and repression of the AMDH in an earlier period attest to the inherent difficulties and to changes that had transpired in the interim. Growing interest in human rights at home was undoubtedly troublesome to the Moroccan authorities, but primarily because a changing political climate both at home and abroad made it difficult to respond with repression. The 1989 releases may have been intended to appease the new OMDH and its international chorus, but subsequent measures of clemency are more directly attributable to international pressures.

Power speaks to power, and only when political partners in Europe and the United States began to make clear their own concerns did the procession of releases commence. The nature of the Moroccan political system and the king's relative insulation from public pressures at home left Hassan II interested only in the moves made by other potent players, and it was these players who were decisive. It is important to note, however, that diplomatic pressures did not arise out of the immediate concerns of Morocco's international partners. The big powers scholars once saw as prime movers in international affairs were themselves subjected to pressures. Internationally as well as in Morocco, actors under scrutiny of the international press were pressed to reduce the gap between word and deed.

The array of actors and interactions that converged to exert pressures on Morocco points up the complexity of contemporary international politics. What the full narrative captures better than a more systematic but fragmented analysis of individual actors is the extent, and sometimes coincidental nature, of interplay between them. Actors variously exerted pressures on Morocco, but they also interacted with one another, sharing information or pressing one another to act. In the end, the actions of noteworthy state and nonstate actors converged to send a single message to Morocco, and in the face of heavy criticism, there was no clear voice able or willing to defend the monarchy's political practices.

CONCLUSION

Consideration of the international forces that have had an impact on the North African politics of human rights illustrates some of the changes that have taken place in world politics in recent decades. Although many of the direct avenues of influence from Western states to the Maghrib identified by dependency theorists and world-system scholars continue to operate, they do not alone capture the complexity of interactions today. In the first place, the powerful states of the West are shown in this study not to be monolithic: within their government apparatuses, multiple forces compete for influence, and when arguments about national security interests are not persuasive, the door opens to moral concerns. As Lars Schoultz has argued in the specific case of U.S. human rights policy vis-à-vis Latin America in the 1970s,[44] a general analysis of the human rights element in Western foreign policies must account for an effect of narrow interest groups and the press out of all proportion to their size and general influence. The study of such international actors has been neglected and their impact generally discounted. Only recently has the role of the international human rights movement in creating pressures for liberalizing change been acknowledged by scholars.[45] Recognition of the role such groups may play in influencing the foreign policy of powerful international actors and in directly conveying human rights concerns to offending governments is overdue, but it is nevertheless important to keep a balanced perspective. With the attention given to new foreign policy rhetoric about human rights in recent years, outside actors have been seen almost universally as supportive of human rights. In fact, they have variously aided or impeded progress, and even when they intend to help, their efforts may produce contrary results. In the Maghrib, international actors—whether states or more amorphous bodies—helped shape the context of concern about human rights, and their actions went into the mix of factors that shaped government responses. In the specific case of Morocco from 1988 to 1991, there was extraordinary collusion among international actors. Even during this period, however, each acted out of its own set of interests, and there is little to suggest that the relationship of complementarity is a necessary one. Considerable progress in the development of international human rights instruments notwithstanding, human rights continues to be seen primarily as a domestic issue, and the direct impact of international forces will necessarily be attenuated.

In any event, indirect effects rather than direct efforts were the most significant contribution of outside forces to the politics of human rights in the Maghrib. All across the region, the actions of outside forces gave credence to and amplified the voices of domestic actors. The emergence of human rights groups in Algeria, for example, made it possible for French socialists to frame their own concerns in terms that were politically sensitive, and in Tunisia, human rights concerns were most effectively addressed by outsiders while the Tunisian League of Human Rights was itself strong. The U.S. government paid homage to the league by citing its reports and inviting prominent members to meet its own leaders. Human rights groups abroad alternatively reinforced charges made locally and prodded the league to do more; moreover, they raised cries of alarm when its members were threatened. Although the league's 1992 dissolution was ultimately rescinded, it has not recovered its earlier élan, and human rights pressures from outside have in the interim lost some of their effectiveness.

The Moroccan account, likewise, establishes the emergence of a domestic group as a cause that crystallized hopes for change, legitimated the concerns of statal and other international actors, and gave new purpose to human rights groups abroad. The egregious nature of the abuses, the personal engagement and deep commitment of certain outside actors, the king's own intransigence, and a long history of close diplomatic ties are all critical elements in the story, but their importance was either established or heightened after the emergence of a strong domestic claim for the respect of human rights. In the series of amnesties and legal reforms, the king appears to have responded largely to outside pressures, but those pressures in turn were stimulated by, and interacted with, domestic concerns for human rights as represented and articulated by the new OMDH. Failure to respond risked diplomatic reprisals for the king, but it also threatened to isolate him from an international dynamic that built solidarity between an important segment of Moroccan society and a broad range of international interests.

If the Maghrib is representative with regard to the role of outsiders in the politics of human rights, it is a mistake to assign either credit or blame for changes in human rights performance to outside forces. International actors have clearly had an impact, but their primary effect has been to supplement, and augment, the efforts of domestic groups.

11 The Changing Face of North African Politics

Neither the emergence nor the development of a human rights movement in North Africa was inevitable. In the first two decades after independence, rebellions and reform efforts alike failed, and the cycle of protest that did finally take shape in the late 1970s contained illiberal elements that in important regards were antipathetic to a doctrine of universal human rights. The movement's development was not always smooth, and its future has at times appeared uncertain. It derived force from a strong sense of purpose rather than from numbers, and its perseverance for more than fifteen years has earned it a place of note in the political landscape.

Across the pages of this book I have identified the several factors that converged to assist development of the human rights movement and ensure its survival. The passion of a few good men and women willing to assume attendant political risks provided the impetus to organize. Their deep commitment either to human rights ideals or to the more tactical—and potentially self-serving—goal of opening up a political system sustained the work. That commitment has variously been driven by moral concerns, the search for political autonomy, and the rejection of a political form that concentrated state powers in the hands of a few, to be exercised arbitrarily.

North African activists are political reformers, and their efficacy has been enhanced by the fact that many of them came from the same social and economic classes as the ruling elites. They understood the workings of power in the local context, and they had both the social and the financial resources to make themselves heard. Their positions of relative privilege within society, moreover, gave them access to communications and transportation technology that facilitated contact among themselves and dissemination of information across the Maghrib and in Europe. The resources and skills they brought as educated elites increased their capacity for effective action, and the interests many shared with ruling elites also made them somewhat less likely candidates for political repression. The path they carved was often treacherous: they were critical without wanting to appear threatening; they cooperated while trying to protect their independence. Individual members and groups as a whole sometimes stumbled on this narrow ridge, but to a remarkable degree, they managed to avoid sliding down either of the slippery slopes.

If individuals supplied the necessary motivation and commitment, structural conditions at home and abroad helped shape an environment in which the human rights movement could grow. As argued earlier, the fact that the movement emerged in Tunisia had ramifications both for its shape and for its spread across the Maghrib. Of the three Maghribi counties, it was Tunisia that initially appeared to have the best chance of achieving a transition to democracy. In its early days the Neo-Destour Party had anchored itself well in society, and levels of participation were fairly high in the polity, even if competition was not tolerated. Democratizing pressures there fed the human rights movement, and the government's fear of reactions at home and abroad helped stay the hand of repression. On one hand, there was concern about the expression of political dissent. Labor unrest in 1978 had dispelled any myths about Tunisia's immunity to popular revolt, and although trade unionism was effectively contained by 1980, Islamic dissidents were gathering force on the horizon. At the same time, the international reputation for political moderation Bourguiba had carefully cultivated was in jeopardy. Tunisia's image had already suffered in the aftermath of 1978, and harassment of those who argued simply but ardently for the respect of human rights threatened to damage it further. By the government's own calculus, there was more to gain than to lose by tolerating a domestic human rights league.

Islamism offered a separate challenge to those who sought an extension of civil and political liberties. Concern about political expression and repression was widely shared across the two groups, but views about the role of women and the secular nature of the state more commonly clashed. Islamists and their sympathizers vastly outnumbered the liberals and leftists who were LTDH mainstays, but Tunisia was a land where much of the ruling class had a vested interest in secularism and the liberal code of personal status, and human rights activists were able to draw on that heritage. Without a human rights movement to temper Islamist rhetoric, I have suggested, Tunisian politics—and by extension, politics across the Maghrib—might look very different today.

From Tunisia, the human rights movement spread across the Maghrib. The LTDH had no direct hand in organizing either the Algerian leagues or the OMDH, but its demonstrated effectiveness was discussed in neighboring countries, and it served as an example of what *could* be accomplished. Maghribi groups maintained contact with one another and jointly pressured their governments to commit themselves to respect and promote human rights. Ben Ali's political endorsement of human rights in 1987 added legitimacy to popular pressures and contributed to the inclusion of human rights principles in the framework of the UMA.

International forces added their own weight to dynamics within the Maghrib. Since passage of the UDHR in 1948, the world of international politics had welcomed many new state and nonstate actors. Western states retained their influence, but on another stage nongovernmental organizations also found ways to register humanitarian concerns. An international human rights movement provided politically independent and credible assessment of human rights practices in the Maghrib, supplied the international press with compelling stories, and organized global society to pressure both local leaders and other governments with influence in the region. North African human rights practices were discussed in newspaper columns, radio broadcasts, international fora, and the hearing rooms of foreign parliaments. By 1990, even special bilateral diplomatic relations were no longer privileged.

Individual commitment, local political dynamics, and international pressures thus helped bolster the profile and advance the work of North African human rights groups. No one of these several contributing factors, though, was alone sufficient to effect change. In the absence of external support, domestic pressure groups would almost certainly have met repression, and strong domestic voices made it difficult to dismiss pressures from outside. Even in Morocco, where external forces had the greatest impact, both the press and foreign governments cast themselves in supporting roles and relied on internal monitors to verify amnesties and evaluate the significance of reforms. The human rights movement arose out of domestic concerns and political dynamics, but its energies were sustained and its impact amplified by an international chorus, whose chant remained audible despite the fact that its several sections did not always follow the same score. Gradually, human rights worked its way into political discourse across the region. Government officials increasingly gave lip service to the idea of human rights, and by the end of 1991, leaders in each of the three Maghribi states had used their powers to create a special office or council to address related concerns.

CONTINUITY AND CHANGE IN
NORTH AFRICAN POLITICS

Returning to the issues raised in the first pages of this book, we have now reached the point where the efforts of the Maghribi human rights groups may be linked to larger questions of democratization and metapolitical change. Democracy is not to be confused with its trappings—elections, multipartyism, parliaments. Democracy, more basically, is a contract between a people and the government it chooses, and democratization is a process by which both participation and accountability are increased. The outcome of a political contest necessarily becomes less predictable, because more degrees of freedom are introduced to the game itself; there are more players, and they exercise greater discretion. Democratization may or may not entail a reduction of state powers: at least in theory, popular recognition of a democratic government's right to rule may reduce the need for coercion and enhance a state's ability to govern.

It is the thesis of this book that human rights groups contribute to the process of democratization by challenging political practices that limit participation and reduce accountability. In the Maghrib, such practices are embedded in the patrimonial (or neopatrimonial) political systems that were constructed in the first years after independence. The state inherited by Tunisian nationalists was put to the service of a single party and the man at its helm; law was used to legitimize power but rarely to limit it. In Morocco political contest was permitted, but the monarch planted himself above the law. The Algerian system vacillated between collegial rule and personal rule in the shadow of the army, and law was mostly inconsequential.

Political systems in the Maghrib are not uniform with respect either to ideology or dynamic processes, but they do share a propensity to patrimonial structures that turn on patronage and personal rule. Patrimonialism is undergirded by pervasive and deep-seated social norms that discourage autonomous political behavior, and leaders have tended to rely on engrained patterns of authority relations and political ideology, rather than bargaining strategies and interest-group politics, to consolidate and legitimate their rule. Nationalism, religious ritual, class linkages, and clientelist networks have served as instruments of political control, but they all involve compliance on the part of society and so appear benign. Such indirect instruments of control are not always effective, and it is when they fail that the arbitrary powers of a personal ruler are most apparent. Repression is an expedient tool of social control, and within a patrimonial framework of governance, the structural constraints are few. Maghribi leaders have occasionally "disappeared" political opponents or had them assassinated; more frequently, torture and long-term imprisonment have been used to muzzle opposition.

By condemning such practices and by linking them to universal moral and legal principles, human rights groups across the Maghrib have chiseled away at the linchpin of personal rule. The preeminence of law on which they have insisted is incompatible with the arbitrary exercise of power, and the moral and humanitarian concerns they have expressed directly challenge the working rules of patrimonial governance. Human rights groups may not explicitly call for democratization, but their efforts are no less important to that process. Through the logic of their arguments, they hold government authorities accountable before the law, and they defend political participation across the rights of expression, assembly, and association.

Human rights activists worked under the cover of domestic and international laws to which their governments had freely subscribed, but the initial formation of civic groups and their subsequent dogged pursuit of human rights concerns made those in power uneasy. In all three countries governments initially tried to intimidate activists and prevent the emergence of the groups. When those efforts threatened to become too costly vis-à-vis international public opinion, the contest shifted to the arena of public discourse, and battles were waged over the control of political ideology. Activists can claim victory in the subsequent war of words about human rights, but to what extent are political rhetoric and legal reforms indicative of far-reaching structural change?

Change at the Surface

It can be argued that human rights groups have opened the door to political change in North Africa, but the question of their immediate and palpable effects on political structures remains. The series of amnesties issued by Ben Ali in 1988 and 1989, and by Hassan II from 1989 to 1992, involved very real changes in thousands of individual lives, but what is the long-term significance of these gestures? While human rights groups can claim much of the credit in altering the fate of thousands of individuals and for inserting human rights into political discourse, Maghribi politics remains patrimonial in essence. There have been some enduring legal reforms in all three countries, but they are overshadowed by continuing patterns of abuse and by practices that violate even the reforms. At the surface, only the face of North African politics has changed. Rhetoric notwithstanding, governments in power have shown little inclination to carry through on their avowed commitment to the rule of law, democratization, and international human rights standards. In Algeria the experiment in democracy was aborted when the FLN lost its bid for a return to power, and in Morocco the constitutional modifications augmenting powers of the prime minister were simply ignored by King Hassan II. Tunisia admitted opposition parties into its legislature for the first time in 1994, but the rule of law is still commonly bent to political purposes.[1]

Those who hold extensive powers are rarely willing to cede them. Even so, concessions in relational politics—including patronage as well as policy choices—are made more easily than metapolitical changes. Relational politics need not challenge a ruler's hold on power or the basis of power. Indeed, in circumstances favorable to the leader, they may enhance power by increasing sentiments of loyalty and legitimacy. Metapolitical pressures, by contrast, call into question fundamental political arrangements and so threaten to alter the way the game itself is played. For those in power the stakes are much higher, and it should be no surprise when they fight ardently to preserve the status quo.

Human rights groups have been engaged in a metapolitical struggle; this book has addressed their efforts to recast—without dismantling—political systems. They cannot be said to have won their battle, but at the outset I argued that there is much to be learned from truncated transitions and from efforts alone. One such lesson is that the success of reform efforts wherever they take place is in part a reflection of existing, and changing, power balances. As discussed in Chapter 9, the "accomplishments" of North African groups have depended not simply on their own cohesion, strategies, tactics, and supporters, but also on the cards held by those in power. The political context has itself colored the struggle over rights-inspired structural reform.

In general, we may expect that advantage lies on the side of those in power. They have vested interests in the status quo, and they have political instruments at their disposition to defend those interests. At times, though, political dynamics may shift as they did across the Maghrib in the 1970s and 1980s. Several decades of economic and social change culminated in widespread discontent and raised the costs of maintaining the status quo throughout the region. Opportunities were thus created for those who sought reform. The greatest advances for human rights groups, human rights victims, and structural reform came at times when governments were seeking support in quarters where these issues were prominent. In Tunisia the Ben Ali government turned for support to liberal critics of Bourguiba, and following the 1988 riots in Algiers, the weakened regime of Chadli Bendjedid sought the backing of professionals shocked at extensive repression. Hassan II responded primarily to political leaders in Europe and the United States, and they were showing increasing interest in human rights issues.

The marginal advantage enjoyed by human rights groups in the late 1980s has by now waned, and hopes for structural transformation have faded. Several factors helped to restore the advantage to those in power. To quiet foreign critics and enhance the king's own image as a statesman, Morocco wooed the attention of prominent businessmen and journalists in Europe and in 1993 launched a media campaign in Europe somewhat more subdued than the ill-fated Temps du Maroc. Despite the Tabet affair and the ardent concern about abuse of power and political accountability it provoked, the Palace emerged from the 1993 elections with its powers intact.

Because the Moroccan king's own legitimacy derives in substantial part from his role as Prince of the Faithful, Hassan II has had little interest in emphasizing an Islamist threat. The demonstrated strength of an Islamist movement in Algeria, however, has been used by the governments of Tunisia and Algeria to strengthen their hands. In portraying Islamism as a revolutionary threat, Tunisian and Algerian authorities developed a rationale for delaying reforms and extending their hold on power. It is probably too late now to know whether Islamists might ever have been incorporated into existing, but reformed, regimes in the region. Through the 1980s, al-Nahda (the MTI), and the FIS alike insisted that they intended to play politics within the bounds of an expanded game with modified rules. Like the human rights groups, they advocated reform, not revolution.

Islamism by the mid 1990s did, however, present a credible revolutionary threat in Algeria, and governments have played on popular fears to counter critics at home and abroad. Promoting fear was an effective strategy in Algeria in January 1993 and again in 1994. Despite the government's disarray and dubious hold on the powers of state, many liberals supported the extension of military rule in 1994 as they supported the decision to suspend the electoral process in 1993. Likewise, the Islamist card continues to play in Tunisia, where the movement is yet "contained" but can still be advanced as a credible threat. Tunisians watch the chaos that engulfs Algeria, where even the army's hold is insecure. That fear enhances Ben Ali's powers and even for many liberal elites justifies extended police powers and excuses the abridgment and abuse of rights.

The political advantage has shifted back to the status quo, and questions of structural transformation have receded from national agendas, but human rights groups remain active, and their work continues to benefit from the support of outside powers and global society. Although the opportunity for momentous change appears to have passed, more subtle pressures continue to be exerted and longer metapolitical effects are not to be discounted.

Change beneath the Surface

Two vantage points remain from which important changes beneath the surface may be discerned. To consider the first of these, attention is directed back to questions of political discourse. I have argued that in addition to expressing concerns about individual cases, human rights groups have energetically promoted human rights principles and successfully engaged governments in a struggle for control of political discourse. From the Driss Commission to the royal Consultative Council to Algeria's human rights Observatoire, Maghribi leaders have inserted human rights into their own rhetoric and have created institutions to symbolize concern for human rights. In creating such bodies, governments have sought to appease critics, for the most part without altering the structures of power that underlie their rule. The dishing out of political rewards, even symbolic ones, is normally a matter of relational politics, a reapportioning of the political pie. In the case of human rights, however, the gradual incorporation of human rights language into official discourse has held more ramifications for fundamental political structures than for relations between components of the existing political game. Political rhetoric does not always translate into political practice, and continuing abuses raise troubling questions about policy and political commitment. At the deeper level, though, the rhetorical embrace of human rights portends more significant change.

Some would dismiss the political rhetoric and symbolic reforms as trifles for public consumption, but that is to underplay their significance. The point is that they *are* for public consumption. In Algeria and Morocco, it is a significant political development for governments to show concern about any public, at home or abroad. In Tunisia, where public opinion has played an important role in politics since the nineteenth century, the innovation is somewhat different. There the shift has primarily been in content, reflecting a change in perceptions of what the public has wanted to hear. Political talk and reality are interrelated, and by using human rights language and incorporating it into official discourse, North African officials imbue it with legitimacy. Talk alone rarely engages leaders, but official discourse does frame political debate and helps shape political structures. In this case it also opens the door to participation—the right to political expression—and legitimates expectations of accountability.

Evidence of the power of human rights rhetoric may be found in all three countries, but the Tunisian case from 1987 to 1992 is the most poignant. Ben Ali's early endorsement of human rights helped establish the legitimacy of the new regime, but it also posed some problems. The new government was neither willing to accommodate Islamists politically nor able to undermine their popular support, and its resort to familiar measures of repression belied its commitment to human rights, and to democratization. Deeds blatantly contradicted words, and not surprisingly, many rose to denounce the new regime as a reincarnation of the old one. The more intriguing fact is that even as it resumed the practices of an earlier era, Ben Ali's government maintained its rhetorical emphasis on human rights. It can only be inferred that the regime judged the price of abandoning rights rhetoric too high. The notion of human rights had clearly become irksome, yet human rights rhetoric was a useful enough political tool that Ben Ali's government was initially willing to make some sacrifices to lend it credibility. When human rights groups in Tunisia and abroad defended the power of human rights rhetoric and pushed the regime to investigate allegations of torture and deaths in detention, the government decided to prosecute those charged with wrongdoing and to compensate victims' families. Clearly such measures do not establish a regime's firm commitment to protecting civil and political liberties: arrests and allegations of ill-treatment continued unabated. Nevertheless, they declare the standard.

The impact of human rights rhetoric in the Maghrib has been limited, not so much by the fact that it is for public consumption, but because the public specifically addressed may not be the one most affected. Several gestures made by Bendjedid were designed primarily to please outsiders of influence, and since 1987 the Tunisian government has published many human rights–related documents and news reports in French and English, for circulation abroad. In 1993—amidst serious criticisms and in the context of an equally serious public relations campaign—it made much ado internationally about the creation of a government-sponsored human rights prize.[2] In similar fashion, the Moroccan CCDH was created to appease Western critics, and several of the most dramatic human rights measures were not even announced in Morocco. Most Moroccans who learned of the release of Tazmamart prisoners in 1991, for example, received the news via Paris contacts and the French press.

The incorporation of "human rights" into political discourse across the Maghrib—even if intended primarily for Western ears—is not without impact, insofar as it creates expectations and reinforces standards to which governments may be held. A visit from Amnesty International and the release of a report on the practice of incommunicado pretrial detention opened the valve of pressure on Morocco in 1990, but it was Hassan II's own efforts to impress Western television audiences in 1989 that turned that visit into a diplomatic necessity for Morocco. Before the world community he could not maintain both professed ignorance of abuses and resistance to impartial scrutiny. The use of human rights rhetoric creates a basis for accountability and the risk of political embarrassment when deeds depart too obviously from words. The official use of human rights rhetoric thus amounts to legitimation and promotion of human rights, extending the process begun within the UN framework forty-five years ago. The promotion of human rights, as Jack Donnelly and others have argued, lays the basis for their implementation.[3]

The second perspective from which official human rights rhetoric and promulgated reforms take on significance despite their obvious practical limitations is that of the citizenry. Without guarantees of civil and political rights, "citizen" has little meaning. As a political concept, human rights points directly to the relationship between governed and government, and the language of human rights nurtures citizenship. Without necessarily inspiring confidence that a government's rhetorical commitment is sincere or raising expectations that reforms will be fully implemented, human rights as a byword and as a political concept has spread widely across the top echelons of society. North Africans are well accustomed to distinguishing between what Michel Camau has called an *état réel* and an *état idéal*,[4] and few mistake the rhetorical ideal for political reality. "Human rights" has nevertheless provided a new framework across which to discuss political relationships and a new avenue for participation in the polity.

Over the past decade, human rights has acquired legitimacy as a political concept in the Maghrib. Leftists who once dismissed it as a bourgeois construct now freely embrace guarantees of physical integrity; Islamists under siege denounce abuses; and official endorsement of human rights opens the door to free—if abstract—discussion among intellectuals across the region. In *Arab Voices* Kevin Dwyer has brought some Maghribi participants to the attention of English-speaking audiences; in French and Arabic other North African intellectuals variously defend human rights, secularism, and Islamic liberalism. The press in the Maghrib must work within narrowly defined political space, but even so, through domestic news stories, news analyses, and reports from within the region and beyond the legitimacy of human rights concerns has been reinforced and discussion has been stimulated. The concept of "human rights" framed Algerian questions about widespread torture following the 1988 riots, Tunisian interest in the Driss Commission's report, and Moroccan outrage at blatant abuse of a police commissioner's power. Citizens of the Maghrib in all these cases held authorities responsible and claimed a right simply to know.

Concerns have been voiced most ardently within the rather small nexus of committed activists who have led rights groups in each of the three countries, but interest in human rights has extended well beyond inner circles. Even after a year-long suspension of its activities, the Tunisian League of Human Rights set about reviving not only its central leadership but the forty-one branches scattered throughout the country. In Morocco, both the AMDH and the OMDH have multiplied their membership and have affiliate groups in most urban communities. At its third congress, held late in 1991, the AMDH elected a 45-member administrative committee from among its national membership. Arguably the most compelling evidence of regional interest in human rights as a political concept lies in the fact that Tunisia and Algeria are two of only three Arabo-Muslim countries to host functioning sections of Amnesty International. AI's working rules prohibit groups from focusing on abuses in their own country, and such a mandate leaves little room for the pursuit of political self-promotion that some have argued underlies the indigenous human rights movement.

If the concept of human rights holds potential for reorienting political thought, groups themselves are instruments through which political activity can be reshaped. Human rights groups provide an alternative to political parties and interest groups (trade unions and student organizations, notably) for engagement in political life. Some activists, in fact, have abandoned relational politics for the high road of human rights: for many of the lawyers, academics, and intellectuals drawn to the Maghribi groups, human rights have offered means to transcend the pointless competition in which partisan politics is mired.[5] The human rights movement has directed its energies to metapolitical issues: according to one activist, it is the mission of Maghribi human rights organizations "to install a democratic ethic in the minds of all those who hold authority in the region."[6]

Human rights groups are committed to recrafting the rules of Maghribi politics, but denunciation of abuses and promotion of law are not the only means by which they have pursued that end. Their activities, as well as the ideals they promote, have created opportunities to recast the elements of political culture. Students of comparative politics have often argued that both the emergence and the sustenance of democracy are affected by the prevailing political culture, and a culture that promotes the maintenance of order and respect for hierarchy while discouraging individual competence is commonly seen as an impediment to democratization and democratic governance.[7] In explaining the recent "third wave" of democratic transitions, though, Samuel Huntington notes that many of the societies that democratized their political systems from 1974 to 1990 had also undergone marked shifts in values and beliefs; accordingly, he cautions against viewing any political culture as immutable.[8] I argued in earlier parts of this book that patriarchal norms that foster heteronomous political attitudes undermine both participation and accountability in North African polities. Economic structures today do not support a political culture of patriarchy to the extent they once did, but the principal ideological response to social and economic change has come in a form that seeks to restore rather than replace the waning moral order. The human rights movement provides an important political counterpoint to that ideological creed; not only does it offer alternative values, but the rights groups have themselves been schools for democracy.

The experiences of the OMDH and the LTDH are of particular relevance in this regard. By contrast to both of the Algerian human rights leagues, which from the outset were subordinated to strong individual personalities and by consequence have tended to replicate familiar political patterns, the explicitly nonpartisan groups in Tunisia and Morocco have on several occasions been obliged to address issues of power sharing, political contest, and leadership rotation. Both organizations have developed mechanisms for regular turnover in leadership, and at least to some degree internal elections have been contested. Each organization, moreover, has dealt with internal strife over personalities and has set limitations on leaders' ability to speak for the group. The Tunisian League of Human Rights, in fact, faced such problems once again late in 1993. The league did not find it easy to reconstitute itself under the 1992 law of association, and for several months it was mired in organizational difficulties. Decision-making in these two organizations has not always been smooth or relations cordial, but in the process of resolving problems, some new variations on old patterns of political interaction and decision-making have appeared. In both groups most decisions have been made by consensus, but only after extended discussion and debate reaching well beyond the inner circle of leadership. Political parties and professional groups within corporatist polities have a regular supply of patronage to offer supporters, but human rights groups have held out little more than the satisfaction of contributing to a compelling humanitarian cause and the collective ownership of an articulate political voice. Under such circumstances, inclusive discussion and decision-making are not political luxuries.

In limited ways they have also crafted new solutions to problems of political division. Despite the formality of pluralism, Tunisia has effectively remained a single-party political system, with corporatist structures controlled from the top. Power dynamics have discouraged the officially recognized opposition parties from uniting their forces, and they remain marginalized. Against that backdrop, the LTDH experience offers a degree of contrast. In biannual congresses its own membership has effectively functioned as a multiparty parliament. At times, majority rule resolved differences within its ranks, but more commonly, extensive consultation and political compromise have led to consensus that accommodated not only the recognized parties but Islamists as well. The league has been tested on several occasions, and although by early 1994 it had not resolved a dispute over new leadership, over the previous fifteen years it had managed to extract itself from other political quagmires that had threatened to pull it under. In those instances, league members ultimately recognized and reaffirmed their common purpose, and the strength of that commitment was sufficient to overcome divisions.

Like the Tunisian league, the Moroccan Organization of Human Rights confronted a tradition of fragmentation within the local political culture. In Morocco, political divisiveness enhances the power of a monarch who sits above most political contest, and from that seat, fragmentation is actively encouraged. In creating a third human rights group, the founders of the OMDH seemed poised to continue rather than resist the tradition. The OMDH failed to merge with the Moroccan Association of Human Rights and/or the Moroccan League of Human Rights, and the partisan struggle that replaced the group's initial élan raised doubts about its ability to overcome fissiparous tendencies. Many of the original, politically unaffiliated members left the organization, and some predicted that the OMDH would lose its political independence. A new cohort of leaders, however, stepped into the breach and made deliberate efforts to steer clear of the snares of partisan rivalry.

As in the Tunisian league, activists of a different political stripe have successfully collaborated within the OMDH, and cross-party cooperation in that context provided experience on which a multiparty coalition, the Kutla, was able to draw in the June 1993 legislative elections. North African human rights groups exist outside the formally defined arena of political contest, but the groups themselves are microcosms of the national political contexts within which they operate. In the political space they occupy, the conventions that govern politics are being modified.

CONCLUSION

Across the Maghrib in the late 1980s, political games that had been constructed in an earlier era were challenged both by Islamists and by liberals, for whom human rights groups served as a vanguard. After an initial period where overarching change seemed imminent, favor has returned to the status quo, and at least for the moment, political games remain largely intact. The times also remain turbulent, however, and pressures continue to be exerted by several contrary interests. Not improperly, attention is riveted on the contest between Islamists and those who would defend the status quo.

In this political context, predictions are hazardous. The role to be played by human rights groups in the struggle over the shape of North African politics is both important and limited, and it should neither be exaggerated nor underestimated. For a brief historical moment, human rights groups occupied center stage and contributed substantially to dramatic political developments. Governments, though, lost little time in planning their own moves to recapture the offensive, appointing human rights officials and adopting new rhetoric. Legislation that temporarily crippled the LTDH allowed the Tunisian government to reassert its own command of human rights discourse, while in Morocco the Tabet scandal increased domestic pressures for the monarchy to treat rights seriously. The Ministry of Human Rights was added to supplement the work of the royal human rights council. In Algeria, however, government authorities and human rights activists alike were overtaken by events.

It seems unlikely that human rights groups will soon reclaim the political spotlight, but they have not left the stage. While changes in the balance of political forces may reduce the likelihood of near-term structural change, they do not have a commensurate effect on the commitment of human rights activists. Human rights groups, in fact, continue to provide foci of political energy, and they are cheered on from the wings by their international counterparts and an assortment of other international actors. Independent of their accomplishments, even the emergence of organized and sustained efforts to achieve structural change is a significant political development in the region, and its importance promises to grow. Interest in human rights has spread within professional classes across the greater Middle East, and the human rights movement has taken root in countries as disparate as Turkey, Kuwait, Egypt, and Sudan.

From the outset, North African human rights activists have shown themselves to be careful tacticians, and there will necessarily be retreats as well as advances in their work. Those interested in charting their progress are well advised to look to the edges of the political game and beneath its surface. The craft of human rights groups is to promote the impartial rule of law, urge enforcement of existing law, propose new legal safeguards, and protest abuses. They carve away at political practices that enshrine arbitrary powers. If to date their efforts have altered only the face of North African politics, tomorrow's work cannot yet be judged.

Epilogue

As he climbed the stairs to his office in the early morning of 18 June 1994, the Algerian notary Youcef Fethallah was shot by assailants at point-blank range. In the circle of North African human rights activists, his death was not simply another fatality in Algeria's civil strife. President of the LADH since December 1990, Fethallah was known as a cautious but principled defender of human rights. At a conference in Vienna just a few weeks earlier, he had asserted that political killings in Algeria were being carried out not only by Islamic dissidents but by government agents as well. His death, for which no group claimed responsibility, pointed up risks that seemed to be growing exponentially.

Political violence combined with social and economic disarray has had a profound impact on Algerians and Algerian political dynamics. "It would seem that God has turned his back on this nation," wrote an acquaintance recently. "We have only the Mediterranean sun for comfort." There is no accurate count of the carnage, but from January 1992 through September 1994, at least 10,000 lives were claimed. The *combattants* are themselves difficult to identify. The Armed Islamic Group (GIA), which in late 1993 issued menacing warnings to foreigners, was recognized by mid 1994 as the principal instrument of terrorist action. In 1992, though, the FIS had begun to develop its own armed corps, the Army of Islamic Salvation, and in 1994 it threatened to coordinate efforts with the GIA and smaller, less organized armed groups to overthrow the Algerian government by force. Government security forces have been heavily engaged, of course, and their activities apparently extend beyond reprisals targeted at armed groups. There is widespread belief that security forces rather than Islamists have been responsible for assassinations of key political figures, including Kasdi Merbah and President Boudiaf. The cloud of political violence and repression is also extensive enough to provide cover for those looking simply to settle old personal scores. In circles that extend beyond the ruling elite to intellectuals and all professionals, fear is palpable.

Matters are only complicated by the fact that structural problems seem insoluble. As noted in Chapter 5, difficulties associated with a flailing economy and high unemployment continue to mount, and arrangements made with external financiers in 1994 to some extent exacerbated basic political tensions. In an effort to demonstrate fiscal responsibility to international creditors, but at considerable political risk at home, for example, the government raised the price of bread in July 1994, and in September it announced that 150,000 people were likely to lose their jobs in the early phases of privatization. The country's "leaders"—including all those who have been in power from the time of independence, whether party leaders, FLN technocrats, military officers or security chiefs—are mistrusted and even despised by large segments of the population. For a time in 1994, government forces successfully routed armed Islamists from major cities, but the security forces' inability to declare a decisive victory (and the Islamists' continued ability to launch attacks) led many journalists and political observers to predict the imminent overthrow of the Zeroual government. Others, noting the serious fragmentation within the ranks of the Islamists themselves,[1] feared a protracted civil war. Then, in September 1994, two surprise moves upset the entire calculus. As a concession to Islamists, but perhaps in hopes of further dividing them, Zeroual ordered the transfer of the FIS leaders Abbas Madani and Ali Belhadj from their prison cells at Blida to house arrest, presumably to facilitate their participation in a "national dialogue." Days later, security forces killed Cherif Gousni, commander of the GIA, in an ambush. Elections have been scheduled for 1995, but major participants in both the political and the armed struggle show little real interest in dialogue, and resolution of the conflict through negotiation—however desirable—remains doubtful.

The effects of civil strife are naturally felt most keenly by Algerians, but political ramifications have been noted well beyond that country's national borders. Elites across the region have registered the fragility of the Algerian state and express a commensurate fear of Islamism. Leaders in Tunisia and Morocco are interpreting the lessons Algeria offers for their own polities, and in elite circles, talk of "liberty," "law," and "civil society" has begun to diminish. The politics of human rights are being renegotiated, and the final pages of this book address the dynamics of that process.

As argued throughout this book, the politics of human rights is essentially a politics of rhetoric. That rhetoric is not to be dismissed for its emptiness, insofar as political discourse ultimately shapes political expectations and political behavior. It is thus significant that as regards the politics of human rights, the primary impact of civil strife in Algeria is the rhetorical revaluation of "order," "security," and "national sovereignty." As might have been expected, by mid 1994, Algerian leaders spoke of little else, but in neighboring countries there was also an apparent shift in emphasis. In Tunisia, officials touted an atmosphere of calm and security, but now insisted there was no longer room for anyone to talk in the name of the people outside the new parliament.[2] Morocco closed its borders with Algeria in August after an explosion at a Marrakesh hotel claimed the lives of two Spanish tourists. The attack was credited to arms traffickers with ties to Algeria; the Moroccans alleged complicity on the part of Algerian security forces and imposed visa requirements on Algerians in Morocco.

Concern for security did not necessarily win new support for regimes in power, but it effectively dampened calls for the respecting of human rights. To some degree the liberal proponents of human rights and structural reform had come to fear the political success of an Islamist movement, and to some extent they now feared government reprisals for continued defense of civil and political liberties. In Algeria, some of the most ardent defenders of civil liberties had been assassinated. Only a handful of lawyers and human rights activists continued to protest the renewed use of torture and executions and defend the rights of Islamists to due process, and even before Fethallah's assassination in June, the activities of the LADH had ground nearly to a halt. Little is left of the independent press that flourished only two years before.

In Tunisia, the LTDH elected a new president and reconstituted itself after an eighteen-month hiatus in activities imposed by the 1992 law of association, but it was not able to reestablish its considerable influence in political life. To many observers, the league's choice of the attorney Taoufik Bouderabala over the outspoken and at times flamboyant Moncef Marzouki signaled a new truce between the league and government authorities. As time progressed, however, it became apparent that even the newly moderated voice of the league would be muffled. The league's cause was no longer so popular, and in view of shifting political winds, association with it was viewed by many as risky. The press's reluctance to publish league communiques further marginalized the once-outspoken body. More dramatic constraints were imposed on its erstwhile chief spokesman. A few weeks before the March 1994 legislative and presidential elections,

Dr. Marzouki had announced his intent to stand as a presidential candidate—an effort to introduce an element of competition into the race and, no doubt, to provoke and perhaps embarrass the RCD. His candidacy was formally disallowed because he could not find the requisite *parrainage* among existing parliamentarians—RCD members—but the move rankled government officials and party leaders alike. An interview with a Spanish paper in which Marzouki allegedly questioned the independence of the Tunisian judiciary was used as a pretext for his arrest, and despite the paper's own retraction of an erroneous quotation, he was held in custody for several months. Considerable domestic and international pressure helped secure Marzouki's release on bail, but in September 1994 he still awaited trial. In the meantime, the expulsion of French correspondents led both *Le Monde* and *La Libération* to withdraw their papers from circulation in Tunisia, and leftists as well as the few attorneys who defended those accused of political crimes came under increasing pressure. Some faced harassment, police questioning, and even imprisonment.

Only in Morocco did the cause of human rights enjoy sustained appeal through 1994. Moroccan human rights groups continued to press for liberalizations and were gratified when King Hassan II declared his intent to "turn the page," inviting the royal Consultative Council on Human Rights to submit a comprehensive list of the country's political prisoners. They cheered the sweeping amnesty that liberated more than 350 political prisoners in July 1994, even if several of the alleged beneficiaries had in fact already been released. (Less publicly, some also noted that the thorny problem of the Saharan disappeared had still not been addressed.) Despite a general euphoria about the far-reaching measure of clemency, however, the popular mood shifted somewhat in late August with growing fears about arms trafficking and terrorist groups. Appeals by human rights groups to rescind visa requirements for Algerians did not resonate as well as had their calls for a general amnesty.

Expression of concern for order and security is the classic rejoinder to popular calls for liberty and expanded participation, and to some degree the present round of rhetorical contest was predictable. Assuring public order is a legitimate function of the state; indeed, some would argue that it is the most legitimate function of a state. Order and security are thus quite naturally the concerns advanced by governments to rationalize and justify the constraints they may impose on political activity and expression. Governments are not always convincing in their claims of threats, however, and in Tunisia at least, the success of the government's effort to shift the rhetorical emphasis was not inevitable. The Islamist "threats" the government had publicized in the early 1980s, again in 1984, and, finally, in 1991, were not fully credible. For Tunisians, the serial assassinations in Algeria accomplished what government propaganda had not, and perhaps could not. To the extent that there must be a trade-off between liberty and security, a belief that the system is threatened—whether the threat be real or contrived—inevitably diminishes concern about political rights and civil liberties, except for the most committed libertarians. Maghribi human rights activists and their supporters are mindful of their stake in the system; throughout this book I have presented them as reformers, not revolutionaries. They have sought change but not revolution, and in the minds of many, "Algeria" has come to represent the threat of an undesired revolution.

Concern for security has risen across the region, and its impact on the politics of human rights has not been limited to government policies, political discourse, public opinion, or political conditions for Maghribi human rights groups. Although international human rights organizations such as Amnesty International, Middle East Watch, and the Lawyers' Committee for Human Rights have continued to release reports and identify human rights issues, there has also been a notable shift in attitudes outside the region. The international press has closely followed events in Algeria and consistently reported attacks on foreigners; particularly in France, public interest in the preservation of a secular government in Algeria has eclipsed concern about the abridgment of democratic process. Most important, the foreign policy stances of both France and the United States have shifted.

As key partners of the Maghribi states, France and the United States have watched the situation in Algeria with some nervousness. Keeping options open, the United States has adopted a relatively neutral posture toward the conflict in Algeria. Formally and publicly, the United States has backed the HCE and the Zeroual government that succeeded it, but it has likewise had indirect contact with FIS leaders abroad and signaled support for a national dialogue to resolve the crisis of state and governance. France has been less sanguine about the possibility of a political solution, and its interior minister made it clear that France endorsed the drive by Algerian security forces to regain control. Despite the wide differences in their positions, however, both countries have emphasized the possible ramifications of the Algerian conflict for their own security concerns in the region, and in so doing have had a similar effect on the politics of human rights. While human rights concerns have not slipped from the foreign policy agendas of the Maghribi nations' international partners, the protection and support that Western democracies have afforded human rights groups and the pressures for reform they continue to exert are somewhat attenuated by their acknowledgment of the need to assure security within the region.

Algeria's short experiment with democracy was widely heralded by those who advocated transitions away from authoritarian rule, and many who observed Algeria from afar were sorely disappointed at the return to old and familiar patterns of governance—not to mention the eruption of civil conflict. In fact, Algerian political culture offered little by way of support to the practice of democracy. Interruption of the democratic experiment in the final hours of an electoral contest that was not going well for those who had been used to control was more in keeping with established patterns than the slow and careful building of a pluralistic polyarchy might have been. Human rights groups who, together with journalists and other brand-new civic and political groups, spearheaded the move toward democratization emerged late in Algeria and were not themselves consolidated.

The chances of structural transition were improved in both Tunisia and Morocco, because in each country some established patterns could lend themselves to democratic practice.[3] Morocco's several political parties each had a long history, even if much of that history was one of fractious division, and if for the most part they had been excluded from any significant role in governance. Tunisia did not have a history of pluralism, but—unlike Algeria—its dominant (and for many years single) party was inclusive rather than exclusive, and it encouraged popular participation within its own framework. In each case, however, only limited changes have been wrought. In Tunisia, the door to participation was not opened to the best organized and most significant opposition, and today even the press is severely limited in the views that can be expressed. As in previous decades, criticism of the regime is not tolerated publicly. In Morocco, King Hassan II continues to tower over the polity. The 1994 amnesty, however welcome, was the discretionary act of a personal ruler. Likewise, the replacement of Prime Minister Karim Lamrani with Abdellatif Filali in May 1994 did not open up the regime, but instead reinforced patrimonial structures. Filali had served as foreign minister since 1985 and was known and respected as a political independent; however, he is also father of the king's son-in-law, who is himself president of the conglomerate Omnium Nord Africain, which dominates the Moroccan economy, and in which the king has a substantial interest.

On the other hand, in appointing Filali, Hassan II this time honored the new constitutional provision that allows the prime minister to appoint the cabinet. Of perhaps greater significance, the summer amnesty followed shortly on parliament's abrogation of the 1935 *dahir* (decree) authorizing repression of demonstrations likely to disrupt public order or threatening respect for authority. The 1935 dahir had frequently served as the legal basis for political imprisonment, and its abrogation may well extend political space. Significantly, the parliamentary measure rescinding it was initiated by two Kutla parties, the USFP and the Istiqlal Party.

If developments in Tunisia are similarly evaluated in terms of the innovations they introduce rather than for continuations of patrimonial patterns, provisions that hold more promise for structural transformation can also be discerned there, despite recent curtailments in civil and political liberties. The elections of March 1994 allowed the RCD to maintain its firm hold on political processes, but it is noteworthy that the Tunisian parliament today seats representatives from five parties rather than one. Although few in number, representatives of opposition parties now have the opportunity to make their voices heard within the formal structures of governance. Furthermore, if current laws are honored throughout the decade, Tunisians will in 1999 choose a new president by electoral processes for the first time since independence.

Measured against the hopes and dreams of those who have fought for structural transformation and the respecting of human rights, these gains are slender and may even appear insignificant. For perspective, however, it is important to consider them in the context of patrimonial structures developed over several centuries. As noted in the first pages of this book, continuity is the lawful expectation of culture, and in the end, the most enduring change may come incrementally. Patrimonial leaders in whose hands power is concentrated have little incentive to change, and patrimonial regimes may in consequence prove exceptionally resistant to efforts to transform them. However small the democratizing changes may seem when compared to initial visions of overarching structural transformation, it is unlikely that such changes as have occurred in North Africa would have come about without the pressures brought to bear, and the risks assumed, by human rights groups. Even in the midst of growing concerns for security, human rights remains prominent in political discourse throughout the region, and in this sense at least, North African regimes have significantly changed.

Notes

1. INTRODUCTION

1. Michael Hudson, "After the War: Prospects for Democratization in the Arab World," *Middle East Journal* 45 (Summer 1991): 407–26, notes that through 1990, the Middle East was overlooked in major surveys of liberalizing transitions and draws attention to efforts at democratization in the region. See, too, John Esposito and James Piscatori, "Democratization and Islam," in the same issue. Two years later, the *Middle East Journal* invited Richard Norton to edit a special issue on civil society. Several contributors to that issue were less than sanguine about the prospects for government- or party-led democratization but noted the rise of civic organizations throughout the region. See, in particular, Augustus Richard Norton, "The Future of Civil Society in the Middle East," *Middle East Journal* 47 (Spring 1993): 205–16, and Saad Eddin Ibrahim, "Crises, Elites, and Democratization in the Arab World," ibid.: 292–306.

2. Leonard Binder, *Islamic Liberation: A Critique of Development Ideologies* (Chicago: University of Chicago Press, 1988); Jill Crystal, *Oil and Politics in the Gulf: Rulers and Merchants in Kuwait and Qatar* (Cambridge: Cambridge University press, 1990); Robert Bianchi, *Unruly Corporatism: Associational Life in Twentieth-Century Egypt* (New York: Oxford University Press, 1989); Mahmoud Hussein, *Versant sud de la liberté* (Paris: Editions de la découverte, 1989). In 1992 the Ibn Khaldoun Center for Development Studies in Cairo began publishing a monthly newsletter entitled *Civil Society*, with Saad Eddin Ibrahim as editor.

3. David Held, *Models of Democracy* (Stanford: Stanford University Press, 1987).

4. Robert A. Dahl, *Polyarchy: Participation and Opposition* (New Haven: Yale University Press, 1971), 27–29.

5. Benjamin Barber, *Strong Democracy: Participatory Politics for a New Age* (Berkeley and Los Angeles: University of California Press, 1984). In his *Models of Democracy*, Held also traces considerable variety and by implication shows the mutable nature of democracy.

6. Guiseppe DiPalma, *To Craft Democracies: An Essay on Democratic Transitions* (Berkeley and Los Angeles: University of California Press, 1990), 9.

7. These terms are borrowed and adapted from Stephen D. Krasner, *Structural Conflict: The Third World against Global Liberalism* (Berkeley and Los Angeles : University of California Press, 1985), 14.

8. Guillermo O'Donnell and Philippe C. Schmitter, *Transitions from Authoritarian Rule: Tentative Conclusions about Uncertain Democracies* (Baltimore: Johns Hopkins University Press, 1986), 6.

9. Harry Eckstein, "A Culturalist Theory of Political Change," *American Political Science Review* 82 (September 1988): 799.

10. Ibid., 794–96.

11. Samuel Huntington, *The Third Wave: Democratization in the Late Twentieth Century* (Norman: University of Oklahoma Press, 1991), 316.

12. Adam Przeworski, "Some Problems in the Study of the Transition to Democracy," in *Transitions from Authoritarian Rule: Comparative Perspectives* ed. Guillermo O'Donnell, Philippe C. Schmitter, and Laurence Whitehead (Baltimore: Johns Hopkins University Press, 1986), 50–53.

2. THE POLITICAL POWER OF HUMAN RIGHTS

1. Jack Donnelly, "International Human Rights: A Regime Analysis," *International Organization* 40 (Summer 1986): 617.

2. As discussed in Chapter 8, a change in the law of association temporarily dissolved the Tunisian League of Human Rights in 1992; it was granted legal status again in 1993.

3. Richard Falk, "Cultural Foundations for the International Protection of Human Rights," in *Human Rights in Cross-Cultural Perspectives*, ed. Abdullahi Ahmed An-Na'im (Philadelphia: University of Pennsylvania Press, 1992).

4. Alison Dundes Renteln, *International Human Rights: Universalism versus Relativism* (Newbury Park, Calif.: Sage Publications, 1990), 12.

5. Rhoda E. Howard, "Cultural Absolutism and the Nostalgia for Community," *Human Rights Quarterly* 15 (Summer 1993), 315–338.

6. Ibid., 320–322.

7. Reza Afshari, "An Essay on Islamic Cultural Relativism in the Discourse of Human Rights," *Human Rights Quarterly* 16 (Summer 1994), 255.

8. Ibid., 249.

9. Falk, "Cultural Foundations."

10. See Ann Elizabeth Mayer, *Islam and Human Rights: Tradition and Politics* (Boulder, Colo.: Westview Press, 1991), who analyzes a number of such texts.

11. The Salafist call for "reopening the door of *ijtihad*" is often cited in this regard. Mohamed-Cherif Ferjani, *Islamisme: Laïcité et droits de l'homme* (Paris: Editions l'Harmattan, 1991) adds to that approach with an extended discussion of the theological basis of secular power that draws on the writings of the theologian Ali Abderraziq.

12. Compare Kevin Dwyer, *Arab Voices: The Human Rights Debate in the Middle East* (Berkeley and Los Angeles: University of California Press, 1991), 90, for example, with Mayer, *Islam and Human Rights*, 64.

13. Hamid Enayat, *Modern Islamic Political Thought* (Austin: University of Texas Press, 1982), 127.

14. Mayer, *Islam and Human Rights,* 123.

15. Binder, *Islamic Liberalism,* 129.

16. Michael C. Hudson, *Arab Politics: The Search for Legitimacy* (New Haven: Yale University Press, 1977), 49.

17. James A. Bill and Carl Leiden, *Politics in the Middle East* (Boston: Little, Brown, 1984), 46.

18. Dwyer, *Arab Voices,* 174.

19. Afshari, "An Essay on Islamic Cultural Relativism," 259–60.

20. Saad Edin Ibrahim. "The Future of Human Rights in the Arab World" (mimeograph, April 1986).

21. James N. Rosenau, *Turbulence in World Politics: A Theory of Change and Community* (Princeton, N.J.: Princeton University Press, 1990); Joseph A. Camilleri and Jim Falk, *The End of Sovereignty? The Politics of a Shrinking and Fragmenting World* (Sydney, Australia: Edward Elgar, 1993), 199–235; and Paul Ghils, "International Civil Society: International Non-Governmental Organizations in the International System," *International Social Science Journal* 44 (August 1992): 417–29.

22. The LADH and AMDH are "correspondent members" of the FIDH. The LTDH, LADDH, and OMDH are full affiliates.

23. *Amnesty International Report, 1978* (London: AI Publications, 1979) and *Amnesty International Report, 1993* (London: AI Publications, 1993).

24. *Human Rights Internet Reporter* 11, no. 3 (September 1986). Also see Lowell W. Livesey, *Nongovernmental Organizations and the Ideas of Human Rights* (Princeton, N.J.: Center of International Studies, Princeton University, 1988).

25. David P. Forsythe, *Human Rights and World Politics* (Lincoln: University of Nebraska Press, 1989), 83–101.

26. Amnesty International, *Torture in the Eighties* (London: AI Publications, 1984).

27. Robert A. Packenham, *Liberal America and the Third World* (Princeton, N.J.: Princeton University Press, 1973), 26–32.

28. See David P. Forsythe, *Human Rights and U.S. Foreign Policy: Congress Reconsidered* (Gainesville: University Presses of Florida, 1988), 9. Lars Schoultz offers an extended account of the origins and evolution of U.S. human rights legislation in *Human Rights and United States Policy toward Latin America* (Princeton, N.J.: Princeton University Press, 1981.)

29. Forsythe, *Human Rights and World Politics,* 110–14.

30. Abraham F. Lowenthal, "The United States and Latin America: Learning from History," in *Exporting Democracy: The United States and Latin America,* ed. id. (Baltimore: Johns Hopkins University Press, 1991), 260.

31. René Lemarchand discusses the perfidious effects of covert operations on democratic processes in "The C.I.A. in Africa: How Central? How Intelligent?" *Journal of Modern African Studies* 14 (1976): 401–26. Harry Howe Ransom, "Covert Intervention," in *Intervention into the 90's,* ed. Peter J. Schraeder (Boulder, Colo.: Lynne Rienner, 1992), 120, reports that according to William Colby, then CIA political operations chief in Rome, intervention in the 1958 Italian elections was the CIA's largest-ever covert program.

32. Laurence Whitehead, "International Aspects of Democratization," in *Tran-*

sitions from Authoritarian Rule: Comparative Perspectives, ed. Guillermo O'Donnell, Philippe C. Schmitter, and Laurence Whitehead (Johns Hopkins University Press, 1986), 25.

33. Forsythe, *Human Rights and U.S. Foreign Policy*, 161.

34. Ibid., 1.

35. This charge was relayed as an amendment to Section 116 of the Foreign Assistance and Arms Export Act.

36. See "Failure: The Reagan Administration's Human Rights Policy in 1983" (mimeograph, 1984), and "... *In the Face of Cruelty*": *The Reagan Administration's Human Rights Record in 1984* (New York: N. p., 1985), both published jointly by Americas Watch, Helsinki Watch, and the Lawyers' Committee for Human Rights.

37. Forsythe, *Human Rights and U.S. Foreign Policy*, 126.

38. Ibid.

39. See Tamar Jacoby, "The Reagan Turnabout on Human Rights," *Foreign Affairs* 64 (Summer 1986): 1082. Jacoby was deputy editor of the *New York Times* op-ed section.

40. "L'Aide, les droits de l'homme et l'Occident," *Jeune Afrique*, no. 1401 (11 November 1987); David P. Forsythe, *The Internationalization of Human Rights* (Lexington, Mass.: Lexington Books, 1991), 119.

41. Przeworski, "Some Problems in the Study of the Transition to Democracy," 48.

42. Nancy Bermeo, "Rethinking Regime Change," *Comparative Politics* 22 (April 1990): 368.

43. Irving Lester Janis, *Groupthink: Psychological Studies of Policy Decisions and Fiascos* (Boston: Houghton Mifflin, 1982); Robert Jervis, *Perception and Misperception in International Politics* (Princeton, N.J.: Princeton University Press, 1976); Graham T. Allison, *Essence of Decision: Explaining the Cuban Missile Crisis* (Boston: Little, Brown, 1971).

3. STATE AND SOCIETY IN THE MAGHRIB

1. Binder, *Islamic Liberalism*, 34.

2. Samir Amin, *The Maghreb in the Modern World*, trans. Michael Perl (London: Penguin Books, 1970).

3. Hussein, *Versant sud de la liberté*.

4. Edward W. Said, *Orientalism* (New York: Vintage Books, 1979).

5. The distinction between the terms *patriarchy* and *patrimony* merits clarification here. *Patriarchy* refers to the domination of elder male relatives over family members in both private and public spheres. *Patrimonialism*, as developed by Max Weber, refers to a political situation where a leader treats the polity as his private domain. In other words, patrimonialism is the application of patriarchal logic on a much larger scale. The terms *neo-patriarchy* and *neo-patrimonialism* have been coined to reflect adaptations of patterns associated with premodern, "traditional" societies, although a general resurgence of *patriarchy* in analyses of both Western and non-Western societies has tended to confuse that distinction. In this book I have attached no particular significance to the prefix *neo-*. See James A. Bill

and Carl Leiden, *Politics in the Middle East* (Boston: Little, Brown, 1984), 148–59; Hisham Sharabi, *Neopatriarchy: A Theory of Distorted Change in Arab Society* (New York: Oxford University Press, 1988); C. Clapham, ed., *Private Patronage and Public Power: Political Patronage in the Modern State* (New York: Pinter, 1982); Gerda Lerner, *The Creation of Patriarchy* (New York: Oxford Univrsity Press, 1986); and Peter R. Knauss, *The Persistence of Patriarchy: Class, Gender, and Ideology in Twentieth-Century Algeria* (New York: Praeger, 1987).

6. Abdelwahab Boudhiba, *A la recherche des normes perdues* (Tunis: Maison tunisienne de l'edition, 1973), 173.

7. Hussain Bendahman, *Personnalité maghrébine et fonction paternelle au Maghreb* (Paris: La Pensée universelle, 1984), 76. Also see Halim Barakat, *The Arab World: Society, Culture, and State* (Berkeley and Los Angeles: University of California Press, 1993), 97–102.

8. Bendahman, *Personnalité maghrébine*, 73.

9. Nefissa Zerdoumi, *Enfants d'hier: L'Education de l'enfant en milieu traditionnel algérien* (Paris: Francois Maspero, 1970), 42 (author's translation).

10. The Moroccan sociologist Fatima Mernissi has treated this subject extensively in several books, the best known of which within the English-speaking world is *Beyond the Veil: Male-Female Dynamics in Modern Muslim Society* (Bloomington: Indiana University Press, 1987).

11. Camille LaCoste-Dujardin explores the power of this relationship in *Des mères contre les femmes: Maternité et patriarcat au Maghreb* (Paris: Editions de la découverte, 1985).

12. Bendahman, *Personnalité maghrébine*, 222.

13. See Hildred Geertz, "The Meaning of Family Ties," in *Meaning and Order in Moroccan Society*, ed. Clifford Geertz, Hildred Geertz, and Lawrence Rosen (New York: Cambridge University Press, 1979), 330–31.

14. Zerdoumi, *Enfants d'hier*, 44.

15. See Dale Eickelman, *Moroccan Islam: Tradition and Society in a Pilgrimage Center* (Austin: University of Texas Press, 1976), 132–33.

16. Mohammed Kerrou, "La Mort au féminin," *Cahiers intersignes*, no. 2 (1991): 71–89.

17. Souad Khodja, *Les Algériennes du quotidien* (Algiers: Entreprise nationale du livre, 1985). See also Zerdoumi, *Enfants d'hier*, 38.

18. Mohamed Arkoun, "Préface: Les Tâches d'une pensée maghrébine," in *L'Individu au Maghreb: Actes du colloque international de Beit al-Hikma* (Tunis: Editions TS, 1993), xi–xx.

19. Gabriel Almond and Sidney Verba, *The Civic Culture: Political Attitudes and Democracy in Five Nations* (Boston: Little, Brown, 1965); Harry Eckstein, *Patterns of Authority* (New York: John Wiley and Sons, 1975).

20. Eickelman, *Moroccan Islam*, 123–54.

21. M. E. Combs-Schilling, *Sacred Performances: Islam, Sexuality, and Sacrifice* (New York: Columbia University Press, 223.

22. Sharabi, *Neopatriarchy*, 132.

23. Clement H. Moore, *Tunisia since Independence: The Dynamics of One-Party Government* (Berkeley and Los Angeles: University of California Press, 1965), 89. In the early years following independence, Bourguiba regularly in-

structed his countrymen about health and hygiene, decent housing, the importance of sports and exercise, and the desirability of a sedentary life (see ibid., 47).

24. Zerdoumi, *Enfants d'hier*, 166–67. See also Bendahman, *Personalité maghrébine*, 222.

25. Germaine Tillon, *The Republic of Cousins*, trans. Quintin Hoare (Thetford, Norfolk: Al Saqi Books, 1983). Positivist methodology dominates the social sciences, and cultural explanations of political phenomena that reach into the psyche are not heavily favored. Omitting them from analysis, however, obscures the potentially perverse impact of symbols and belief frameworks, which at times may overshadow physical reality. M. E. Combs-Schilling illustrates this point in an analysis of Moroccan first marriage rites by which men become the cultural usurpers of the natural birth process. She notes: "Culture has at its disposal a convincing mechanism for a great sleight of hand. Culture can make its elaborations appear true by embedding them within the body's most basic biological truths. . . . When a 'body politic' exists, it becomes difficult to bring the system of political domination to the level of self-conscious scrutiny without doing real damage to oneself, without bringing the system as a whole, internal and external, into question, for it is precisely the whole that is at stake. Embedding a system of domination within the male-female division of the world, and within the acts of human reproduction, is, to borrow from Bourdieu, "the best founded of collective illusions'" ("Etching Patriarchal Rule: Ritual Dye, Erotic Potency, and the Moroccan Monarchy," *Journal of the History of Sexuality* 1, no. 4 [1991]: 678–79).

26. See James C. Scott, *Weapons of the Weak* (New Haven: Yale University Press, 1985), and id. *Dominance and the Arts of Resistance* (New Haven: Yale University Press, 1990).

27. Sharabi, *Neopatriarchy*, 131. In the months following Tunisian Prime Minister Zine el Abidine Ben Ali's accession to power, journalists did not cloak their admiration for a head of state who appeared to work. See "Tunisie: Un Homme nouveau," *Jeune Afrique*, no. 1331 (7 July 1986).

28. Robert H. Jackson and Carl G. Rosberg, *Personal Rule in Black Africa: Prince, Autocrat, Prophet, Tyrant* (Berkeley and Los Angeles: University of California Press, 1982).

29. Cf. Joel Migdal, *Strong Societies and Weak States: State-Society Relations and State Capabilities in the Third World* (Princeton, N.J.: Princeton University Press, 1988).

30. See, e.g., Sophie Bessis and Souhayr Belhassen, *Femmes du Maghreb: L'enjeu* (France: J. Clattès, 1992), as well as Aziz Krichen, "La Fracture de l'intelligentsia: Problèmes de la langue et de la culture nationales," 326–27, and, more generally, Soukeïna Bouraoui, "Ordre masculin et fait féminin," 343–71, both in *Tunisie au présent: Une Modernité au-dessus de tout soupçon?* ed. Michel Camau (Paris: Editions du CNRS, 1987).

4. TUNISIA: STRONG STATE, STRONG SOCIETY

1. Moore, *Tunisia since Independence*, 41.

2. Clement H. Moore, "The Era of the Neo-Destour," in *Tunisia: The Politics of Modernization*, ed. Charles Micaud (New York: Praeger, 1964), 127.

3. Kenneth J. Perkins, *Tunisia: Crossroads of the Islamic and European Worlds* (Boulder, Colo.: Westview Press, 1986); Abdallah Laroui, *L'Histoire du Maghreb: Un Essai de synthèse* (Paris: François Maspero, 1982); Jamil M. Abun-Nasr, *A History of the Maghrib in the Islamic period* (New York: Cambridge University Press, 1987).

4. Perkins, *Tunisia*, pp. 63–67. Leon Carl Brown, *The Tunisia of Ahmad Bey, 1837–1855* (Princeton, N.J.: Princeton University Press). Also see Lisa Anderson, *The State and Social Transformation in Tunisia and Libya, 1830–1980* (Princeton, N.J.: Princeton University Press, 1986), and Lucette Valensi, *Tunisian Peasants in the Eighteenth and Nineteenth Centuries* (Cambridge: Cambridge University Press, 1985).

5. Brown, *Tunisia of Ahmad Bey*, 7 and 353–78.

6. Anderson, *State and Social Transformation*, 143–44.

7. Ibid., 146.

8. Private *habus* constituted 1.5 million hectares in 1956. Whereas the yields of public *habus* directly served religious or social purposes, *habus* set up as the indivisible property of private families continued to benefit their owners, reverting to the public domain only at the extinction of blood heirs. In practice, *habus* was one effective tool for denying women access to their share of inherited property.

An 1898 law made provision for the gradual transfer of public *habus* property to the State Domains administration for resale to colonists. Private *habus* was less vulnerable, but even there a provision of perpetual annuity known as *enzel* gave unscrupulous settlers a means of transforming *habus* lands into *mulk*. The state in some cases acquired tenancy through *enzel*, registered the lands, and resold them as *mulk* (private or freehold property) to settlers. See Leon Carl Brown, "Stages in the Process of Change," in *Tunisia: The Politics of Modernization*, ed. Charles A. Micaud (New York: Praeger, 1963). For a general treatment of the Maghribi system of land tenure, see John Ruedy, *Land Policy in Colonial Algeria* (Berkeley and Los Angeles: University of California Press, 1967), 1–12, and Valensi, *Tunisian Peasants*, 61–71.

9. Anderson, *State and Social Transformation*, 152–57. For a discussion of the traditional sharecropping contract (*khammasat*)—which was itself subject to exploitation—see Valensi, *Tunisian Peasants*, 107–9. While formally defined as an "associate," the *khammas* was in fact a hireling paid in kind from the produce of his harvest, and a beylical decree in 1874 had served further to reduce his limited freedoms—including the conditions under which the *khammas* could change occupation.

10. Beys were under pressure from both the nationalists and the French colonial rulers, and their political position became increasingly difficult during the final decades of the protectorate. Moncef Bey's nationalism was unacceptable to the French, and he was deposed on the pretext that he had collaborated with the Germans. His successor, Lamine Bey, was more conciliatory to the French, but on several occasions Neo-Destour leaders threatened to expose him for collaborating with the colonial overlords.

11. Both Bourguiba and Ben Youssef were among the Neo-Destour leaders arrested in April 1938 and subsequently interned in Marseille. Both were released by Axis forces in December 1942.

12. Sophie Bessis and Souhayr Belhassen, *Bourguiba*, vol. 1: *A la conquête d'un destin (1901–1957)* (Paris: Groupe Jeune Afrique, 1988), 120.

13. Ibid., 122–24.

14. Bourguiba had presented the Neo-Destour's seven-point program for independence in 1950. His banishment first to Remada and then to Galîte from January 1952 to May 1954, however, took him temporarily out of political circulation. When Mendès-France sought to open negotiations with Tunisia, Bouguiba was transferred to Brittany and made accessible to political figures in both France and Tunisia. (The Tunisian bey had effectively been stripped of both power and credibility and was never involved in independence talks.) Several Tunisians were included in the early talks, but according to Charles-André Julien, *Et la Tunisie devint indépendante* (Paris: Editions Jeune Afrique, 1985), 150–79, Bourguiba saved the negotiations at a critical moment by lending support to a process of incremental moves toward independence. In consequence, he was generally seen by the French as the only viable negotiator for the nationalists.

Ben Youssef had served in a national government headed by M'Hamed Chenik from 1950 to 1952, but according to Bessis and Belhassen (*Bourguiba*, 1: 162), he was not regarded favorably by the less nationalist Tunisians who served in the bey's cabinet from 1954 on. Ben Youssef was less willing than Bourguiba to negotiate with France, and in the French view, his association with Nasser and Ben Bella counted as additional liabilities.

15. See Moore, *Tunisia since Independence*, 69, and Dwight L. Ling *Tunisia: From Protectorate to Republic* (Bloomington: Indiana University Press, 1967), 177–81.

16. Bessis and Belhassen, *Bourguiba*, 1: 158–59. Public news of the decision was suppressed for several days, and Ben Youssef was apparently informed only on 13 October.

17. Norma Salem, *Habib Bouguiba: Islam and the Creation of Tunisia* (London: Croom Helm, 1984), 157. Tunis's total Tunisian population in 1956 numbered only 232,000.

18. Bessis and Belhassen, *Bourguiba*, 1: 159

19. Ibid., 170–71.

20. Ibid., 122–23.

21. Although voter participation nationwide was 84 percent, in Djerba more than two-thirds of the voters stayed home. Yet more significant, in the capital city, Youssefists contributed strongly to a 41 percent abstention rate (Moore, *Tunisia since Independence*, 74).

22. Ibid., 143–45.

23. Charles Debbasch, *La République tunisienne* (Paris: Librairie générale de droit et de jurisprudence, 1962), 44.

24. Tahar Belkhodja, for example, was a member of the PSD central committee and director of national security at the time of his arrest in 1968 for "abuse of power." He was released a few months later without trial. In 1973, he became minister of interior and accumulated considerable power until 1977, when at the apogee of his career he was removed as a political rival to the Tunisian embassy in West Germany. John Entelis, *Comparative Politics of North Africa* (Syracuse, N.Y.: Syracuse University Press, 1980), 169, presents a litany of many similar personnel

changes that illustrate the importance of personal considerations in political appointments.

25. As a member of the Tunis bourgeoisie, Wassila Ben Ammar was ready and able to wield her own power. Bessis and Belhassen trace her considerable involvement in several momentous political events, including the dismissal of Ahmed Ben Salah, the labor unrest of December 1977 and January 1978, efforts to unseat Prime Minister Hedi Nouira, electoral fraud in 1981, and the bread riots of 1983. Habib Bourguiba, they claim, was not duped by the machinations of his wife but instead generally appreciated them as an added element of complexity in the game he controlled. His decision in 1983 to retain Prime Minister Mohammed Mzali and fire Interior Minister Driss Guiga was, however, partly intended to stem her impressive power. See Sophie Bessis and Souhayr Belhassen, *Bourguiba*, vol. 2: *Un si long règne (1957–1989)* (Paris: Japress, 1989), 144, 202, and passim.

26. See "A quoi sert un premier ministre," *Jeune Afrique*, no. 1504 (30 October 1989).

27. Moore, *Tunisia since Independence*, 188–94.

28. Asma Larif Beatrix, "L'Etat tutélaire, système politique et espace éthique," in *Tunisie au présent: Une Modernité au-dessus de tout soupçon?* ed. Michel Camau (Paris: Editions du CNRS, 1987), 132.

29. *Le Monde*, 28 July 1990.

30. Bessis and Belhassen, *Bourguiba*, 1: 161.

31. According to Bessis and Belhassen, in 1954, Bourguiba issued formal orders to the Neo-Destour from his prison on Galîte to assassinate the bey's prime minister, Mohamed Salah Mzali (*Bourguiba*, 1: 142).

32. Harold Nelson, ed., *Tunisia: A Country Study*, U.S. Government Area Handbook Series (Washington, D.C.: Government Printing Office, 1987), 311.

33. "Tunisie: Un Homme nouveau," *Jeune Afrique*, no. 1331 (7 July 1986).

34. Amnesty International, *Tunisia: Summary of Amnesty International's Concerns* (London: AI Publications, 1990).

35. Moore, *Tunisia since Independence*, 80.

36. Ben Youssef served as minister of justice in the 1950 Chenik government. See Julien, *Et la Tunisie devint indépendante*, 27.

37. Keith Callard, "The Republic of Bourguiba," *International Journal* (1961), cited by Moore, *Tunisia since Independence*, 89.

38. *Le Maghreb*, 26 December 1981.

39. U.S. Department of State, *Country Reports on Human Rights Practices for 1990* (Washington, D.C.: Government Printing Office, 1991), 1661. See also Lawyers' Committee for Human Rights, *Critique: Review of the U.S. Department of State's Country Reports on Human Rights Practices for 1992* (New York: N. p., 1993), 386–87.

40. The incident is recounted more fully in Susan Waltz, "Clientelism and Reform," in *Political Economy of Reform in Tunisia*, ed. I. W. Zartman (Boulder, Colo.: Lynne Rienner), 40. In 1990, Tunisian lawyers observed a two-hour strike to protest interference with the practice of law and due process (*Le Monde*, 1 November 1990).

41. Moore, *Tunisia since Independence*, 80.

42. Bessis and Belhassen, *Bourguiba*, 1: 171.

43. Ling, *Tunisia*, 188.
44. See Clement H. Moore, *Politics in North Africa* (Boston: Little, Brown, 1970), 174–75, and Eqbal Ahmad, "Trade Unionism," in *State and Society in Independent North Africa*, ed. Leon Carl Brown (Washington, D.C.: Middle East Institute, 1966), 146–91.
45. "Mzali-syndicats: Le Bras de fer," *Jeune Afrique*, no. 1207 (22 February 1984).
46. *Cases of Trade Unionists Imprisoned in Tunisia* (London: AI Publications, 1986).
47. See Khalil Zamiti, "La Question syndicale: Contradictions sociales et manipulations politiques," in *Tunisie au Présent: Une Modernité au-dessus de tout soupçon?* ed. Michel Camau (Paris: Editions du CNRS, 1987), 287–96.
48. See *Africa Contemporary Record*, vols. 2–8 (New York: Holmes & Meier, 1969–76), for a detailed account of these events.
49. In an unconventional decision, Bourguiba allowed parties not yet approved to "try" themselves at the ballot boxes, with promises that parties showing more than 5 percent of the popular vote would be rewarded with recognition. The Tunisian Communist Party, however, was allowed to contest the elections as a formally recognized party, on the grounds that it had once been legal.
50. "La Fin de l'ère Mestiri?" *Réalités*, no. 377 (11 December 1992), and "Le Congrès de rupture," *Réalités*, no. 392 (2 April 1993).
51. The ban on the Tunisian Communist Party was lifted in 1981; and two left-wing parties, the Socialist Progressive Rally (RSP) and the Popular Unity Party (PUP), were recognized in 1988. Two other leftist parties, the "PUP2," led by Ben Salah, and the Tunisian Communist Workers' Party, remain unauthorized, as does the large Islamist party, al-Nahda.
52. See Anderson, *State and Social Transformation*, 249, and for a historical perspective, Clement H. Moore, "Politics in A Tunisian Village," *Middle East Journal* 17 (1963): 527–40.
53. See Lars Rudebeck, *Party and People: A Study of Political Change in Tunisia* (Stockholm: Almqvist & Wiksell, 1967).
54. Henri de Montety, "Old Families and New Elites in Tunisia," in *Man, State and Society in the Contemporary Maghrib*, ed. I. William Zartman (New York: Praeger, 1973), 176.
55. Abdelkader Zghal, "The New Strategy of the Movement of the Islamic Way: Manipulation or Expression of Political Culture?" in *The Political Economy of Reform*, ed. I. William Zartman (Boulder, Colo.: Lynne Rienner), 205–17. Also see Krichen, "La Fracture de l'intelligensia," in *Tunisie au présent*, 297–341.
56. See Elbaki Hermassi, "L'Etat tunisien et le mouvement islamiste," *Annuaire de l'Afrique du nord* 28 (1989): 297–308, and for background, Abdelkader Zghal, "Le Retour du sacré et la nouvelle demande idéologique des jeunes scolarisés" *Annuaire de l'Afrique du nord* 18 (1979): 41–64; and Mohammed Elbaki Hermassi, "La Société tunisienne au miroir islamiste," *Maghreb, Machrek*, no. 103 (Spring 1984): 39–56.
57. Several key figures, Ghannouchi among them, remained in exile.
58. I have argued this in "Islamist Appeal in Tunisia," *Middle East Journal* 40 (Autumn 1986): 651–70. See also Zghal, "New Strategy of the Movement of the

Islamic Way," and François Burgat and William Dowell, *The Islamic Movement in North Africa* (Austin, Tex.: Center for Middle Eastern Studies, 1993).
59. Migdal, *Strong Societies and Weak States*, 206–37.

5. STATE VERSUS SOCIETY IN ALGERIA

1. John Ruedy, *Modern Algeria: The Origins and Development of a Nation* (Bloomington: Indiana University Press, 1992), 41–42.
2. Abdallah Laroui, *L'Histoire du Maghreb* (Paris: François Maspero, 1982), 248.
3. There is some dispute about the appropriate characterization of this relationship, which some have identified as feudal. In *State and Revolution in Algeria* (Boulder, Colo.: Westview Press, 1986), Rachid Tlemçani argues against this claim on several grounds, but his own presentation of the communal nature of Algerian society is also open to interpretation. At least by 1871, local social harmony had been undermined. As Peter von Sivers notes, the difficulty some notables had in rousing peasant support for resistance suggests that differences in interest were widely perceived ("Rural Uprisings as Political Movements in Colonial Algeria, 1851–1914," in *Islam, Politics, and Social Movements*, ed. Edmund Burke III and Ira M. Lapidus [Berkeley and Los Angeles: University of California Press, 1988], 39–59).
4. Laroui, *L'Histoire du Maghreb*, 250; see also Tlemçani, *State and Revolution*, 29.
5. Ruedy, *Modern Algeria*, 46–48.
6. Laroui, *L'Histoire du Maghreb*, 277–78.
7. Ruedy, *Modern Algeria*, 55–57.
8. Laroui, *L'Histoire du Maghreb*, 279–81, and Ruedy, *Modern Algeria*, 59.
9. Tlemçani, *State and Revolution*, 34–37, and Laroui, *L'Histoire du Maghreb*, 280. See also René Gallisot, *Maghreb-Algérie: Classes et nation* (Paris: Arcantère, 1987), 1: 107–56.
10. Pierre Bourdieu, *The Algerians* (Boston: Beacon Press, 1962), 125–26.
11. Ibid., 139; Eric Wolf, *Peasant Wars of the Twentieth Century* (New York: Harper & Row, 1969), 214–17.
12. Bourdieu, *Algerians*, 139.
13. Elbaki Hermassi, *Leadership and National Development in North Africa* (Berkeley and Los Angeles: University of California Press, 1972), 136.
14. Ironically, Ahmad Pasha's concerted efforts in Tunisia to raise an army and implement fiscal reforms were partially inspired by the recent installation of the French in Algeria. With more time, Ruedy argues, an Algerian state apparatus might have emerged. Drawing on Vatin and others, he directs attention to several developments in the early nineteenth century. In addition to tribal or religious leaders who, like Abd-al-Qadir, controlled local political structures with potential for expansion, either of the two Ottoman offices of dey and bey might have provided the foundation for an eventual Algerian state. From 1817 to 1930, the office of dey was gradually being converted into a monarchy, and the beys of both Oran and Constantine were consolidating links with the local elites on whom they de-

pended to legitimize their authority. French colonization, of course, truncated such developments. See Ruedy, *Modern Algeria*, 32–37 and 42–44; Jean-Claude Vatin, *L'Algérie politique: Histoire et société* (Paris: Presses de la Fondation nationale des sciences politiques, 1983), 96–104.

15. Quoted by Alastair Horne, *A Savage War of Peace: Algeria, 1954–1962* (New York: Viking Press, 1977), 40.

16. William B. Quandt, *Revolution and Political Leadership: Algeria, 1954–1968* (Cambridge, Mass.: MIT Press, 1969), 25–42.

17. Hermassi, *Leadership and National Development*, 132.

18. Mohammed Harbi, *Le F.L.N.: Mirage et réalité* (Paris: Editions Jeune Afrique, 1980), 389.

19. Quandt, *Revolution and Political Leadership*, 92. The nine *chefs historiques* were Ahmed Ben Bella, Hocine Ait Ahmed, Mohammed Khider, Mohammed Boudiaf, Mustapha Ben Boulaid, Larbi Ben M'Hidi, Mourad Didouche, Rabab Bitat, and Belkacem Krim. Ben Boulaid, Ben M'Hidi, Didouche, Bitat, and Krim were *wilaya* leaders.

20. Tlemcani, *State and Revolution*, 62–63. Harbi, *Le F.L.N.*, 143–62.

21. Quandt, *Revolution and Political Leadership*, 134–38.

22. Provoking some controversy, Ben Khedda left the conference early, before any decision on the Political Bureau had been made. Ben Bella would later claim that the Political Bureau had been supported by a majority of the CNRA at Tripoli, but regardless, it was not invested by a formal vote of two-thirds majority as required by the CNRA statutes. Further undermining the Political Bureau's legitimacy, or at least its ability to perform, two of the proposed members (Mohamed Boudiaf and Hocine Ait Ahmed) refused to be part of it (Quandt, *Revolution and Political Leadership*, 165–67).

23. See, e.g., Mohammed Harbi, *Les Archives de la révolution algérienne* (Paris: Editions Jeune Afrique, 1981); id., *Le F.L.N.*; Quandt, *Revolution and Political Leadership*; Gallisot, *Maghreb-Algérie*;.

24. Quandt, *Revolution and Political Leadership*, 164.

25. Ramdane Redjala, *L'Opposition en Algérie depuis 1962* (Paris: Editions L'Harmattan, 1991), 45.

26. See Bourdieu, *Algerians*; LaCoste-Dujardin, *Des mères contre les femmes*.

27. See Moore, *Politics in North Africa*, 285.

28. An appendix to Harbi's *Le F.L.N.* lists many such noms de guerre and reveals how extensive the practice was. See also Benjamin Stora, *Dictionnaire biographique de militants nationalistes algériens* (Paris: Editions L'Harmattan, 1965). According to the journalist Hamza Kaïdi, even after Chadli Bendjedid became president, few knew that his given name was Khemaïs and Chadli a nom de guerre ("Chadli: Pouvoir, famille, et farniente . . . ," *Jeune Afrique*, no. 1622 [6–12 February 1992]).

29. Only four of the *chefs historiques* played active roles in the guerrilla war, and three of them died in the conflict (Ben Boulaid, Ben M'Hidi, and Didouche). The other five—including Ben Bella, Ait Ahmed, and Boudiaf—were arrested when their plane was intercepted by the French; they spent the entire war in French custody.

30. Jean Leca and Jean-Claude Vatin, *L'Algérie politique: Institutions et régime* (Paris: Presses de la Fondation nationale des sciences politiques, 1975), 393.

31. Quandt, *Revolution and Political Leadership*, 241–45.

32. Ibid., 246–51.

33. Cf. Zartman, "The Algerian Army in Politics," in *Man, State, and Society in North Africa*, ed. I. William Zartman (New York: Praeger, 1973), 211–24.

34. John P. Entelis, "Algeria: Technocratic Rule, Military Power," in *Political Elites in Arab North Africa*, ed. I. William Zartman (New York: Longman, 1982), 94.

35. "Les Petits pas de Chadli," *Jeune Afrique*, no. 1099 (27 January 1982).

36. "Qui tient la barre?" *Jeune Afrique*, no. 1345 (15 October 1986).

37. "A la tête de l'Algérie: Deux généraux et deux civils," *Jeune Afrique*, no. 1619 (16–23 January 1992), 8.

38. Soldiers were called in to reestablish order in Algiers in 1988, and in 1991 a protracted general strike initiated by Islamists ended in the imposition of martial law. Previously the army had preferred a position on the sidelines, "observing the process carefully, with a discreet but always present eye" (Entelis, "Algeria: Technocratic Rule, Military Power," 97).

39. David Ottaway and Marina Ottaway, *Algeria: The Politics of a Socialist Republic* (Berkeley and Los Angeles: University of California Press, 1970), 199.

40. I. William Zartman, "Algeria: A Post-Revolutionary Elite," in *Political Elites and Political Development in the Middle East*, ed. Frank Tachau (New York: Schenkman), cited by Entelis, "Algeria: Technocratic Rule, Military Power," 97.

41. All of these men were "rehabilitated" into the FLN posthumously in 1984, as were Belkacem Krim and Mohamed Khider (*Le Monde*, 25 October 1984). It is estimated that as many as one-half of the leaders who survived the war of liberation were subsequently murdered by instruments of the FLN in power (Khalid Duran, "The Second Battle of Algiers," *Orbis* 33 [Summer 1989], 413).

42. Moore, *Politics in North Africa*, 123–25.

43. Quandt, *Revolution and Political Leadership*, 195.

44. In an FFS memorandum written by Ali Mecili and reproduced in Redjala, *L'Opposition en Algérie*, 194–202, allegations are made of military responsibility for the assassination of Khider. According to Redjala, Mecili was a member of the military intelligence forces before joining the FFS. He later became an attorney and close associate of Hocine Ait Ahmed; he was assassinated in Paris in 1987. See Hocine Ait Ahmed, *L'Affaire Mecili* (Paris: Editions de la découverte, 1989). Harbi notes several victims of repression, listing the assassinations of Krim, Khider, and Cheikh Mesbah but also several "suicides" and "accidents" (Mohammed Harbi, "Sur les processus de relégitimation du pouvoir en Algérie," *Annuaire de l'Afrique du nord* 28 [1989], 134).

45. "Pas de condoléances pour la SM," *Jeune Afrique*, no. 1554 (10–16 October 1990). See also Redjala, *L'Opposition en Algérie*, 170.

46. "Pas de condoléances pour la SM." See also Harbi, "Sur les processus de relégitimation."

47. Harbi, "Sur les processus de relégitimation," 134.

48. The entry on Algeria in the U.S. State Department's 1990 *Country Reports on Human Rights Practices for 1990* notes: "In late 1990 the Government announced the abolition of the Algerian internal intelligence services, although this 'abolition' seems to represent a transfer of intelligence functions to other agencies rather than the end of governmental intelligence-gathering activity."

49. The *wilaya* of Kabylia was one of the last holdouts in the 1962 conflict, and FLN candidates from that region were among those excluded when electoral lists for the Constituent Assembly were revised.

50. See Redjala, *L'Opposition en Algérie*, 161.

51. Ait Ahmad was condemned to death in April 1965 but was subsequently pardoned by Ben Bella. Before the Boumediene coup, he escaped from prison and went into exile, returning to Algeria only in December 1989.

52. Redjala, *L'Opposition en Algérie*, pp 155–58.

53. These included the Organization of Popular Resistance and the Clandestine Organization of the Algerian Revolution. See Leca and Vatin, *L'Algérie politique*, 405–10.

54. "Faible et divisée: L'Opposition algérienne," *Jeune Afrique*, no. 1350 (19 November 1986).

55. Redjala, *L'Opposition en Algérie*, 164–67.

56. Ibid., 109.

57. Ibid., 128–32.

58. Ibid., 73, 171. From 1969 to 1975, democracy was not favored by the PRS (ibid., 109). See also Leca and Vatin, who note that Boudiaf's leadership within the PRS was commonly criticized for its authoritarian character and for the arbitrariness of decisions (*L'Algérie politique*, 403).

59. Ibid., 122.

60. Kasdi Merbah, for example, head of the SM from 1962 to 1979 and prime minister from 1962 to 1979, founded the Algerian Movement for Justice and Democracy. (He was assassinated in 1993.) In a separate effort Cherif Belkacem invited other figures prominent in the Boumediene era, including Abdel Aziz Bouteflika and Mohammed Salah Yahiaoui, to form a party.

61. World Bank, *World Development Report, 1988* (New York: Oxford University Press, 1988), 275, 281. By 1990, postsecondary education had reached 11 percent, and population had also grown, to 25 million (*World Development Report, 1992*).

62. Duran, "Second Battle of Algiers."

63. "Algeria: Sectarian Clashes," *Africa News*, 11 April 1983.

64. "Chadli face aux intégristes," *Jeune Afrique*, no. 1296 (6 November 1985).

65. Several of his lieutenants survived and after a brief imprisonment would again take up armed struggle. In 1991, Abdelkader Chebouti revived the Armed Islamic Movement, which in 1992 under his direction became the backbone of the Army of Islamic Salvation (AIS, the armed branch of the Islamic Salvation Front, FIS), while Mansouri Meliani led an armed group near Blida from 1989 until his capture in 1992 (he was executed in 1993).

66. Duran, "Second Battle of Algiers," 405.

67. "Que vont faire les islamistes de leur victoire?" *Jeune Afrique*, no. 1538 (20–26 June 1990).

68. Ibid.

69. "La Dernière croisade des islamistes algériens," *Jeune Afrique*, no. 1568 (16–22 January 1991).

70. Several hundred Algerian Islamists served alongside Afghani rebels after 1980, and many of them have advocated armed struggle against the government.

Four radical groups were said to have surfaced, or resurfaced, by the end of 1991. One such group attacked military barracks in Guemmar in late November 1991 and in April 1992 were condemned to death by hanging. Although the FIS had a "hard" wing that advocated open confrontation with the government, it was not an armed movement at the time of its dissolution in February 1992.

71. See, e.g., Benjamin Storer "Huit clés pour comprendre," *Jeune Afrique*, no. 1539 (22 June–3 July 1990).

72. See "L'Arroseur arrosé," *Jeune Afrique*, no. 1588 (5–11 June 1991). In Djendel, Bir Oulad Khelifa, and Ben Allal, FIS municipal governments had actually been displaced.

73. "Kidnappers Give Foreigners '1 Month' to Leave," FBIS-NES-93–212 (4 November 1993). The statement accompanied the release of three French hostages kidnapped by a group calling itself the Armed Islamic Group, Jama'a al-islamiyya al-mussallah.

6. MOROCCO: GOD AND KING

1. Robert H. Jackson and Carl G. Rosberg, "Why Africa's Weak States Persist: The Empirical and the Juridical in Statehood," *World Politics* 35 (October 1982): 1–24.

2. On the general connection between ritual and the construction of political relationships, see David L Kertzer, *Ritual, Politics and Power* (New Haven: Yale University Press, 1988).

3. These dynasties were the al-Murabitin (Almoravids: 1069–1147); the al-Muwahhidun (Almohads: 1147–1269), and the Banu Marin (Merinids: 1258–1420). Their successive empires spanned the length of Morocco and large parts of the Iberian Peninsula and stretched across the breadth of the Maghrib. Berber dynasts presided over a centralized state apparatus, developed an administrative corps, and promoted a celebrated educational and judicial system. Fez, home to Ibn-Khaldun and Ibn-Rushd (Averroës) was renowned as a center of learning, and the architecturally exquisite residential colleges surrounding the Qarawiyin (Kairouine) mosque were monuments to Islamic scholarship, as well as to the rulers who commissioned them.

4. Jamil M. Abun-Nasr, *A History of the Maghrib in the Islamic Period* (New York: Cambridge University Press, 1987), 208.

5. Ibid., 209.

6. Combs-Schilling, *Sacred Performances*, 157–74.

7. Ibid., 180.

8. See Jacques Berque, *Ulemas, fondateurs, et insurges du Maghreb* (Paris: Sindbad, 1982), 81, 122–23, 149.

9. Abun Nasr, *History of the Maghrib*, 227–30.

10. Berque, *Ulemas, fondateurs, et insurges*, 266–67.

11. Ibid., 235 and, more generally, 221–32.

12. Combs-Schilling, *Sacred Performances*, 249.

13. Ibid., 277, citing Charles-André Julien, *Le Maroc face aux impérialismes* (Paris: Editions Jeune Afrique, 1978), 90.

14. Clifford Geertz, *Islam Observed* (New Haven: Yale University Press, 1968), 81.

15. I. W. Zartman, "King Hassan's New Morocco," in *The Political Economy of Morocco*, ed. I. W. Zartman (New York: Praeger, 1987), 1–58.

16. Mark A. Tessler discusses this image of Morocco in "Image and Reality in the Moroccan Political Economy," in *Political Economy of Morocco*, ed. Zartman (cited in preceding note), 218–42.

17. Omar Bendourou treats the general relationship between monarch and parties in *Le Pouvoir exécutif au Maroc depuis l'indépendence* (Paris: Publisud, 1986).

18. These parties are often identified as the parliamentary opposition. They include the Istiqlal Party, the USFP, the OADP, the PPS, and the very small remnant of the UNFP.

19. Aherdane in turn formed a new party, the National Popular Movement, which won 14 of the 222 directly elected seats in the June 1993 parliamentary elections, as compared to the MP's 33.

20. In the first decade after independence, ministers from outside the royal coalition occasionally succceeded in depriving the king of a policy victory, but more commonly they got only enough rope to hang themselves. Unempowered, but seeming responsible to the electorate, many ultimately resigned. See I. William Zartman, *Morocco: Problems of New Power* (New York: Atherton Press, 1964), 208, and John Waterbury, *The Commander of the Faithful* (London: Weidenfeld & Nicholson, 1970), 218.

For concerns underlying more contemporary ministerial appointments, see Mustapha Sehimi, "Les Elites ministérielles au Maroc: Constantes et variables," in *Le Maroc actuel: Une Modernisation au miroir de la tradition?* ed. Jean-Claude Santucci (Paris: Editions du CNRS, 1992), 209–31.

21. Alain Claisse, "Le Makhzen aujourd'hui," in *Le Maroc Actuel*, ed. Santucci (cited in preceding note), 296.

22. Waterbury, *Commander of the Faithful*, 262–63.

23. Frank H. Braun, "Morocco: Anatomy of a Palace Revolution That Failed," *International Journal of Middle East Studies* 9, no. 1 (1978): 63–72, and John Damis, "The Moroccan Political Scene," *Middle East Journal* 26 (Winter 1972): 25–36.

24. Combs-Schilling, *Sacred Performances*, 306–9.

25. Constitutional changes allowed a greater proportion of parliamentary seats to be filled by direct election. Hassan II's disdain for parliament is well known; cf. Waterbury, *Commander of the Faithful*, 157. With a certain amount of arrogance, he has frequently reiterated the basic position. In a speech to parliament in 1978 cited by Mohamed Tozy, he claimed that at that point his role as Prince of the Faithful made him equally responsible for executive and legislative functions of government (Tozy, "Représentation / Intercession: Les Enjeux de pouvoir dans les 'champs politiques désamorcés' au Maroc," *Annuaire de l'Afrique du nord* 28 [1989]: 157). To European audiences he put it differently. It is generally recognized, he told French journalist Jean Daniel, that modernity requires the efficiency of a presidential regime ("Hassan II s'explique," *Le Nouvel Observateur*, 18 December 1989.) Also see Bendourou, *Le Pouvoir executif*.

26. Zartman, "King Hassan's New Morocco," in *Political Economy of Morocco*, ed. id., 6–18.

27. Waterbury, *Commander of the Faithful*, 220.

28. Max Weber, *Theory of Social and Economic Organization* (New York: Oxford University Press, 1947), 347; cited in Reinhart Bendix, *Max Weber: An Intellectual Portrait* (Garden City, N.Y.: Doubleday, 1962), 340.

29. In June 1991, plans to publish an exposé of Moroccan finances won Moumen Diouri expulsion from France to Gabon, under a little-used French legal procedure and despite earlier recognition of his status as a political refugee. Following public outcry, Diouri was returned to France a month later. The book was eventually published, and in it Diouri makes prominent note of Article 168 of the Moroccan Penal Code, forbidding investigation into the finances and private affairs of the king and the extended royal family (Moumen Diouri, *A qui apartient le Maroc?* [Paris: Editions L'Harmattan, 1992], 19).

30. Will D. Swearingen, *Moroccan Mirages: Agrarian Dreams and Deceptions, 1912–1986* (Princeton: University of Princeton Press, 1987).

31. Waterbury, *Commander of the Faithful*, 150.

32. See Tessler, "Image and Reality," and Gilles Perrault, *Notre ami le roi* (Paris: Gallimard, 1990).

33. In theory the constitutional reforms of 1992 altered this by giving the prime minister powers to appoint the ministerial cabinet, although the king retained power to appoint the prime minister. In practice, after the 1993 elections, Hassan II made direct offers of ministries to Kutla parties, apparently bypassing the prime minister.

34. The patronage system in Morocco has been extensively described. See John Waterbury, "Endemic and Planned Corruption in a Monarchical Regime," *World Politics* 25 (July 1973): 533–55, and Kenneth Brown, "Changing Forms of Patronage in a Moroccan City," in *Patrons and Clients in Mediterranean Societies*, ed. Ernest Gellner and John Waterbury (London: Duckworth, 1977), 309–27. Also see Alain Claisse, "Makhzen Traditions and Administrative Channels," in *The Political Economy of Morocco*, ed. I. W. Zartman (New York: Praeger, 1987), 51.

35. "Par-delà la fête royale," *Jeune Afrique*, no. 1380 (17 June 1987).

36. "Subventions pour l'opposition au Maroc," *Jeune Afrique*, no. 1357 (7 January 1987).

37. See Driss Basri, *L'Agent d'autorité: Mémoire du diplome d'études supérieures* (Rabat: Imprimerie royale, 1975), and interview with the labor leader Mohammed Noubi Amaoui, "On ne négocie pas avec le roi," *Jeune Afrique*, no 1566 (2–8 January 1991).

38. Claisse, "Makhzen Traditions," in *Political Economy of Morocco*, ed. Zartman, 54. The Ministry of the Interior has taken over an office of rural affairs from the Ministry of Housing, and since 1985 Driss Basri has also held the Ministry of Information porfolio.

39. Remy Leveau, *Le Fellah marocain, défenseur du trône* (Paris: Presses de la Fondation nationale de science politique, 1985), 54. Also see Claisse, "Le Makhzen aujourd'hui."

40. Harold Nelson, ed., *Morocco: A Country Study*, U.S. Government Area Handbook Series (Washington, D.C.: Government Printing Office, 1986), 357–69.

41. Many Moroccan Arabs, and in particular the urban elite, have historically viewed themselves as culturally superior to the Berbers, and in a society where

bonds of lineage are primordial, cultural identification may be strong. The importance of ethnic identity can easily be overstated in the Moroccan case, however, as numerous authors have argued. See, e.g., Dale F. Eickelman, *The Middle East: An Anthropological Approach* (Englewood Cliffs, N.J.: Prentice-Hall, 1990), 220; Ernest Gellner and Charles Micaud, *Arabs and Berbers: From Tribe to Nation in North Africa* (London: Lexington Books, 1972); and Lawrence Rosen, "The Social and Conceptual Framework of Arab-Berber Relations in Central Morocco," in *Meaning and Order in Moroccan Society*, ed. Clifford Geertz, Hildred Geertz, and Lawrence Rosen (New York: Cambridge University Press, 1979), 155–74.

42. Claisse, "Makhzen Traditions," in *Political Economy of Morocco*, ed. Zartman, 39.

43. "Moulay Ahmed Alaoui: Le Ministre anti-ministre," *Jeune Afrique*, no. 1417 (2 March 1988).

44. Ann Elizabeth Mayer, "Moroccans—Citizens or Subjects? A People at the Crossroads," *New York University Journal of International Law and Politics* 26 (Fall 1993): 63–105.

45. The March 23 Movement derived its name from the 1965 riots in Casablanca that resulted in the declaration of a state of emergency and suspension of the constitution.

46. The PPS claims to have about 40,000 members.

47. "Les 'Gauchistes' de Sa Majesté," *Jeune Afrique*, no. 1306 (15 January 1986), and "Un Parti pas commes les autres," *Jeune Afrique*, no. 1364 (26 February 1987).

48. Waterbury, *Commander of the Faithful*, 218–19.

49. Ibid., 295.

50. "Maroc: Les Révélations explosives du 'Fqih' Basri," *Jeune Afrique*, no. 1383 (8 July 1987).

51. See Amnesty International, *Amnesty International Briefing on Morocco* (Nottingham: Russell Press, 1977). There were eight major trials in July–August 1976 alone.

52. Perrault, *Notre ami le roi*, 153.

53. Ibid., 198–205, and Amnesty International, *Briefing*, 4.

54. Saïd Ihraï, *Pouvoir et influence: Etat, partis et politique étrangère au Maroc* (Rabat: Edino, 1986), 190–98.

55. USFP leaders publicly protested the king's endorsement of a proposal that emerged at the 1981 OAU summit in Nairobi, calling for a referendum on the disputed territory. They argued that the Sahara's link to Morocco was not debatable. Over the past ten years the Palace has approved a series of UN-negotiated terms, but without apparent enthusiasm. John Damis has discussed the Moroccan position in several articles, including most recently "The U. N. Settlement Plan for the Western Sahara: Problems and Prospects," *Middle East Policy* 1 (1992): 36–46." Also see "The Western Sahara: The Referendum Process in Danger. A Staff Report to the Committee on Foreign Relations of the United States Senate" (Washington, D.C.: Government Printing Office, 1992).

56. Lawyers' Committee for International Human Rights, "Morocco Briefing Memo" (photocopied, n.d. [c. 1984]), 51.

57. "On s'en sortirait créait son partie: Interview avec Mohamed Elyazghi," *Jeune Afrique,* no. 1728 (17–14 February 1994).

58. See "Les 'Gauchistes' de Sa Majesté."

59. "Le Procès des intégristes de Casablanca: Treize des soixante et onze accusés sont condamnés à mort," *Le Monde,* 2 August 1984.

60. "Le Procès des intégristes de Casablanca: Deux observateurs français protestent contre 'la disproportion du réquisitoire,'" *Le Monde,* 27 July 1984.

61. "Dix-neuf intégristes condamnés à perpétuité à Marrakech," *Jeune Afrique,* no. 1296 (6 November 1985). Enaamani led a group called "the Moudjahidin Movement" until his disappearance in September 1985. According to friends, he was "picked up" while living in France; followers of Muti claimed he was the victim of internal squabbles. Also see Henry Munson, Jr., "Morocco's Fundamentalists," *Government and Opposition* 26 (1991): 331–44.

62. "Le Temps de la clémence," *Jeune Afrique,* no. 1602 (11–17 September 1991).

63. Several arrests were made, but the security forces apparently did not intervene to stop the attacks. By contrast to the death sentences handed out to Islamists engaged in political protest in 1984, Islamists convicted of civil crimes resulting in death received penalities ranging from only six months to four years. See "23 Injured, 130 Arrested in University Clashes," FBIS-NES-91-211 (31 October 1991), and *La Lettre de l'ASDHOM,* no. 24 (20 November 1991).

64. Hassan II's own views on Islamism were made clear in an interview with Jean Daniel, "Je ne laisserai pas l'intégrisme déformer l'islam," *Le Nouvel Observateur,* 28 March–3 April 1986.

65. Amnesty International publications have covered these issues extensively. See the annual *Amnesty International Report* (London: AI Publications), 1978–92, as well as reports specific to Morocco: *Briefing on Morocco* (1977); *Report of an Amnesty International Mission to the Kingdom of Morocco* (1982); *Torture in Morocco* (1986); *Human Rights Violations in Garde-à-Vue Detention* (1990); *"Disappearances" of People of Western Saharan Origin and Submission to the United Nations Human Rights Committee* (1990); and *Morocco: A Pattern of Political Imprisonment, "Disappearances" and Torture* (1991).

66. Mustapha Sehimi, "Depuis un an . . . le Maroc," *Grand Maghreb,* no. 55 (2 February 1987): 45–46.

7. THE EMERGENCE OF A MAGHRIBI HUMAN RIGHTS MOVEMENT

1. Mohsen Toumi, *La Tunisie de Bourguiba à Ben Ali* (Paris: Presses universitaires de France, 1989), 102–6; 118–19, gives a less sympathetic account of the LTDH, which Toumi saw at its inception as the handmaiden of the MDS and the Tunis bourgeoisie.

2. See Bessis and Belhassen, *Bourguiba,* 2: 175.

3. See Dwyer, *Arab Voices,* 143, and Susan Waltz, "Tunisia's League and the Pursuit of Human Rights," *Maghreb Review* 14, nos. 3–4 (1989): 214–25.

4. See Dwyer, *Arab Voices,* 143–44, and "Interview: Khemais Chemmari," *Réalités,* no. 77 (2 August 1985).

5. "Mise en garde contre la Ligue des droits de l'homme," *Le Monde,* 12–13 April 1987.

6. Hamza Kaidi, "La Revendication berbère" *Jeune Afrique,* 30 April 1980.

7. See Salem Chaker, "Les Droits de l'homme, sont-ils mûrs en Algérie?" *Annuaire de l'Afrique du nord* 24 (1985): 489–503.

8. See Ramdane Bababji, "Le Phènomène associatif en Algérie: Génèse et perspectives," *Annuaire de l'Afrique du nord* 28 (1989): 239–41.

9. A third and more serious charge, that of conspiring against the security of the state, was dropped. See "The Imprisonment of Prisoners of Conscience in Algeria" (mimeo; London: AI Publications, August 1986).

10. Ibid.

11. U.S. Department of State, *Country Reports on Human Rights Practices for 1987* (Washington, D.C.: Government Printing Office, 1988), 1100.

12. Later Brahimi would grant several interviews to the Algerian press in which he relayed arrangements that had been made with the government. Authorization was granted speedily to Brahimi's group, and in response to those that questioned its political independence, Brahimi replied that the group's terms had been negotiated before formal recognition was sought. Bababji, "Le Phènomène associatif en Algérie."

13. See ibid., 240, and Brahim Brahimi, *Le Pouvoir: La Presse et les intellectuels en Algérie* (Paris: Editions L'Harmattan, 1989), 135–36.

14. Bababji, "Le Phènomène associatif en Algérie," 240.

15. "La Ligue des droits de l'homme fait le bilan de son action," *Le Monde,* 19 July 1988.

16. The Algerian press began to grow in 1985, with the FLN adding a French-language newspaper and several regional papers appearing. As chronicled by Brahim Brahimi, however, prior to 1987, debates within the press were largely confined to disputes between "the government" and "the party." He credits not simply the 1987 conference but the general emergence of concern about human rights with freeing the press. See Brahimi, *Le Pouvoir,* 130–37.

17. Much of this discussion was previously published in Susan Waltz, "Making Waves: The Political Impact of Human Rights Groups in North Africa," *Journal of Modern African Studies* 29, no. 3 (1991): 481–504. Also see Ahmed Ben Othman, "Les Organisations non-gouvernementales: Maroc," *Les Cahiers de l'Orient* 20 (October 1990): 231–35.

18. In Europe, the Comité de lutte contre la répression au Maroc had been founded by the French wife of one of these prisoners, Abraham Serfaty. Some of the AMDH's early communiqués involved these prisoners and their families.

19. Lawyers' Committee for Human Rights, "Morocco Briefing Memo" (photocopied, n.d.), 89.

20. See "Communiqué de l'Association marocaine des droits de l'homme au Maroc concernant l'arrestation de Maître Abderrahmane Ben Ameur, membre du Bureau central et celle de membres des familles de détenus politiques" (Rabat, 12 December 1980), and *Le Monde,* 25 July 1981.

21. OMDH, "Rapport de la Commission préparatoire" (mimeographed, 10 December 1988), 4–5.

22. Ibid., 5.

23. OMDH, Commission préparatoire, "Une Nouvelle Association des droits de l'homme: Pourquoi et comment?" (mimeographed, n.d.), 3–4.

24. Morocco has signed and ratified the International Covenant on Civil and Political Rights and the International Covenant on Economic, Social and Cultural Rights. In 1993 it ratified the Convention against Torture and Other Cruel, Inhuman and Degrading Treatment or Punishment, with the proviso on Article 28 that it does not recognize the competence of the Committee against Torture to carry out investigations.

25. OMDH, "Une Nouvelle Association," 4.

26. OMDH, "Rapport de la Commission préparatoire," 6.

27. *Le Monde*, 1 June 1988. The government later clarified this objection; more than a decade earlier, the government had made charges against one individual, but these were dropped in 1976; the other individual had been pardoned in 1980 (*Le Monde*, 27 July 1988).

28. *Le Monde*, 5 October 1988.

29. OMDH, "Déclaration à l'occasion du 100ième jour de l'organisation" (mimeographed, 20 March 1989).

30. *Le Monde*, 28 March 1989.

31. This incident is recounted more fully in Waltz, "Making Waves."

32. Jill Crystal, "The Human Rights Movement in the Arab World" (paper presented to the American Political Science Association, San Francisco, 1990).

33. Amnesty International's rule preventing national groups from addressing violations in their own country puts these groups beyond the scope of this book.

8. CHALLENGING THE POLITICAL ORDER

1. Robert Wuthnow explores these ideas in *Meaning and Moral Order: Explorations in Cultural Analysis* (Berkeley and Los Angeles: University of California Press, 1987), 155–56.

2. Ibid., 159.

3. Burgat, *Islamic Movement in North Africa*, 183. Also see the autobiographical accounts of Rached Ghannouchi and Tareq al-Bishri reproduced in ibid, 53–62 and 49–53 respectively.

4. Some groups within the Islamist movement fall outside this characterization, locating the central problem in the believers. As a result, such groups are less politicized. See Douglas K. Magnuson, "Islamic Reform in Contemporary Tunisia: Unity and Diversity," in *The Political Economy of Reform*, ed. I. William Zartman (Boulder, Colo.: Lynne Rienner), 169–92.

5. Scholarly work on the politics of human rights commonly differentiates between the activities of promotion, implementation, and enforcement. Of the three, promotion regimes require the weakest degree of commitment. See Donnelly, "International Human Rights," 603–5, and Forsythe, *Internationalization of Human Rights*, 57–58.

6. See "Présentation du dossier de presse relatif aux prisonniers politiques," in OMDH, *L'Organisation marocaine des droits de l'homme à travers ses communiqués et déclarations* (Casablanca: Imprimerie Editions maghrébines, 1991), 67–68.

7. William A. Gamson, "The Social Psychology of Collective Action," in *Frontiers in Social Movement Theory*, ed. Aldon D. Morris and Carol McClurg Mueller (New Haven: Yale University Press, 1992), 68.

8. John D. McCarthy and Mayer Zald, "Resource Mobilization and Social Movements: A Partial Theory," *American Journal of Sociology* 82, no. 6 (1977): 1212–41; Bert Klandermans, "Mobilization and Participation: Social-Psychological Expansions of Resource Mobilization Theory," *American Sociological Review* 49 (October 1984): 583–600; and Jean L. Cohen, "Strategy or Identity: New Theoretical Paradigms and Contemporary Social Movements," *Social Research* 52 (Winter 1985): 663–716.

9. Carol McClurg Mueller, "Building Social Movement Theory," in *Frontiers in Social Movement Theory*, ed. Aldon D. Morris and Carol McClurg Mueller (New Haven: Yale University Press, 1992), 17, and Claus Offe, "New Social Movements: Challenging the Boundaries of Institutional Politics," *Social Research* 52 (Winter 1985): 839–56.

10. Susan Eckstein, "Power and Popular Protest in Latin America," in *Power and Popular Protest: Latin American Social Movements*, ed. Susan Eckstein (Berkeley and Los Angeles: University of California Press, 1989), and Gamson, "Social Psychology of Collective Action," 61.

11. David Snow, E. Burke Rochford, Steven K. Worden, and Robert D. Benford, "Frame Alignment Processes, Micromobilization, and Movement Participation," *American Sociological Review* 51 (August 1986): 464–81.

12. Sidney Tarrow, "Mentalities, Political Cultures, and Collective Action Frames: Constructing Meanings through Action," in *Frontiers in Social Movement Theory*, ed. Aldon D. Morris and Carol McClurg Mueller (New Haven: Yale University Press, 1992), 189.

13. David A. Snow and Robert D. Benford, "Master Frames and Cycles of Protest," in *Frontiers in Social Movement Theory*, ed. Aldon D. Morris and Carol McClurg Mueller (New Haven: Yale University Press, 1992), 144.

14. Eckstein, "Power and Protest," 39.

15. David Laitin, "Political Culture and Political Preferences," *American Political Science Review* 82, no. 2 (1988): 589–93, has argued that opposition traditions as well as traditions lending support to the regime in power must be included in consideration of political culture.

16. Wuthnow, *Meaning and Moral Order*, 198–99.

17. Ibid.

18. Susan Waltz, "Clientelism and Reform in Ben Ali's Tunisia," in *Political Economy of Reform in Tunisia*, ed. I. W. Zartman (Boulder, Colo.: Lynne Rienner), 31–33. Also see Michel Camau, "Tunisie au présent: Une Modernité au-dessus de tout soupçon?" in *Tunisie au présent: Une Modernité au-dessus de tout soupçon?* ed. id. (Paris: Editions du CNRS, 1987), 11–49.

19. Erving Goffman, *Frame Analysis* (Cambridge, Mass.: Harvard University Press, 1974); also see Snow et al., "Frame Alignment Processes."

20. From at least 1980 to 1993, Hadj Mohamed Mustafa Tabet, *commissaire principal de police*, had raped literally hundreds of Moroccan women, some of them minors, and had kept extensive videotaped records. Questions were raised about inproprieties in 1980, but the victim committed suicide and the story was sup-

pressed. Tabet was transferred to headquarters of the Sûreté nationale in Rabat, where his career continued to advance. In 1985 he was made chief police superintendent of a Casablanca prefecture, one of the four largest in the country. A complaint of rape was lodged in 1990 but was suppressed. In 1993, however, the story could not be contained. Tabet was swiftly tried; he was sentenced to death and executed in August. See "Sexe, pouvoir et vidéo," *Jeune Afrique*, no. 1681 (25–31 March 1993).

21. See the annual *Amnesty International Report*, 1981–84.

22. Mueller, "Building Social Movement Theory," 15.

23. Ligue tunisienne pour la défense des droits de l'homme (LTDH), *Premier congrès national, Tunis, 14 février 1982* (Tunis: Maghreb-Editions), 14.

24. Ligue tunisienne pour la défense des droits de l'homme, "2ᵉ Σ= congrès national, Amilcar, 23–24 Mars 1985. Rapport Moral" (photocopied), 4.

25. *L'OMDH à travers ses communiqués*, 88, 110.

26. The FIDH, like most other human rights groups, has maintained neutrality on the Western Sahara, occasionally referring to a right of self-determination. See Hurst Hannum, *Autonomy, Sovereignty, and Self-Determination* (Philadelphia: University of Pennsylvania Press, 1990).

27. From August 1990 to May 1991, nine of the LTDH's thirteen communiques addressed some aspect of the Gulf conflict.

28. Following the onset of protests in September, the league issued a communique expressing concern about reports of political brutality, arrests, and illegal searches, and in December, an LTDH delegation visited the minister of interior to discuss these concerns. In general, however, concern over the Gulf greatly overshadowed domestic issues.

29. "Conférence internationale sur les droits des Palestinéens: Le coup de la ligue," *Réalités*, no. 319 (18–24 October 1991).

30. Albert O. Hirshman, *Getting Ahead Collectively: Grassroots Experiences in Latin America* (New York: Pergamon Press, 1984).

9. HUMAN RIGHTS AND POLITICAL DISCOURSE

1. Tunisia and Algeria both acceded to the covenants in 1968. Morocco signed the treaties in 1977, ratifying them in 1979.

2. In 1983 the member from Tunisia led efforts to put pressure on Zaire, Forsythe notes (*Internationalization of Human Rights*, 64).

3. Theda Skocpol, "Bringing the State Back In: Strategies of Analysis in Current Research," in *Bringing the State Back In*, ed. Peter B. Evans, Dietrich Rueschemeyer, and Theda Skocpol (New York: Cambridge University Press, 1985), 3–37, and esp. 20–21.

4. It is important to recognize here that relinquishing arbitrary powers does not necessarily and automatically result in a net loss of power for the state (see A. Stepan, "State Power and the Strength of Civil Society," in *Bringing the State Back In*, 317–43). Raw force constitutes only one of the state's several bases of power and by curtailing political repression, states can arguably increase their popular support. Arbitrary powers that translate into repression nevertheless remain an

important source of control and the patrimonial regimes of North Africa relied heavily on their use (see Chapters 2–5).

5. "Hassan Speech on Human Rights Council Creation," FBIS-NES-90–091 (10 May 1990).

6. See Khalil Zamiti, "La Société tunisienne: Absolutisme et démocratie après la déposition du 'president à vie,'" *Peuples méditérranéens*, no. 47 (1989): 125–35.

7. See Article 19, *The Press in Tunisia: Plus ça change* (London: International Centre against Censorship, 1993).

8. An open letter widely circulated in April 1990 is reproduced in *Annuaire de l'Afrique du nord* 29 (1990): 804–9.

9. The League's communiques circulated freely at this time, and they elicited government response. See "La Guerre des communiqués," *Le Maghreb*, no. 198 (20 April 1990); "Des vagues qui s'apaisent," *Réalités*, no. 224 (26 April 1990); and "Interior Ministry Rebuts the League," FBIS-NES-90–073 (16 April 1990).

10. See "Reportage on President Ben Ali's U.S. Visit," FBIS-NES-90–097 (18 May 1990); "Ben Ali Interviewed on Results of U.S. Visit," FBIS-NES-90–101 (24 May 1990); and "Bush Meets with Leader of Tunisia," *Washington Post*, 16 May 1990.

11. "Ben Ali: Le Discours des quatre ruptures," *Réalités*, no. 260 (17–23 August 1990), 15.

12. Habib Boulares, then minister of foreign affairs, had a few years earlier authored a book on the dangers of militant Islam, *L'Islam: La Peur et l'espérance* (Paris: J-C Lattes, 1983).

13. According to Amnesty International, more than five hundred people were arrested in this manner from September 1990 to March 1991. "Tunisia: Update on AI Concerns" (Amnesty International, MDE 30/11/91 [15 March 1991]). Also see Zakya Daoud, "Chronique tunisienne," *Annuaire de l'Afrique du nord* 29 (1990): 794–95.

14. Not surprisingly, the Tunisian government was quick to broadcast Ghannouchi's words, and its Washington news bureau did so in a new publication, *Issue Brief*. See "The Failed Tactics of Religious Extremism in Tunisia," *Issue Brief* 1, no. 1 (June 1991): 4.

15. In less than six months, their cases were heard and appealed to two higher courts. Irregularities abounded in each of the hearings—perhaps most egregiously in the appeals court's statement that two of those allegedly involved had confessed to the crime, when in fact they remained fugitive and had been tried *in absentia*. The Supreme Court was apparently not troubled by such irregularities, and in fact, increased sentences from life to capital punishment when it issued its decision in July. The three defendants in custody were executed in October.

16. The stakes were raised even higher in this case when in September 1991 the government claimed that Islamists had procured a Stinger missile intended for use in assassinating Ben Ali and overthrowing the government. Even absent that claim, however, evidence to support government charges is subject to dispute: on display at an eventual trial were only a collection of guns, hand-made grenades, and miscellaneous office equipment, exhibits that in fact were never cited in the proceedings (Amnesty International, *Tunisia: Heavy Sentences after Unfair Trials,*

AI MDE 30/23/92 [October 1992]). The Stinger missile was apparently not produced as evidence (see Lawyers' Committee for Human Rights, *The Mass Trial of Islamists before Military Courts in Tunisia* [21 August 1992], and Human Rights Watch, *Military Courts That Sentenced Islamist Leaders Violated Basic Fair-Trial Norms* [October 1992]).

17. In general, the LTDH addressed its admonitions to all parties, although many of its complaints were made on the direct behalf of al-Nahda members. On 5 October 1989, however, it issued a stern rebuttal to a statement of political position published by al-Nahda three days earlier. Specifically, the league made clear its objection to validating the notion of heresy, to narrowly defining the concept of *umma* (community), and to the general attempted monopolization of Islam by al-Nahda.

18. *La Presse,* 19 February 1991.

19. "Ben Ali Praises Progress in Human Rights," FBIS-NES-91–069 (10 April 1991). Also see Daoud, "Chronique tunisienne," 794.

20. From 1989 to 1990, the size of the Public Order Brigade alone increased from 2,000 to 3,500 (International Institute of Strategic Studies, *Military Balance, 1988–1989* and *Military Balance, 1989–1990* (London: Brassey's, 1989 and 1990).

21. LTDH, "Communique," 14 June 1991. The thread of this developing conflict may be traced through LTDH communiques dated 18 May, 14 June, 29 June, and 26 July, as well as in "Les Droits de l'homme en Tunisie," *Réalités,* no. 304 (28 June–4 July 1991). Also see "Ben Ali Praises Progress in Human Rights," FBIS-NES-91–069 (10 April 1991), and "Ben Ali Chairs Meeting on Rights Violations," FBIS-NES-91–121 (24 June 1991).

22. These included Hassib Ben Ammar, president of the Arab Institute of Human Rights, and Mahmoud Ben Romdhane, from the Tunisian section of Amnesty International. See "Les Droits de l'homme en Tunisie," 7, and "Ben Ali Chairs Meeting on Rights Violations.".

23. "Des agissements individuels ont provoque des abus," *Le Temps* (Tunis), 10 October 1991. See also Lawyers' Committee for Human Rights, *Promise Unfulfilled: Human Rights in Tunisia Since 1987* (New York, 1993), 40–47.

24. Amnesty International, *Prolonged Incommunicado Detention and Torture,* MDE 30/04/92 (4 March 1992); Government of Tunisia, "Truth About Human Rights in Tunisia: A Response to Amnesty International" (photocopied, n.d.); Amnesty International, *Tunisia: Amnesty International Welcomes Cooperation, Responds to Government Inaccuracies,* MDE 30/WU 02/92 (2 April 1992).

25. Higher Committee for Human Rights and Basic Freedoms, *Report to the President of the Republic on the Implementation of the Recommendations of the Commission of Enquiry* (Tunis: Republic of Tunisia, 1992). The report did not enjoy full credibility. Despite eyewitness accounts and an independent autopsy attributing one death to beating and torture, the second Driss Report maintained that the victim had died in a traffic accident (U.S. Department of State, *Country Reports on Human Rights Practices for 1992* (Washington, D.C.: Government Printing Office, 1993), 1096.

26. U.S. Department of State, *Country Reports on Human Rights Practices for 1991* (Washington, D.C.: Government Printing Office, 1992).

27. Republic of Tunisia, "The Military Court Examines the Case of the Plot against Internal State Security," and "The Guarantees for Those to Be Tried in Military Courts in Tunisia" (Tunis, photocopied, n.d.).

28. "La LTDH en équilibrise," *Réalités*, no. 321 (1–7 November 1991), 5.

29. "Polémique entre le gouvernment et la Ligue des droits de l'homme," *Le Monde*, 18 December 1991.

30. "Précision," *Réalités*, no. 335 (14 February 1992), 10.

31. See Saloua Ben Youssef-Charfi, "La Ligue tunisienne pour la défense des droits de l'homme" (mémoire pour la Diplôme d'études approfondies des sciences politiques, Université de Tunis, Faculté de droit et des sciences politiques, June 1987), 277–82. An exchange of letters between Interior Minister Ben Ali and the LTDH is published as Annexes X and XI.

32. "Bataille autour d'une réforme," *Réalités*, no. 341 (27 March 1992), 12.

33. Arab Organization for Human Rights, *Newsletter*, 8 May 1987.

34. See U.S. Department of State, *Country Reports on Human Rights Practices for 1989* (Washington, D.C.: Government Printing Office, 1990), and *Country Reports on Human Rights Practices for 1990* (Washington, D.C.: Government Printing Office, 1991).

35. Amnesty International, "Algeria: Deteriorating Human Rights under the State of Emergency," MDE 29/04/93 (March 1993).

36. Haroun was initially appointed as minister delegate for human rights, but in October 1991 the position was given full cabinet status and he became minister of human rights.

37. *Foreign Broadcast Information Service*, 17 January 1992, quoted in *Human Rights in Algeria since the Halt of the Electoral Process* (New York: Middle East Watch, 1992).

38. *Algeria: Deteriorating Human Rights under State of Emergency*, MDE 28/04/93 (London: AI Publications, 1993).

39. News item, Agence France Presse wire service, 6 June 1992; "Human Rights Watchdog Group Condemns Excesses," FBIS-NES-93–023 (5 February 1993).

40. "Les Conditions de détention dans le camp d'Ouargla sont 'extrêmement mauvaises,'" *Le Monde*, 11 March 1992.

41. "Les Médias reprochent au pouvoir de vouloir les domestiquer," *Le Monde*, 19 March 1992.

42. News item, Agence France Presse wire service, 2 June 1992.

43. "Thousands Participate in Marches against Terrorism," FBIS-NES-93–055 (24 March 1993).

44. "Hassan Speech on Human Rights Council Creation," FBIS-NES-90–091 (10 May 1990).

45. Among these were many individuals whose integrity was recognized and respected; questions were raised about the role of others, including Minister of Interior Driss Basri and Ahmed Afazaz, who was the presiding judge in the 1977 political trial in Casablanca.

46. "Discours historique de sa majesté le roi Hassan II à l'occasion de l'installation du Conseil consultatif des droits de l'homme, 8 May 1990" in *Conseil consultatif des droits de l'homme* (Rabat: Royaume du Maroc, 1992), 14.

47. Amnesty International, *Morocco: Continuing Human Rights Violations*,

MDE-29/06/92 (October 1992). In one of these cases, the Moroccan government conducted an inquiry and charged two police officers with assault.

48. See "Memorandum adressé à la haute attention de sa majesté le roi Hassan II," in *Conseil consultatif des droits de l'homme,* 83; and "Council for Human Rights Outlines 1993 Program," FBIS-NES-93–035 (24 February 1993).

49. Their communique was then circulated by the Istiqlal Party paper *L'Opinion.* See "Un Memorandum demande la 'suspension immédiate' des procès,'" *Le Monde,* 2 January 1991, and "Human Rights Council Urges Suspension of Trials," FBIS-NES-91–001 (2 January 1991).

50. "Discours historique," 15–16.

51. Article 19, *The Press in Tunisia: Plus ça change.*

10. THE INTERNATIONAL DIMENSION

1. See Packenham, *Liberal America,* and, more recently, Lowenthal, *Exporting Democracy.*

2. Rosenau, *Turbulence in World Politics.*

3. This was true not only of North African exiles but of Latin Americans as well. See Iain Guest, *Behind the Disappearances* (Philadelphia: University of Pennsylvania Press, 1990), 63, 67.

4. Redjala, *L'Opposition en Algérie.*

5. Watch Committee reports on the Maghrib were limited until the formation of Middle East Watch in 1990, but prior to that Maghribi countries were treated in the Watch Committees' more general reports. Following a mission in 1984, the Lawyers' Committee for Human Rights prepared a report entitled "Morocco Briefing" (photocopied, n.d. [c. 1984]), and a second one in 1990 entitled *Cleaning the Face of Morocco: Human Rights Abuses and Recent Developments.* A report on Tunisia, *Promise Unfulfilled: Human Rights in Tunisia since 1987,* was released in 1993.

6. An exception is Henry J. Steiner, *Diverse Partners: Non-Governmental Organizations in the Human Rights Movement. The Report of a Retreat of Human Rights Activists* (Cambridge, Mass.: Harvard Law School Human Rights Program and Human Rights Internet, 1991).

7. Association internationale des juristes démocrates and International Association of Democratic Lawyers, *La Faim pour la justice* (Leiden, Netherlands: 1989).

8. "Tunis Expels Reporter over Rights Story," *San Francisco Chronicle,* 12 April 1991.

9. Schoultz, *Human Rights and United States Policy toward Latin America.* See also Kathryn Sikkink, "The Power of Principled Ideas: Human Rights Policies in the United States and Western Europe," in *Ideas and Foreign Policy: Beliefs, Instituions, and Political Change,* ed. Judith Goldstein and Robert O. Keohane (Ithaca, N.Y.: Cornell University Press, 1993), 139–70.

10. *Tunisia Digest,* a newsletter published intermittently by the Tunisian Information Office in Washington, D. C., for example, regularly prints news items concerning official promotion of human rights or rights-related activities.

11. In 1965, for example, William Coplin predicted that neither regional nor

international organizations would effectively challenge the assumptions of sovereignty embedded in the state system ("International Law and Assumptions about the State System," *World Politics* 17 [July 1965]: 615–35). Forsythe offers argument and evidence to show shortsightedness in these predictions (*Internationalization of Human Rights*, 33–48).

12. Farrokh Jhabvala, "The Practice of the Covenant's Human Rights Committee, 1976–82: Review of State Party Reports," *Human Rights Quarterly* 6 (February 1984): 81–106.

13. See Robert Mortimer, "Maghreb Matters," *Foreign Policy* 76 (Fall 1989): 160–75, and Ahmed Aghrout and Keith Sutton, "Regional Economic Union in the Maghreb," *Journal of Modern African Studies* 28, no. 1 (1990): 115–30.

14. Participating groups dismissed that concern as the FIDH's fear of seeing its own influence eclipsed in the region.

15. Quoted by Jacques de Barrin, "Royal Privilege and Human Rights," *Manchester Guardian*, 18 December 1990.

16. U.S. Congress, House, Committee on Foreign Affairs, *Arms for Morocco: U.S. Policy Toward the Conflict in the Western Sahara. Report of a Study Mission to Morocco, the Western Sahara, Mauritania, Algeria, Liberia, Spain and France, Aug. 5–18, 1979* (Washington, D.C.: Government Printing Office, 1979).

17. "Peuvent-ils s'entendre?" *Jeune Afrique*, no. 1101 (10 February 1982).

18. "Morocco Emerging as Closest Arab Ally," *New York Times*, 1 February 1983.

19. Lawyers' Committee for Human Rights, "Morocco Briefing Paper," 5. Shortly after presenting his credentials in November 1981, Reed declared, "The leadership of the Reagan Administration has stated that your country's concerns are my country's concerns. The United States will do its best to be helpful in every area of need that may arise. Count on us. We are with you." See "King Hassan Moves against His Foes," *New York Times*, 19 November 1981.

20. "Chronique d'une crise annoncée et contenue," *Jeune Afrique*, no. 1560 (21–27 November 1990).

21. *Africa Research Bulletin*, 15 August 1987.

22. Resolution B2–1128, 1136 and 1145/88, passed 15 December 1988.

23. "Le Maroc du silence" *Le Monde diplomatique*, December 1988.

24. *Le Monde* published at least seventeen articles directly relating to the OMDH and its concerns over a 15-month period spanning 1988 and 1989.

25. "L'Organisation des droits de l'homme s'inquiète du sort de grévistes de la faim," *Le Monde*, 17 June 1989.

26. U.S. Congress, Senate, *Foreign Operations, Export Financing, and Related Programs Appropriations Bill*, report 101–131 (18 September 1989), 47–48.

27. AI, press release, "Morocco: Amnesty International Welcomes King's Invitation," MDE 40/WU 01/90 (5 January 1990).

28. *Amnesty International Report, 1991*, 161.

29. J.-C. Santucci and M. Benhlal, "Chronique marocaine," *Annuaire de l'Afrique du nord* 29 (1990): 716. The Moroccan government also prepared, and circulated widely, a document entitled "Réponses au points soulevés par Amnesty International" (photocopied, n.d.). Inter alia, it included copies of instructions circulated to local authorities on penal legislation and *une fiche réfutant la notion de 'détenus*

politiques' que ne cesse d'évoquer Amnesty International ("a file refuting the notion of 'political detainees' incessantly raised by Amnesty International").

As a nonstate actor, AI apparently did not see its voice muffled by "dialogue" with the Moroccan government. The Moroccans, however, were outraged that the organization had published a report drafted before the first meeting without making any changes (*Human Rights in Garde-à-Vue Detention*, MDE/29/01/90 [20 February 1990]). AI argued that its concerns had not been addressed, and that no changes were in order. See "Expulsion de deux représentants d'Amnesty International," *Le Monde* 17 March 1990; "Statement on Expulsion of Amnesty Representatives," released by the Moroccan Press Agency (MAP) and printed in FBIS-NES-90–053 (19 March 1990); and Amnesty International press release, "Moroccan Government Orders Amnesty International Delegates to Leave" (16 March 1990).

30. Santucci and Benhlal, "Chronique marocaine," 718.

31. *Jeune Afrique*, in a rare critical piece on Morocco, ran a 6-page cover story on the human rights angle of the exposition, citing Jobert's admonitions. The glossy cover of the 16 April 1990 edition showed a document stamped "Amnesty International" and emblazoned with the headline "Droits de l'homme: Maroc sous haute surveillance" (*Jeune Afrique*, 16 April 1990). The "Temps du Maroc" exhibition was cancelled by Morocco in October 1990 following publication of Gille Perrault's *Notre ami le roi*, which squelched any hopes of containing criticisms of the monarchy's human rights abuses.

32. "Une affaire de trop?" *Jeune Afrique*, no. 1558 (November 1990); "Culture, droits de l'homme et irritation royale" *Le Monde*, 12 September 1990; and "Rabat-Paris: Les Raisons d'une crise," *L'Express*, 16 November 1990.

33. "Morocco Seeks Ban on Perrault Book," FBIS-WEU-90–216 (7 November 1990).

34. "Rabat-Paris: Les Raisons d'une crise."

35. "Le Gouvernement français appelle Rabat au respect des droits de l'homme," *Le Monde*, 21 December 1990.

36. OMDH, *Observations de l'Organisation marocaine des droits de l'homme au sujet du rapport gouvernemental au Comité des droits de l'homme des Nations-Unis* (Rabat: Editions maghrébines, 1990), 87.

37. "Human Rights Committee Begins Consideration of Report from Morocco" and "Human Rights Committee Will Pursue at Later Session Its Consideration of Report from Morocco" (UN press releases HR/2673 [7 November 1990] and HR/2674 [8 November 1990]).

38. "La Délégation marocaine refuse que la télévision filme les débats," *Le Monde*, 13 July 1991.

39. "Statement of Amnesty International USA on Human Rights Abuses in North Africa before the Foreign Affairs' Subcommittees on Human Rights and Africa" (photocopied, 19 June 1991).

40. Abraham Serfaty was one of the few political prisoners ever individually identified by Hassan II, who publicly denounced his advocacy of Western Saharan self-determination as traitorous. To rationalize the release, a diplomatic loophole was crafted. Serfaty was not, it seems, Moroccan at all, but Brazilian . . . by virtue of his father's work-related travels at the time of his birth ("La Libération de Serfaty," *Jeune Afrique*, no. 1603 (18–24 1991).

41. Pamela Brogan, *The Torturers' Lobby* (Washington, D.C.: Center for Public Integrity), 17–19.

42. J. de Barrin, "Royal Privilege and Human Rights."

43. "Le Roi Hassan II assure qu'il n'y a plus de détenus politiques dans le pays," *Le Monde*, 7 July 1992. Less than a year earlier, Basri had recited for French television audiences: "As concerns the prison at Tazmamart, and I repeat what His Majesty the King said recently, it exists only in the mind and imagination of those who would malign Morocco" ("Déclaration de M. Driss Basri à 'TF-1,'" *Le Matin du Sahara et du Maghreb*, 19 September 1991.

44. Schoultz, *Human Rights and United States Policy Toward Latin America*, passim.

45. The Free South Africa movement is now commonly acknowledged to have had an impact on events in South Africa, and a similar effect for Argentina is documented by Alison Brysk, "From Above and Below: Social Movements, the International Situation, and Human Rights in Argentina," *Comparative Political Studies* 26 (October 1993): 259–83. In more general works—from quite different perspectives—two prominent theorists have recently recognized the influence of the international human rights movement (Rosenau, *Turbulence in World Politics;* Huntington, *Third Wave*).

11. THE CHANGING FACE OF NORTH AFRICAN POLITICS

1. In a well-publicized case in 1993, for example, a Tunisian professor at the Sorbonne in Paris was arrested while on a family visit to Tunisia and charged with belonging to al-Nahda. According to the FIDH, which sent observers to the original trial and an appeal trial, the court refused to examine the real circumstances of Taoufik Rajhi's arrest, and it accepted arrest documents whose dates had been modified to make the period of incommunicado detention conform to the law. Papers provided by Tunisian police showed that Rajhi was arrested on 11 August, whereas France Libertés had received a letter from his sister postmarked 30 July. In the course of the appeals trial on 8 October 1993, a defense attorney pointed out that several of the alleged offenses were committed exclusively in France and by provisions of Tunisian law could not be prosecuted unless the offenses were also punishable by French law. The appeals court upheld the conviction of the lower court but reduced the sentence (Fédération internationale des droits de l'homme, "Missions d'observations judiciaires: Procès de Taoufik Rajhi" [November 1993]). On 22 November the Tunisian parliament approved a modification of the penal code permitting prosecution of infractions committed outside Tunisian territory, even if the acts are not punishable in the country in which they take place (Law 93–113 of 22 November 1993).

2. Tunisian Information Office, *Tunisia Digest* 3, no. 1 (1994).

3. Jack Donnelly, *Universal Rights in Theory and Practice* (Ithaca, N.Y.: Cornell University Press, 1989); and Forsythe, *Human Rights and World Politics*.

4. Camau, "Tunisie au présent."

5. "La Politique autrement," *Jeune Afrique*, no. 1588 (5–11 June 1991).

6. "Il y a une conscience nouvelle de la problematique des droits de l'homme,"

interview with Khalid Naciri, president of OMDH, *Réalités,* no. 259 (10 August 1990).

7. Almond and Verba, *Civic Culture;* Huntington, *Third Wave.*

8. Huntington, *Third Wave.*

EPILOGUE

1. "FIS, GIA, AIS . . . Où en sont-ils? Que veulent-ils? Une interview de Séverine Labat," *Jeune Afrique,* no. 1755 (25–31 August 1994).

2. "Interior Minister Calls for Respect for Law," FBIS-NES-94–106 (2 June 1994). Interior Minister Kallel's remarks echoed those made by Ben Ali to parliament a few weeks earlier ("Souveraineté, souveraineté," *La Presse* [Tunisia], 10 April 1994).

3. Cf. Michael Bratton and Nicholas Van de Walle, "Neopatrimonial Regimes and Political Transitions in Africa," *World Politics* 46 (July 1994): 487. They argue that democratic transitions from neopatrimonial regimes are impeded by low levels of participation and competition.

Index

Compositor: Graphic Composition, Inc.
Text: 10/13 Aldus
Display: Aldus
Printer: Maple-Vail Book Mfg. Group
Binder: Maple-Vail Book Mfg. Group